FINDING HEAVEN
IN THE DARK

First published by Dog Ear Publishing
4011 Vincennes Road
Indianapolis, IN 46268
www.dogearpublishing.net

ISBN: 978-1-4575-4827-7

This book is printed on acid free paper.
Printed in the United States of America

Dedication

To Roy Masters and The Foundation
of Human Understanding

Table of Contents

Finding Heaven in the Dark

FOREWORD

L ife is beautiful and perfect. We are surrounded by intelligence and excellence at every level of existence, and yet throughout history, mankind has suffered. Why is human life such a puzzling mystery?

All of the philosophies and religions throughout the ages endeavor to explain what mankind is. The answers are everywhere, and so are the clues. If we only knew that the purpose of this life is to seek the purpose of this life, we would experience the joy of solving life's mystery and fulfilling its purpose.

The trials of my early life were mixed blessings. A confused life view, weak character, and bad choices trapped me in a world of secret pain and dark imagination. I was a quiet rebel without a cause, blindly searching for a real purpose to life that no one else shared.

My secret rage fostered a rejection of responsibility. I deserted the US Marine Corps for a cross-country trek to oblivion. I was a black, seventeen-year-old fugitive in a Los Angeles, skid-row rescue mission when I began discovering the true purpose of life.

The God and Savior that I blindly accepted as an adolescent, slowly and gently became real to me, as I embarked on a journey of self-discovery. The challenges of living a secret life of lies and unfolding inwardly to the truth of myself is my story.

I am not the hero of my story, but I am a willing and joyful participant. I learned and believe that God's Life is always trying to give us happiness, which we reject and settle for pleasures.

The Gospel of Jesus Christ challenged me to discover what we are as human beings and who I was as an individual. As I learned how to "be still and know" I found my true identity.

Loving the gift of awareness through a Judeo-Christian Meditation I learned 50 years ago, has blessed my life in ways that continue to this day.

PART I:
DARK JOURNEY

CHAPTER 1

HARD TIME

Summer 1970

The handcuffs locked around my wrists. I had been tried, convicted, and sentenced.

I was twenty-one-years old, as I stood shackled and ready to be transported to the Camp Lejeune Regional Brig of the US Marine Corps in Jacksonville, North Carolina.

This military prison was where I wanted to be. My entire focus for the prior three years had been directed toward getting me to this point. This place was the only one where I could end a bad beginning. Silently, I searched for that quiet center of my being that gave me the strength to get this far. My heart pounded. My swirling emotions calmed when I focused my attention on my hands. The handcuffs threw me; they were not part of my anticipated scenario. After all, I had been back on the base and in uniform for several weeks. In a weird way, I had become a curiosity, a minor celebrity. I had a temporary job. I went to chow. I socialized with fellow marines.

My sorrow was deep. Not for myself, but for others for whom I caused pain and suffering through my actions. I asked myself, "My God, why hadn't I grown up sooner?" The answer was unknowable to me at that time. It was what it was.

Spring 1970

I could barely squeeze my swollen feet into my unlaced sneakers. After a two-day bus ride from Los Angeles, we reached St. Louis. I walked stiffly to a telephone booth in the terminal. I plopped onto the seat and closed the door. My heart pounded so hard that my ears throbbed. I felt the beginnings of a tension headache.

In all the time I had been gone, I never forgot the number: NE6–5512. It was nana's phone number. I learned my grandmother's phone number when I was a child in New Rochelle, New York. Her phone number had been my only safety line. Whenever I thought I might be completely lost from my family, I remembered that number. The last time nana saw me or heard my voice was January 1967.

"William Lloyd, is it you?" she cried, not quite wanting to let herself believe it. "Where are you? Are you all right?"

"Yes, nana," I said. I heard my voice break and tasted my tears. "I'm okay. I'm at a bus station in St. Louis, but I'm on my way back to Camp Lejeune to turn myself in."

I could hear the muffled sound of the loudspeaker, announcing boarding times in the background, so I rushed my story. I heard myself say I would be all right. I told her that I had grown up, and I was turning myself in for the punishment I deserved. I said I was sorry I deserted everyone, and that at this point, there was nothing I could do except ask for forgiveness. It was time to put this episode behind me. I couldn't talk too long, because the bus would be leaving soon. Yet, I had one more call to make before turning myself in. I asked grandma for the other phone number I needed.

The number nana gave me was unfamiliar. She knew my mother's latest phone number, because she helped get the service restored after ma missed a payment. The phone rang once, and before the second ring, the receiver was snatched from its cradle. I heard a familiar voice say, "Hello, Mary Rose speaking."

Her greeting threw me for a second. With all the kids around, it seemed unlikely that ma would answer the phone herself. "Hi, ma, it's William," I said with a shaky voice. At first, there was total silence; and then, screaming. She was shrieking like only a mother, whose child had been missing for more than three years, could make.

As we spoke, her tears flowed freely. I knew they were tears of joy. (Only she knew the bittersweet taste of those tears.) Her prodigal son had returned, at last. I spoke to this woman through my own tears. I grasped how much we were alike, how much she was a part of me. Over the past three years, through prayer and greater understanding, I learned to love her. In the future, I planned to love her with the calm and patient love she never had—from any man—in her life.

———— • ◆ • ————

"INDOC! Attention!" the NCO shouted. Everyone came to attention. This was indoctrination or "INDOC." It was a type of shock treatment to get convicted marines prepared for military incarceration.

As we stood at attention, at the intake for INDOC, we certainly looked like a motley bunch. We were the losers—the non-hackers—as we used to say of those who couldn't make it. We each joined the Marine Corps, survived and graduated basic training, and were assigned an MOS (Military Occupational Specialty). What went wrong after this point was each man's story.

Some of my peers had gone to the war in South Vietnam (the "Nam"), and returned broken and confused. Others were struggling with (or surrendered to) addictions to drugs or alcohol. Then, there was the usual complement of "bad eggs." Those guys had a knack for staying in trouble by fighting or stealing.

Then, there was me. Perhaps the only convict who wanted to be there. I was the oddball of the group. I was a black marine, who was obviously fat and out of shape. My large Afro hairstyle was cut to regulation length several weeks earlier. With my soft, mushy features and relatively placid expression, I didn't look anything like a US Marine. I was twenty-one-years old, and one of the oldest in the group. I was more civilian than marine.

I made lots of wrong choices in my young life. Now, my maturity gave me a different life view from most others. I wanted to be there, because I had done the crime and must do the time.

Even with the right attitude, it didn't take long for me to screw up. That first morning at INDOC, we stood at attention before the first light of day. All of us in white t-shirts and boxer shorts stood perfectly still with our toes on the line that stretched the length of the squad bay. It was just like boot camp.

The sergeant walked down one side and up the other with a permanent scowl etched on his face. He was looking for any reason to berate and punish. As soon as he spotted an infraction, real or imagined, he flew into a rage and issued punishment. "Drop and give me twenty!" he commanded. Then, he moved on to his next victim. In his wake, he would leave underwear-clad marines loudly counting out their push-ups.

I found the whole scene comical, but only smiled inwardly. Suddenly, the sergeant was in front of me, only inches from my face. I had left my shower shoes (flip-flops) under my bunk. The sergeant spotted them, and he went berserk. He ordered me to turn and see the infraction. I realized that in my rush to get on line, I had left them on the floor.

"Give me twenty," he yelled automatically, as he glared and waited for me to start my push-ups.

"I can't do that, sir," I heard myself saying calmly. "I respectfully decline."

The NCO continued to look at me, but the scowl fell from his face. All the counting stopped. After guys finished their punishment, they returned to attention.

"What did you say?" he asked quietly, as he put his lips next to my cheek.

The staff sergeant stuck his head out of his office, and when everything went silent, he walked toward us quickly.

"What did he say?" the staff sergeant queried before I could answer the NCO's question.

"I said, I respectfully decline, sir," I restated softly, yet forcefully. "I refuse to go through boot camp again."

"What are you talkin' about, boy?" he asked in a tense whisper. I figured he threw the "boy" in to anger me, but I remained calm.

"I refuse to go through boot camp again, sir. The corps doesn't require former marines to go through basic training a second time," I stated. "I see the error I made—leaving my shoes on the floor. I'll correct it."

They were both stunned. Even I was a little stunned. Everything and everyone was silent. Without any obvious movement, I knew every eye was looking in our direction.

The sergeant spoke quietly. "Are you tryin' to stir up some shit? Are you one of those agitators, boy?"

"No sir, I'm not," I emphasized softly. "I turned myself in to get the punishment I deserve, but I don't need to be broken down."

"Why are you talking like some kind of text book? Are you supposed to be a psychologist or somethin'?" the sergeant asked sarcastically.

"No, I'm just being me," I answered. I relaxed and put myself at ease. I began to use my hands to gesture as I spoke.

I stated my case: "I know that my shower shoes shouldn't be under the rack, but I think the punishment is excessive."

"Do you think that you're better than everyone else here?" the staff sergeant asked, as he folded his arms across his chest.

We were all fully engaged and only inches apart. The game was on. It was like a chess match—move and countermove. It was quite eerie.

"No, sir, I know I'm not better," I said sincerely, "but I don't need to be further humiliated to get me to respond to you. I'm responsive to my own awareness and understanding, and I will correct my behavior accordingly."

"Oh, so you don't need discipline," the sergeant jumped back in, mockingly. "Or you're jus' gonna discipline yourself whenever you think you need it?"

"Self-discipline is more important than forced discipline to bring about a desired response," I argued. "That's what boot camp was for—to get us to a point where outer discipline awakens our inner discipline. Once that's done, self-discipline is the prime directive," I said passionately, pleading for them to see my point.

The staff sergeant listened attentively to my last comment. He was the older of the two. They were both white men, and I (one of a handful of blacks) had suddenly become an unanticipated problem. Ideally, there wasn't any black or white in the Marine Corps—just green.

"He's got you listening to him!" the sergeant disgustedly said to the staff sergeant. "He's talkin' like some kind of lawyer, tryin' to baffle us with bullshit! Don't pay any attention to him!" he spat.

The staff sergeant looked at the sergeant and motioned for him to step aside. Then, he looked me in the eye and barked, "Follow me!"

I followed him into the hallway and stood at attention as ordered. Here I was again. My first day in the brig, and I was already in serious trouble. It was like déjà vu of my boot-camp days. Was my pride leading me down the wrong path again? Did I still resent authority? Why didn't I simply go along with the program? No, I had to show them how insightful and tough minded I was. As I stood, waiting, I didn't feel so self-righteous anymore. The rest of the platoon went about its morning activities. Finally, the command came. "Come into my office, private."

The staff sergeant leaned forward in his chair from behind his desk. His hands were folded across an open file folder. The folder was mine. "Stand easy," he said. "I can't have you refusing to accept discipline, private. No matter how you cut it, that's why you're here," he said in a calm, matter-of-fact tone.

"I know that, sir," I said sincerely. "I didn't mean to be such a problem, but I just can't do boot camp again." He looked surprised by my confession.

"Nobody's asking you to do boot camp again. This is to get your mind right—back to the military—the Marine Corps way of thinking. You were out there in the world for a long time, and I know a lot of what you say is right, but most of these others have serious problems and some are gonna go back to their units. We can't have you doing your own thing until your time is up."

He leaned back in his chair, and I could see a copy of my sentence: Eight months hard labor, forfeiture of all pay and allowances, and a Bad Conduct Discharge.

"No sir," I uttered after a pause. "I understand." I genuinely understood the dilemma I created.

"Look, it comes down to this. I need you to be an example. They've all got discipline problems, or they wouldn't be here. I want you to show them that you're no better than them and can accept punishment," he reasoned.

Checkmate. He had moved and boxed me in, brilliantly. Was it planned strategy or experience? He clearly had me at a disadvantage, but he had given me a way out.

I decided to take that way out. I wanted to be a team player and help him do his job. Even my pride swelled a little at the thought of being an example to the other marines. And essentially, he was right. Whatever point I thought I had to make was made.

"I don't think I can do twenty push-ups, sir," I said.

He pointed toward the door. "Go outside this office into the passageway and do as many as you can, but I want to *hear* you count out twenty push-ups. Is that clear?" he asked.

"Sir, yes sir," I shouted and snapped to attention.

"Count them out real loud, private" he added, as I exited the office.

I got down on my hands and knees. The staff sergeant came to the door and shouted, "Now give me twenty, private!"

"Aye, aye sir," I responded and started my count. "One, sir; two, sir; three, sir…."

Reason had prevailed.

————— ◆ ·—————

The morning rituals continued. "INDOC, attention!" the staff sergeant growled. We were doing daybreak PT (physical training) in the exercise field. Most of the guys struggled in the early-morning heat. I felt awkward, and must have looked it, too. During my earlier punishment episode, I resolved to be the best and do the best I could.

We began to march around the large dirt oval track in the middle of the field. The sun suddenly seemed hotter as small clouds of dust began to rise. "Double time, march!" came the command. Like a large human engine, we fell into cadence and leaned forward into our double-time jog. 'Round the track we went to the sing-song tempo of the NCOs' commands. We were a sea of white and green as our arms pumped, and our dusty black boots thumped rhythmically around the track.

The gaps among the guys started widening. Any hint of a breeze was welcome, as our faces glistened with sweat. The salt burned into the corners of my eyes, and my tongue tasted of salt and dirt. My left side began to hurt. I fell back a bit, and others began to pass me.

"Birdie, birdie in the sky, drop a little white wash in my eye," we repeated after the NCO.

I kept jogging along to my own rhythm, just slightly off the pace. Some had dropped out and were panting along the sides of the track. The three NCOs were berating the drop-outs, challenging them to continue, and urging them not to quit. The well conditioned were moving around the track—dodging stragglers and slowpokes—as they sang and kept cadence. After a shaky start, I was surprised when I passed a few guys.

I knew everyone was wondering how I would do. After the earlier confrontation between me and the sergeants, they were curious to see what I was made of. And so was I. I was more shocked than anyone by my early-morning defiance. In the light of reason, I changed my actions, but not my belief. As I moved through the dusty clouds hovering over the exercise track, I wanted to show everyone that I was a "hacker." I would take whatever was thrown at me and not break!

I was glad I quit smoking years earlier. Younger and better-conditioned marines lay on their backs on the grass beside the track, gasping for air. Others were doubled over—with mouths open and arms flailing—as they sucked wind. I kept shuffling along, rhythmically. I was in a zone, and I felt like I could barely keep going. Finally, the long drawn-out command came: "Quick time, march!"

It was over, and I didn't quit! I thanked God, as I fell into marching formation behind the others. We were still moving around the track. How ironic. I was the worst-looking specimen of a marine imaginable, but I finally exhibited the commitment to perseverance.

When I returned to Camp Lejeune that Spring of 1970, word spread like wildfire. Everyone heard how a black marine—who had been UA (Unauthorized Absence) for three years—walked up to the main gate and told the guards that he was turning himself in.

I was overweight—with swollen feet stuffed into size-twelve sneakers—and dressed in thrift-store clothing that was woefully out of fashion. I had a large Afro-style hairdo with long sideburns and a mustache. I appeared rumpled after the three-day bus trip to the base, but carried myself with dignity and calm determination to right the wrong that I had done. I was a completely different person from the angry and frightened boy who ran away years earlier. The "colored" boy had become a man. I was thankful for the opportunity to return to where I had started.

As I sat in Division Headquarters, being reprocessed back into Marine Corps life, I was the curiosity factor of the base. Some of the passing officers looked at me, as if I was a leper. Other staff peaked around corners or stuck their heads out of offices. Young, black, enlisted men tended to nod and smile in my direction.

My paperwork was updated, and I got a new unit assignment, new ID card, payroll number, and the uniforms I would need until my court-martial. The rest of my life couldn't be updated that easily. I was not only out of style, I was out of touch in many ways. I watched as America changed. I was a fugitive—lost in the American dream. I had lived like a monk and a recluse, desperately searching for answers to life's questions.

During the previous years, I had little contact with "regular folk"—a fact that became glaringly evident when I was placed among fellow marines. I must have seemed like I was from another planet by the way I thought and spoke. Like Marco Polo, returning to Italy from China, I lost touch with customs and mannerisms of my former world. I spoke the same language, but sounded like a foreigner, using uncommon phrases and terminology.

I was a deserter! I deserted my fellow marines during a time of war. I was genuinely ashamed of what I did. Desertion proved to be just another self-inflicted wound. That's why I was determined to turn myself in. It was the most telling statement I could make. It said that I realized what I did was wrong, and I was prepared to accept my punishment.

I didn't deserve the respect of my fellow marines. I didn't deserve their understanding, either, but most offered it. Perhaps they extended empathy, because I didn't come back in chains like others. Or it could have something to do with the ties that bind US Marines—once a marine, always a marine. Most likely, though, it was the strains of war that led my fellow marines to relate to me. The Marine Corps—with its rich history of successful combat and heroes—was trapped into playing a role in a war that politicians couldn't resolve. For good or bad, we were bonded.

The Vietnam War was becoming more unpopular every day. It had become an open and running sore in the American consciousness. Its toxicity oozed into every facet of American life, and poisoned our relations with each other and our government leaders.

It wasn't that way when I joined the corps in 1966. The Vietnam War was definitely on the radar screen, as antiwar protests and draft-card burnings were increasing. In addition, student deferments or "escapes" to Canada were encouraged by antiwar activists. However, by 1970, much of the pride that Americans held for their armed forces was eroded by guilt-ridden, self-hating Americans. These citizens took delight in accusing our military of hideous deeds and atrocities. They gave no allowance for understandable over-reactions by our troops to horrors committed routinely by the enemy. More than ever, the war divided the nation.

Before Dr. Martin Luther King, Jr. publically denounced the war—and its disproportionate impact on black Americans—he and many other courageous Americans (of all colors and religions) demanded that the nation live up to its creed and guarantee all citizens equal rights under the law. All Americans witnessed the horrors of forced racial segregation; the images were thrust into our living rooms. We watched peaceful civil-rights marchers sprayed with water hoses and attacked by club-wielding police and their dogs. The scenes shocked and disturbed us. Those who grew up outside the Deep South were especially horrified to see the ugly racial hatred in the eyes and faces of fellow Americans.

While he was respected and admired for his civil-rights positions, Dr. King's patriotism was questioned when he spoke out about the war and the negative way it was changing America. Even his strongest supporters in the government resented his outspokenness. They did not want him "meddling" in international politics. They condemned his denouncement of the war and questioned his motives.

Dr. King hit a nerve, which the Black-Power movement leaders, black separatists, and Afrocentric thinkers and agitators tapped. Why was the poor and black underclass doing a disproportionate amount of the "heavy lifting" in this war when they didn't have full rights at home? The outrage at this injustice changed the Marine Corps' atmosphere during the time that I was gone. The espirit de corps still existed, but a big, black-and-white elephant was in the room. It was impossible not to notice it.

I was assigned to an H & S Company (Headquarters and Supply) in the Eighth Marines while I awaited my court-martial. I was an assistant to the company supply sergeant, who was a corporal named Clayton. As he issued supplies and completed paperwork in his small office, Corporal Clayton loved to play his favorite music at high-decibel levels. He was a laid back, easy-going white guy. Clayton gave me little to do, and I had lots of time free time.

We both liked all types of music so that became our basis for friendship. We enjoyed Blood, Sweat & Tears with its lead singer, David Clayton Thomas. We dug Chicago and other bands that fused jazz riffs with rock and soul.

The first night on the base—after I went to mess hall with Corporal Clayton—a couple of the black marines from my new unit called me over to them. "What's happenin', my brother?" one asked, as I approached.

"Hi," I said and extended a hand. They looked at each other and laughed.

"Look, brother man, you got to get with it. You don't give a brother that lame white boy handshake. Ricky, show my man."

A tall, light-skinned–black marine tapped me on the shoulder. "Where you from, brother?" he asked.

"I grew up in Connecticut," I answered, "but I just came here from California."

"We know that my man! Everybody in Camp Lejeune knows that! Let me show you how to shake hands with a brother." Ricky and another marine proceeded to perform an elaborate series of clenched and open-fist maneuvers. After I watched a couple more times, it was my turn to practice with Ricky. I had the movements and gestures down in short order, and they were all proud of themselves for having enlightened me.

By 1970, the brotherhood "handshake" was as much exclusionary as inclusionary. Even the few white marines that were "honorary brothers" didn't get to do the "handshake." A definite color line was drawn; this division wasn't there in the mid '60s. The macrocosm of the United States and the Vietnam War affected the microcosm of the Marine Corps.

Once I had the "handshake" down, I was welcomed like a new lodge brother. It was very amusing to have a group of "brothers," standing around talking. As each new fellow joined the group, he would approach each guy and perform this elaborate handshake. Then, as each member left the group, he did the same thing. I thought the ritual was humorous, but I kept that thought to myself. I knew the "handshake" was a symbolic gesture to signify black unity and solidarity. It made me feel good to be accepted so easily by my fellow black marines.

The good feeling of acceptance didn't last long. The US Marine Corps—like other branches of the military—knit our unit together in a way that made us stronger. The city kids were paired with country kids, the northern with southern, the eastern with western—and since 1952—black soldiers with white soldiers. These combinations strengthened our forces. Combining opposing energies taught us who we were, and why we were such a unique country.

As recruits in basic training, whenever we congregated by race, the senior drill instructor ordered us to "checkerboard." We knew what he meant. As fissures opened along the fault lines of racial discontentment in society, these disagreements impacted every aspect of America—including military life. As desegregation occurred in the United States, so did desegregation result from a command by our drill instructor.

I always rejected white *or* black racism. One of the few traits I liked about myself was my ability to mingle and respect people of any race or ethnic background. Corporal Clayton wasn't my only white acquaintance. In our squad bay, my bunkmate was a white fellow—I'll call "Lester"—who played the guitar. I played guitar a little while in Los Angeles. We formed a natural friendship when we learned we both liked folk songs.

I was curious and interested in everything. For the past few years, I lived almost as a recluse—a fugitive. Now, I was excited to take every opportunity to interact with—and learn from—anyone. During on-duty and off-duty hours, I could be seen in animated conversations with different people all over the base.

About a week after my return to the base, the same group of black marines called me to their table during evening chow. "Look here, 'Brother Heavy,'" Ricky said, as I sat down. "I got to pull your coat about something." He stressed each word. ("Brother Heavy" was given to me as a nickname.)

"What's that?" I asked innocently.

"You been hangin' with them 'gray' dudes too much. That's bad form, my brother."

I had an uncomfortable suspicion that I knew what he was talking about, but I acted clueless."What are you talkin' about?"

"The white dudes, man," one of the other guys said, as Ricky rolled his eyes.

"Look man, white guys are 'gray' dudes. We got to work with 'em, but we don't have to hang with them."

My face and ears were on fire. Suddenly, I was burning up. History was repeating itself. Racism was always the same—whether spoken from white lips or black lips—and I always rejected it.

"You're wrong, brother," I said calmly. "I don't play that stuff. I talk to everybody. I grew up with all kinds of people. Almost every brother you see has some white blood in his veins from slavery days. I can't get into that way of thinking. Life is too short," I stated emphatically.

"We've got to come together as a people, bro," Ricky said and gestured around the table. "The white man is the enemy. First, he sold us; then he killed our leaders and raped our women! That's why the Black Muslims call 'em devils, man. They're like a disease. We always end up fightin' their wars, and then we come home and catch hell, brother. That shit is tired!"

"I know where you're comin' from, but you can't hate people without that poison choking you," I said passionately. I was moved more by fear than courage. I feared that their attitude would devour them, if not challenged. I was prepared for the consequences. Yet, there were no consequences. There were no threats. That group of "brothers" just wanted their disapproval noted.

I stood firm, because I couldn't be dictated to on that topic. Not all blacks felt like they did. From that moment, they counted me among those who felt differently than they did. I followed my own spirit and spent time with white and black marines. I was an individual who happened to be in a plain, brown wrapper. I had no desire to be "white," nor to be judged by others with a "blacker than thou" attitude.

I was black enough to know the landscape of prejudice and bigotry. The undertones and overtones of racial life in America were a reality, but I knew the common bonds of all people were greater than the sum of their differences. Maybe it was the blessing of a painful and introspective childhood that encouraged me to seek the humanity and goodness in others. When you remove race, culture, religion, and politics, all you have left is a person.

I spent the majority of my free time alone. I discovered an isolated and quiet spot next to a body of water within walking distance of the H & S Company. I sat there for hours at a time, reading or watching the tiny fiddler crabs strut along the sandy beach, performing their calisthenics.

During this time, I reconnected with my family. Collect calls to my mother and grandmother helped ease me back into the family dynamics. I learned of my brothers' and sisters' lives, hopes, and dreams. I tried to remember names from the old neighborhood and faces from a faded past. It was necessary memory work. These are the ties that bind.

As I recall, my best talks were with my Uncle Buddy. He was my mother's only sibling, and we shared the same first name of William. He should have been my role model. I always looked up to and respected him. Uncle Buddy was a tall, handsome, intelligent, strong, black man with a cool demeanor and quick wit. He had a baritone voice and a keen and easy smile. When we talked, I wished I got to know him better when I was growing up. I really could have used his calm insight and clear thinking.

My mother was the oldest and daddy's little darling. Yet, Uncle Buddy was the son that every father wanted. Both my mother and uncle were intelligent, personable, and talented. They were credits to their race and their family. Still, I believe my mother resented Uncle Buddy's maleness and eventually, his success.

My Uncle Buddy, also known as William Leroy Ingram, joined the US Navy after leaving college, but quickly became disenchanted.

During that era, the navy was mired in institutional racism that limited blacks to certain jobs and offered narrow opportunities for advancement. Somehow, Uncle Buddy was able to end his navy service honorably; then, he joined the US Air Force. He used intellect, courage, and skill to become one of the few black jet pilots in the US Air Force. What an amazing accomplishment for any American! Uncle Buddy had every right to be proud, as the "Golden Boy" of the family, but he took it all in stride with his typical humility. Sadly, his father didn't live to see William Leroy's achievements. My maternal grandfather died in a tuberculosis sanitarium in 1946.

My uncle married a beautiful woman named Evor Lee Bradford. Her charm and intelligence were the perfect complement to his handsome good looks. In time, they had three beautiful daughters.

When I talked to my uncle from Camp Lejeune, he was taking classes in engineering for his job at the telephone company. He loved flying jets. However, the limited opportunities for black pilots and the economic pressures of raising a family demanded that he secure a good-paying job.

I reached out to my uncle for the first time as an adult. I told him that I wished that I had talked to him before I decided to enlist. His perspective would have been helpful. (Unknowingly, I inherited my mother's anger towards men, so I still might have gone wrong.) Uncle Buddy liked the manliness I had shown by returning, and he encouraged me to believe that there would be a better life on the other side of this situation. The upcoming challenges would strengthen me, and he would be there if I needed him.

January 1967

I was home for Christmas, and I watched the new year of 1967 begin with a dark shadow. I lied when I told my mother that I had taken an "indefinite leave" until my unit was sent to Guantanamo Bay, Cuba. I explained that we were being sent to "Gitmo" for training, and I would receive my orders by mail and depart directly. That was a lie. It was one of the only things I said to my mother during my visit.

I spent most of my time in my room—brooding. I contemplated dark and dangerous thoughts. Through a thin haze of cigarette smoke, I watched my hands as they quivered involuntarily. My nerves showed as I sat on the edge of the bed and wondered what to do next. I was drowning in quiet desperation.

"William, daddy's here," I heard my mother's muffled voice through my closed door.

I jumped up and looked out the window. My father's car was parked beside the curb. As I peered at him, he returned to his car.

"What does he want, ma?" I asked from the top of the stairs.

She stuck her head around the corner from the kitchen. "He wants to see you outside, he said." Her voice revealed obvious tension. My mother's hackles were up, as usual, whenever my father was around. I put on a coat and walked carefully to the car as the walkway had icy patches. The car was running with the heater on. It was a typically cold day for early January. I climbed beside him. The look on his face told me something serious was going on.

"The marines wrote me, and they say you're overdue to go back," he said with his Jamaican accent. He unfolded an official-looking letter, glanced at it, and folded it again.

"They say you must report back right away. What's going on?" he asked.

What could I tell this virtual stranger? He was my stepfather, but we really didn't know each other. Although he and my mother signed my enlistment papers (because I was only seventeen at the time), he never pressed me for my reasons for enlisting. How could I explain to him that I was tricked and trapped into enlisting without looking like a total fool? Besides, escaping the hell of my life was the ultimate goal.

"You know, I wanted to adopt you, make you my son, and give you my name," he said sincerely. I never heard this intention before. My silence and troubled mood must have worried him. Then, I remembered the letter he clutched. My company commander must have sent it to him. This commander was the only one who knew that I tried to get discharged for fraudulent enlistment after my last leave home.

I returned to the base and requested to see my captain. I showed him a copy of my birth certificate from New Rochelle hospital. It read "William Lloyd Ingram," clearly different from the name William Lloyd Rose that I grew up with and enlisted as. My commander didn't think the name error was a big problem; he didn't believe it was an intentionally fraudulent enlistment. That news would have been good, if I was interested in staying in the marines at that time. However, I was beginning to unravel, looking for a way out.

"I'm sorry I didn't adopt you years ago," I heard my stepfather saying again. I knew he liked me and thought a lot of me. His apology was his way of telling me. "You have to go back, you know?" he said cautiously. "They want me to tell them when you're coming."

"I'll go back tomorrow," I sighed, as I found my voice. There wasn't anything else to say. I was ashamed the mess had gotten to that point.

I couldn't talk to him or divulge the thoughts that swirled in my head. Since he and my mother separated four years earlier, we only tried to get close once—when I moved in with him to hurt her. She became our mutual enemy. Our anger toward her united us for a short time. Then, I moved back home and ended up enlisting after quitting school.

I was a seventeen-year-old boy who had bluffed his way through life. I clung to my fantasy world. I never finished anything that I started, and now, I was faced with a commitment I couldn't walk away from.

I told daddy I would report back to base, but even as I spoke, I hatched a plan in my fevered brain. I already decide not to return to the military. Then, I lied when I said I didn't need any money, although I only had enough cash to get to my grandmother's home in New Rochelle, New York.

Only my stepfather knew that I was UA (Unauthorized Absence) from my Marine Corps unit. So, when I told nana that I was heading back to the base after stopping by for a visit, she didn't think anything of it. My grandmother was a Christian woman who wanted to see the good in people, especially in her family. She was proud of me, her eldest grandson. She didn't understand why I quit high school after my junior year, or how difficult life had become for me in Hartford before I went to boot camp. She was pleased that I seemed to be the fine young man she'd always believed I would be.

Grandmother displayed my graduation photo from boot camp (August 1966). I was in Marine Corps dress blues. The image reflected only the heads and shoulders of our young faces; dress blues are the marines' equivalent to a college's graduation cap and gown. Grandmother had the photo, but was unable to attend my graduation. Not one member of my family showed for my graduation ceremony, and that was how I wanted it. Honestly, I didn't think I would make it through boot camp, and by the time I did, I thought the family couldn't afford a trip to Parris Island, South Carolina.

I spent that night at grandmother's on the same convertible sofa I slept on as a little boy, whenever we visited nana. She fed me well and gave me a little money. I pretended everything was fine.

———————•◆•———————

My next stop was with my Aunt Bertha who lived in Trenton, New Jersey. Aunt Bertha wasn't close with the rest of the family, but she loved my mother and my Uncle Buddy. (My maternal grandfather was her brother.) Aunt Bertha was a childless widow who looked forward to any contact with her favorite niece and nephew or their children.

On the way to her home from the bus depot, we realized that we had not seen each other since she spent two weeks with us in Hartford after ma delivered a stillborn baby some years earlier. I remarked that I never visited Trenton before, and I was excited to see the row houses Aunt Bertha and her late husband, Uncle Wes, owned.. (My aunt lived in one of the two-story apartment houses and rented the other one.)

I didn't know Aunt Bertha well, but she was always a kindly lady to me. She sent birthday and holiday cards with money inserted, and gave us big hugs and wet kisses. She was a dark-skinned woman with facial features that reflected a hard life with much heartache. Her emotions were always exposed. She was a hard worker who was proud of what she had and took care of it. She stayed mostly to herself in those years of widowhood—with only cigarettes and alcohol to ease her through each day.

This lonely and vulnerable lady was one I did not want to hurt at all, but I was about to hurt her the most with my lies. Lying never came easy to me, yet, I still became pretty good at it. I was likeable, and therefore, believable.

When I told Aunt Bertha I didn't have enough money for a one-way ticket to Jacksonville, North Carolina, she gladly volunteered the amount. At the Trenton bus depot, she paid cash for my ticket at the ticket window. She wanted to wait with me for the bus, but I desperately worked at convincing her that I would be fine. She should go off to work, I insisted. I would let her know I arrived safely, so that she could report the news to nana and my mother. Aunt Bertha eventually agreed, and soon I found myself alone with my plans for escape.

The same clerk was at the ticket window when I took the ticket back. I explained to him that my aunt had made a mistake, and I needed a ticket for Washington, DC. In short order, I boarded the DC bus with a one-way ticket and extra cash in my pocket.

————— ◆ —————

The adventure and romance that I loved when watching the TV show, *Route 66,* beckoned me. US Highway 50 stretched from the nation's capitol, across the United States, and ended in Northern California. My interest was drawn to where US 50 met Route 66 near St. Louis, Missouri.

I was now committed to my personal path of self-destruction. My entire course of action was virtual suicide. My US Marine Corps unit was shipping out for Guantanamo Bay, Cuba. But not me. I was running away again. Failing again! Giving up on myself and embracing defeat. My usual life's pattern had reemerged. I still hadn't learned that I couldn't run from myself!

As the bus moved down the highway toward DC, I fought off any second thoughts. I was determined to reject, cancel, and erase all of my life to that point. I would give up family, friends, obligations, and promises. I would wrap myself in my dreamworld and escape the agony of my life.

The bus was only half full when it pulled into the terminal in DC. I descended the steps and walked past the driver and other passengers, as they gathered their luggage from the hold of the bus. The temperature was noticeably warmer than in Trenton, so I put my light jacket over my arm and went directly to the lunch counter.

I wanted a cigarette, but with only a half pack of Camel Filters left, I decided to wait until I ate something. I went over my plan in my mind. I saw the road signs for US 50 West, as we approached the bus station. I was both anxious and nervous to start my journey—as I hitchhiked only one time before—from New York City to Connecticut with a fellow marine. We were in uniform at the time; in the dim light of dusk, we were able to get rides rather quickly.

The waitress put the plate and the bill in front of me at the lunch counter. Suddenly, I was aware of my surroundings. I started stuffing food into my mouth, eager to get started and well on my way before dark. I had no uniform on to help me now.

As I ate, I glanced beyond the waitress service area into a mirror. I noticed something was amiss. I turned my stool to glance around the room, and I slowly turned back. The blood gradually drained from my face. I wasn't looking into a mirror at all, but at the other side of the terminal dining room. In the other area, there were "colored" people. Behind and beside me, there were white people. "Wow," I thought to myself. "Oh, my God, this is it! This is the reality of segregation, and I'm sitting right in the middle of it—and on the wrong side!"

Suddenly, I became very self-conscious and uncomfortable. I had the surreal feeling of being in someone else's nightmare. "What are they thinking?" I wondered. "Do the whites think I am an agitator? What do the "colored" people think? Or is it obvious to all that I am an ignorant traveler who is clueless about the city's racist customs and laws?"

It was 1967 in Washington, DC, the nation's capital, and I had stepped into a time warp; the segregated lunch counter in the recent news became real. The signs were gone now. ("COLORED ONLY" and "WHITES ONLY") They didn't need signs anymore. The laws were abolished that once required restaurants to segregate. However, ingrained habits are hard to break. I smiled inwardly as I recalled one of our drill instructors constantly telling recruits to "checkerboard" whenever we were ordered into formation. They didn't want to see a small cluster of blacks in a company of white faces.

I hurriedly finished my lunch, as I felt the warmth of self-consciousness on my face and neck. I slid off my stool and deliberately avoided any eye contact, as I left the money on the counter. The lunch crowd was mostly gone. I decided I needed a smoke.

After my cigarette, I gave in to the urge to walk into the other side of the bus-terminal restaurant. A few brown faces were scattered around the room. The waitresses served both sides from a busy center island. I looked at where I had been sitting only a short time earlier. I still couldn't quite believe what I experienced. So, this was it—a relic of segregation. Apartheid—American style!

I stood there for a moment, as if silently apologizing for my ignorance. Also, I offered a moment of silence for those forgotten souls with black, white, and brown faces who worked and sacrificed for the changes I hoped to witness. The wheels were starting to turn, ever so slowly. Bigoted and power-hungry elected officials were desperately trying to restore or hold onto the old ways. But the nation was on a course to change. America was forced to realize that to deny any citizen his or her full rights was to deny *all* citizens their full rights!

I stood in the skeletal remains of the once "colored" half of the bus terminal and glanced at the big clock on the wall. Time to go. My rendezvous with history was over. Within an hour I was riding in a car on US 50 West, heading into the sunset.

CHAPTER 2

DARK JOURNEY

On February 21, 1949, I was born. No father's name was listed on the birth certificate. I was the bastard son of an unwed mother. However, I was wanted, welcomed, and loved. My grandmother, although ashamed of her daughter's transgression, rejoiced at my birth. She would tell the story of how she hurried to the New Rochelle hospital, from the funeral for a dear friend, and found me with my eyes wide open. She made that day sound so special and significant that I never forgot her story. One soul had departed life, and another had begun.

Grandmother was a deeply religious woman, a child of the South with African roots. She was devoted to African folklore, "colored" superstitions, and Negro Christianity. These influences combined to form a "mystical stew" of sayings and beliefs that guided "black folks" through life in America for many generations.

* ◆ *

"You're only as sick as your secrets," the saying goes. Mother kept secrets from grandmother— who often was a willing co-conspirator. In turn, grandmother kept secrets from the family outside of Hartford. Nana found out what was going on with her daughter's family, because her daughter's children could not maintain secrets. A slip of the tongue here, and a pregnant pause there, and our grandmother read between the lines. And ma herself—the greatest indicator of how things were going—gave away our circumstances when she swallowed her pride and asked grandmother for money.

Mary Elizabeth Ingram had been proud of her girlhood achievements in New Rochelle. Music and academics were her passion. With her talents at piano, organ, and choir she was lauded, and her bubbly personality made her well liked. She nurtured glorious ambitions for her future.

Things did not work out the way she dreamed. When difficult circumstances overcame us in Hartford, she had to ask for help. We didn't usually know why there wasn't food in the house. We didn't make connections regarding the comments we overheard until daddy was gone. ("Daddy doesn't make enough money." "Daddy's job is on strike." "Daddy's a strike breaker.") After he was gone, most of the shouting and finger pointing stopped. However, food supply was a constant concern. It was either feast or famine.

We knew when ma received some money to buy food for the icebox. A letter or package from nana or a "love offering" from ma's church (where she played piano) would keep our cupboard stocked for a while. Sometimes, daddy came by and gave ma a "little something." This was before the monthly welfare checks became a staple of our lives.

Nana was a disciplined Christian woman who was always ready to respond to a need. She never had a great deal herself, yet, she was willing to share whatever she could. Her daughter wanted nana's help without questions or criticisms. We knew we were never to give nana any bad news unless there was no alternative.

———————— • ◆ • ————————

Charter Oak Terrace was situated in the south end of Hartford. The sprawling complex of multi-family dwellings consisted mostly of two-storied, four- or six-family units housed in long, painted cinder-block buildings. Each structure featured concrete walkways and porches and front and rear entrances. Chimneys towered over each flat roof, emitting smoke from the coal furnaces. We moved into unit D202, and it was like living in the suburbs. No high-rise apartment buildings in sight; no unit was over two stories.

Three of the six-family buildings were arranged around a common area called the "court." All the back doors led to yards with clotheslines and galvanized garbage cans. Narrow cement walks emptied into large black-topped parking areas. Three buildings formed a big horseshoe around the "court" which left one open area as an entrance. This single opening made for a fairly safe cul-de-sac where the neighborhood kids could play when few cars were around. (In the 1950s, most families were usually one-car families.)

Each three-building horseshoe grouping formed a micro-neighborhood. The three buildings were separated by grassy areas, and the front doors of each unit opened onto cement porches, narrow cement sidewalks, and ample yards where kids could play. It was the projects. —separate from the single-family homes of working-class people located on nearby New Britain Avenue. Most of those homes were well maintained, and all were occupied by white families. Contrastingly, the projects were fully integrated; Charter Oak Terrace resembled a small United Nations.

We had whites from Italy, Germany, Greece, the Ukraine (as we called it), Poland, and Ireland. Also, our neighbors were blacks (or "colored" people) from the South, North, West Indies, and (the newly arrived) Puerto Rico.

I was thankful for our little unique place in the world—a village of struggling families searching for the American Dream and the pursuit of happiness. Charter Oak Terrace was a 1950s' version of a mixed generational, multi-ethnic, cultural, and religious neighborhood of working families located in the formally all-white south end of Hartford. Within easy commuting distance to jobs and good schools—and a world away from the older, meaner projects of Hartford's north end (from which some of our neighbors had fled)—we grew up in a country setting with green grass and fresh air. Because we weren't surrounded by crime, drugs, and gang violence, our parents were able to nurture new dreams for us; ones with hope for brighter futures.

Wafting out the windows of each home in my old neighborhood, you could hear the sounds of radio or television. Radio served us well through the Great Depression and war years, but television was making its presence felt. The power of images flickering across TV screens transfixed the nation—one home at a time. America began to see itself, daily. TV was etching itself into the American consciousness. This small black-and-white medium was rapidly becoming a sort of connective tissue for all strata of our society. We could simultaneously experience its wonder as it entertained, informed, inspired, and above all, encouraged consumption.

Rich, poor, black, white, and everyone in between—growing up during these years, we were called the "baby-boom" generation. We were the evidence of hope and the resilience of humanity after World War II. Experts writing books and lecture on this era and its transformation of America and the world

Information and entertainment shot into our homes via the airways, yet, in the mid-1950s, children weren't pressured to grow at a faster pace than what came naturally to them, and there was no great need to socialize young children outside the home or family. Most families were large enough or had relatives living close by, so children had siblings or cousins to play with as well as neighborhood kids.

Turning to the beginning of my life at Charter Oak Terrace, my mother told me that I nursed at her breast for nearly a year. This practice wasn't uncommon at that time, and it is still acknowledged as a superior way of transferring to the child, the mother's resistance to infection and disease. (Is there a tenderer scene among mankind than a mother offering her full breast to the searching mouth of her baby? The child is nourished, and so is the mother.) My mother fed off the vocal praise or silent admiration of family and others as she fulfilled her role of life giver.

And my mother also drew life from me. I was the evidence of her womanhood, her avenue to respect, and her self-esteem, even though she had no husband. My small presence—cradled in her arms and nursing at her breast—validated her as a person.

————— ◆ • —————

As a toddler I suffered through rheumatic fever. After making the ultimate "mistake" for a young girl, my mother was determined to keep me alive and healthy. She had experienced her own trails and tribulation, and now she found herself single, unwed, and the parent of a sick child. Having her first child struggle through such a serious illness created a bond between us—a special one that probably is only experienced by those having been near death. As a result of my near-fatal illness, I was probably a clingy child, reluctant to leave my mother's shadow. In addition, I became anxious to please her and ease her fears. (And she was full of fears!)

Although I do not recall any trauma at leaving my mother's side, I'm sure I suffered the usual separation anxiety that children do when their mothers place them in someone else's care. Basically, I think I adjusted easily to the kindergarten experiences of sandbox, blocks, naps, juice, and crackers. There was no expectation of achievement, and the only requirement was to "play nice."

———— • ◆ • ————

My first walk to elementary school was fraught with danger. In an attempt to avoid passing a vicious dog's yard, I changed direction; I became lost, frightened, and ashamed to ask for help. I walked along confidently, wiping my tears and pretending I knew where I was going. Eventually, my family found me, and I returned home safely.

My next perilous encounter was with the milk-money bully. This nameless white kid was older, and he recognized me an easy mark. I reluctantly handed over my nickels and pennies to this intimidating little highwayman. I remember being overcome by a helpless feeling whenever I saw this kid crossing the street to collect his extortion payment. I kept this secret humiliation to myself. I became a thief to satisfy this bully's craving, and found myself pilfering pocket change from my mother's purse or snatching loose change lying about. I specifically remember trying not to be too obvious with my thefts; I'd rearrange the remaining coins to make them appear undisturbed. I knew stealing was wrong, but I feared being beat up more.

Around this time, our small apartment was bustling with children. My younger brother, Jasper Jr. (born in 1953), was a toddler, and our first sister, Dorcas, was the new baby. That would change soon, because ma was pregnant with our brother, Duncan. Meals were already stretched pretty thin. Seldom was there enough food for seconds, and rarely did we have any leftovers. Money was tight; when a large loaf of bread cost seventeen cents, even nickels and pennies became important. Daddy gave mommy a limited amount for groceries, and the food had to last or we went hungry.

My first lesson in childhood intimidation occurred when I couldn't steal or find any money to carry to school. I was panicked, but I had to go to school. I silently prayed that this day would be one when the bully didn't show up. I resolved in my fevered brain to get beat up. I had no alternative, and the tormenter always implied the threat—your money or your life.

Soon, the moment of truth came as my personal troll strode up to me with his hand outstretched. I steeled myself and said, "I don't have any money."

"You better," he spat, making a fist with the same hand.

"No! I can't give you any more money," I said firmly, bracing for impact.

Then, just like a phantom, he was gone. I was ready to fight, but he wasn't. He was all bluster; he figured it would be easier to find another mark to pick on. The lesson learned was to confront bullies. Yet, I was a slow learner. I continued to avoid confrontation as much as possible. I sought to gain victory through avoidance of conflict.

When you're small, everything seems big. Our new "house" seemed huge with three bedrooms, closets, a hall, an upstairs bathroom, a living room with a closet, a large kitchen, and a small area with stairs to the basement. We had moved one unit over, next door to my best friend.

Our new home was a virtual "kids world." Every area in the house, except our parents' room, was our territory. We had cubby holes and hiding places in closets and behind furniture. We loved sliding down the banister or making tents with blankets straddled across chairs when we couldn't go out to play.

Out the back door was a forest of clothesline poles and pulleys, reaching out from each unit. Some days the lines would be loaded with washed clothes, and kids had to play in the small backyards; our mothers could watch us as they talked with each other.

The bedroom I shared with my brother, Junior, was in the front of the unit; it had a common wall with the bedroom of the Pitt boys next door. Outside our bedroom window was a roof that extended over both units' front entrances. It was forbidden for kids to climb out the window and play on that roof, which meant that the temptation was always great to do so.

Once we were old enough to cross the street (with permission), we enjoyed countless hours in our own enchanted forest. The area was undeveloped, probably the size of two house lots. The location was across the street from the projects, but we embraced it as our own. A large tree stump sat on a knoll. Low bushes and spindly tree sprouts covered the uneven ground. After a winter snow, we sled down the gentle slope from the tree stump and made it all the way to the garage of the house that bordered the property. What a world!

We were always in sight or earshot of our parents, yet, we were on our own planet. Our folks did not see us unless we were hungry or had to go to the toilet. We played around the stump the bugs or our toy soldiers. We made forts with branches and used natural dugouts to fight mock battles. And we talked about whatever kids talk about. It was magical.

This time in my life was when summer seemed like a year. My concept of time only revolved around play. Play was interrupted by meals and other sundry things, but play was the driving impulse of my childhood days.

As the oldest child of a growing family, I had work to do as well. I watched my younger brother and sister while ma bathed the new baby in the kitchen sink. I could be helpful, while the other kids napped, by warming and testing a bottle of baby formula.

And yes, I wanted to be helpful. Daddy was usually working, and even then, I sensed ma felt overwhelmed at times. Even more than empathy, I was driven by guilt. My conflict over paying my miniature tormentor turned me into a thief and liar, and I hated him for that. I had displayed a weakness of character, but I couldn't understand that frailty at that time. I just wanted to feel better about myself and make up to my mother for stealing from her, and lying about it when asked.

Mary Elizabeth Ingram Rose may not have held all the young-girl fantasies of being carried off to live happily ever after by a Prince Charming, but she surely dreamed of having a devoted marriage partner. Perhaps Mary imagined someone who would be a lover, help-mate, and friend; a man who would cherish her and their family. Yet, my mother was trapped. She probably felt helpless and corned at times, but her stubborn pride and willfulness (the same characteristics that put her in this position) would not allow her to admit it.

———————•◆•———————

She would deny that she was in a loveless marriage to a foreign man. The fact that she was the mother of a bastard son and three children with another man within five years was undeniable. My mother tried to keep it together, to accept the bitter with the sweet. She longed to be the wonderful mother of wonderful children and the loving wife of a loving husband. The reality of her life wounded her. She felt disappointment and frustration—toxic emotions; they are poison to the heart that holds them. Sadly, bitter disappointment and frustration morph into anger and hatred.

Mary Rose was no shrinking violet or mousy housewife. She was a proud, intelligent, strong-willed African American woman who had the sting of a scorpion! Most of her "stings" were for the man she married, Jasper Rose. He was a proud, handsome, intelligent, and strong-willed Jamaican immigrant. Like two opposing weather systems, storm warnings sounded as their unavoidable clashes neared. We would feel the tremors of faint rumblings and distant thunder during the week. Then, like a sudden storm on a hot summer day, the twister would release its pent-up ferocity.

I hated hearing and seeing them argue. The lashing out at each other in verbal rage wounded *me* more than it seemed to either of them. I cowered within myself as I tried to avoid these running battles of words and insults. Up and down the stairs, from kitchen to living room, their voices echoed everywhere. Although I witnessed no physical violence, I always feared for my mother. I wanted her to back down, to stop confronting him, but she wouldn't stop until she made her point, and then some.

While my mother didn't use profanity, daddy used curse words like seasoning with his Jamaican accent. Often, the profanity was all I could understand when he was shouting. "Fuck you!" would explode with a calypso accent; it cracked the air like lighting across a darkening sky.

Usually, my daddy was dressing to go out for the evening. Ma had limited time to make her argument. She didn't follow him as he went from bathroom to bedroom and up and down the stairs. Instead, she hovered in the kitchen or at the bottom of the steps where her voice would carry the most.

"My people are intelligent and creative! My mother went to college, and my father wrote plays," she'd shout.

"Fuck you" was his final response as he determinedly got in the last word before slamming the door on his way out.

Jasper Rose resented his wife who was never submissive and openly felt superior to him, and Mary resented her husband who enjoyed making babies, but not caring for them. When he wasn't working, he was involved in the West Indian Club and the Masonic Lodge. The attraction that these organizations held for her Jamaican husband was as foreign to her as he was. To Jasper, these affiliations were necessary to his identity.

His Lodge brothers and drinking buddies at the club sympathized with him over the problems of having an American spouse. They offered aid and comfort as he sought to survive the demands of a young family and an angry wife. The times between their furious, stormy outbursts were like uneasy ceasefires. Looking back, perhaps they tried not to argue around us, but I doubt it. Both parents were proud and angry with explosive temperaments and completely different world views.

———— ◆ • ————

Sunday school was another occasion for me to be surrounded by strangers. We were still clean from our Saturday night baths as we scurried around, half awake, getting dressed. I always felt awkward and uncomfortable as we got ready and waited for the bus to pick us up. Only the three of us attended Sunday school at that time: Dorcas, Jasper Jr., and me. We were scrubbed and shiny, sporting our Sunday best.

My blotchy complexion stood out. The ointment ma used on my pale blotches did not help, and I felt more self-conscious because of it. Only Jasper Jr. seemed comfortable in his suit and bow tie. He was handsome and cute with his dark brown baby face and engaging smile.

The Sunday-school bus arrived at Charter Oak Terrace from Shiloh Baptist Church in the north end of Hartford. It was quite a distance and a world away from where we were growing up. My mother became associated with this church soon after moving to Hartford. She had been raised in the Shiloh Baptist Church in New Rochelle.

Reverend Moody, the church's pastor, was a force in the black community. As his Negro flock dispersed throughout traditional white sections and suburbs, he reached out to all in his congregation via buses. Reverend Moody ensured parents that their children would remain members of the Sunday school. Classes were taught across the street from the church on Albany Avenue. During sessions, we colored pictures of David and Goliath, heard stories of Daniel in the lion's den or Jacob's coat of many colors, and of course, viewed images of Jesus surrounded by little children like us.

After Sunday school we stayed for church services, because our mother often had to accompany the choir on the piano or organ. Her playing paid the little extra money she needed to keep us from being penniless. I was proud to see her sitting at the piano and playing during services.

Church was the haven where ma felt comfortable. We would go there whenever we visited nana. My mother was highly thought of there. Now that she had a family, she was determined that her children reflected well on her. This admiration gave her a sense of worth that she wasn't getting from anywhere else in her life.

"I'm not sorry I had you kids," she'd confess to me, "but when you're older I'm going back to my piano lessons, so I can perform recitals." I was her confidant, the only one she revealed her desires to without criticism.

"My father, your grandfather, wrote plays. Nana's got them in a box under the bed. I want to publish them—get them performed," she stated emphatically, as she looked off into the distance. "I'm writing poems again," she would continue, "and I'm gonna publish them. I can give a recital and read some of my poetry." She'd smile as she wrapped herself in the image.

For those few moments, every so often, she would be happy. We would be happy. I wanted her to be happy so that I could be happy. Her relationship with her mother was strained, the girlfriends she had were in New Rochelle, and her husband was from another world. It fell to me (and eventually, my siblings) to comfort this lonely woman who had lost her dreams.

———— • ◆ • ————

Ma was always up long before her kids, down in the kitchen, listening to the radio. She was raised as one of the radio generation, so it felt completely natural for her to get local news and information from the radio we had on the kitchen counter. I could hear the low baritone of Bob Steele's voice; Steele was a Connecticut personality whose easy and friendly delivery made you feel comfortable as he talked.

The stairs creaked in warning as I descended. Ma greeted me and offered me some juice or tea as I sat at the table. These moments we shared were our time together, while everyone else was still in bed. If she had been writing poetry, she'd lay it aside. We didn't always talk, just sit, sipping our beverages, and listening to Steele on the radio.

Bedwetting is the scourge of many a male youth, and I suffered through it during my early years. I was so ashamed of myself. I knew the instant I awoke if I would have a good day or not. That familiar cold wetness around my middle meant I betrayed myself again. I agonized over the imagined memory of getting out of bed to go to the toilet. Then, I recalled a warm essence that enveloped me. It was painfully embarrassing for me to wake up with urine-soaked pajamas. These accidents proved that I needed the rubber sheet, hidden beneath the linen one.

I hated bedbugs, so I'd get into my pajamas and pull on my socks with the pajamas stuffed into them. I must have looked comical. I fastened all the buttons and slid another pair of socks over my hands and wrists. This was war! Sometimes, as I laid there in the dark between the sheets, I imagined those little, reddish-brown bugs crawling over me, searching for an opening to invade on my body. Then, I'd fling back the covers and turn on the lamp. Sometimes, the sensation was nothing but my skin crawling with the memory of my fears. But usually, the bugs were there.

They scurried to their hiding places once exposed to the light, and I maddeningly attacked all I found, squeezing them between my thumb and fingers. Many bedbugs would pop as I squeezed them, indicating that they had eaten their blood meals; they stained my fingers and bed clothes. Most of these bloodsuckers got away. I would perform this exercise a few times, but eventually I would fall asleep and suffer my fate in unconscious silence. "Sleep tight, and don't let the bedbugs bite?" No such luck! Ma sprayed the mattress before remaking the bed, but soon the ravenous bugs were back—and our war would resume.

———— • ◆ • ————

Our mother was the gravitational center of our universe. We rarely saw daddy at home except to eat and sleep. We knew he worked at various times for Sealtest Dairy Company, and later for Pratt & Whitney Aircraft Company. Daddy also worked side jobs for extra cash. He usually worked nights and slept days. No matter his work schedule, though, he never relaxed at home. He never had any active interest in enjoying or playing with his young family.

———— • ◆ • ————

Jasper Milton Rose was the youngest child of ten, born to his parents on the island nation of Jamaica. The island was still a colony of Great Britain at that time, and a vibrant jewel in the Caribbean. Jasper was representative of many of the island's immigrants who came to the US and Canada for employment. These settlers arrived (with temporary visas or permits) to work the various agricultural industries along the East Coast.

Their own Jamaican version of the Queen's English helped the new immigrants assimilate and rapidly acquire citizenship status. Sometimes, native Hartford residents had difficulty understanding them. American English was their second language. Frustrated listeners displayed flashes of anger due to trouble comprehending their Jamaican-accented speech. Daddy rarely showed any angry emotion towards us unless we prompted him to repeat himself several times. We became reluctant to ask him to reiterate his thoughts, and we were left with only a partial understanding of what he had spoken.

With his handsome features and friendly smile, it was easy to imagine that this youngest of ten children was spoiled. Daddy had a keen intelligence and a quick wit that served him well in Jamaica, where he became an expert in beekeeping. He was usually on the receiving end of attention and affection from his family and friends. Consequently, the under-appreciation of his strong-minded American wife left a bitter taste in his mouth.

Another dynamic was at play here, and it deserves some mention—the clash of two black cultures. The West Indian/Caribbean Island blacks and the African Americans found their ways of life colliding. To understand the discord, a little history is necessary.

The legacy of slavery in the United States created a completely different mind-set among both black and white descendents. Whites demonstrated a consistent determination to devalue and demoralize the black male and reduce his stature from his place in the family structure and society as a whole.

It was a numbers game. In America, blacks of all shades of color were considered a minority in the overall population. After slavery ended, the wreckage of shattered families, lost heritages, and fear of the white male, especially in the South, eventually negated the equality of the Negro male.

During and after Reconstruction, countless impediments were placed in the paths of Negro citizens, hampering their evolution to fully functioning members of society. Voting rights and jim crow laws pervaded the statutes of Southern legislators in order to keep blacks "in their place"—in effect, at the bottom.

Throughout the post-slavery years, many valiant efforts were made by people and groups of all colors to elevate the black male through justice and education in spite of resistance and indifference. As blacks were only twelve percent of the US population, the struggle of "colored" people barely registered on the national consciousness.

Just the reverse was true of the Caribbean Island nations. The black descendants of slavery were often a majority of the island populace. And, as in America, their bloodlines frequently flowed with those of native tribes and their European colonizers. On most of these island nations, slavery was outlawed decades before it was prohibited in the US; thus, a different mind-set evolved among younger generations of these peoples. This enabled Caribbean blacks to act more independent than African Americans.

Black islanders tended to be highly motivated, proud, and upwardly mobile. Through some subtle psychological process of association and osmosis, they appeared to have absorbed their former colonial masters' arrogance and sense of superiority. This behavior was especially true of former slaves of the British and French colonial islands.

These island men were attractive to females wherever they mixed. Their accents and self-assured manners seemed exotic; their motivations and ambitions were admirable. These men seemed different than the marginalized African-American men. They appeared to be achievers and potentially good providers. A different spirit or attitude resonated about them and conflicted with the predominate belief that island people were slow moving and without ambition.

It was an open secret that West Indian blacks resented being considered African Americans; they were intensely proud of their own people's heritage. They were also painfully aware of the low esteem that the Negro male endured in the American culture.

Jasper Rose wanted respect. He probably wanted love too, whatever his concept of that was. However, I think he wanted respect more. Jasper Rose was proud by nature and proud of his accomplishments. He sought his own kind, others who were strangers in a strange land. They formed bonds in the cold climate of Hartford, seeking nurturing and support.

As a member of the Freemason's Lodge in Hartford, daddy invested in the long-term friendship and respect of his lodge brothers. This commitment, among others, assured that he would be absent from his growing family most of the time. Seldom seen by us and never seen by the neighbors, daddy was like a phantom in Charter Oak Terrace. In a time when intact families were the rule and not the exception, our daddy was sleeping or absent.

CHAPTER 3

BOY IS FATHER TO THE MAN

Nothing came easy for me as a child. Every day was a silent struggle to avoid embarrassment. I was stutterer and a bed wetter during those pre-adolescent days. I don't even remember how long these problems plagued me. My mother proved to be a great help in my overcoming those two major childhood problems. Her patience with my difficulties helped me, and now, those struggles are only memories.

My poor nutrition and lack of professional oral attention was reflected in my misshapen teeth and gap-toothed smile (which I hated). I hid my unattractive teeth behind my big lips. That feature was one the neighborhood kids tortured me about. "Big Lips," they teased when I was young. My response was shame, self-hatred, and withdrawal.

My tongue seemed too large and thick for my mouth, and the gaps and uneven bite of my teeth made it impossible for me to correctly make "s" sounds. Therefore, I had to take a speech therapy class. Twice a week, I sat one-on-one with a speech therapist and practiced making these sounds. Eventually, I began to develop a technique of pronouncing "s" that my therapist felt was an improvement.

---◆---

The outside world burst into my awareness in 1957. That year was the one when the Soviet Union launched an orbiting satellite called Sputnik. The race for dominance in space was on. The ripple effect from that launch was like the aftershocks of an actual earthquake. Adults became disquieted and fearful of the future.

At school we practiced survival drills. The fire-alarm bell rang during classes, and we dutifully laid our pencils or crayons aside. Quickly and orderly, we filed into the corridors and sat on the floor along the walls. We wrapped our arms around our heads and buried them in our laps. This position reduced our vulnerability to being permanently injured by flying debris.

———— • ◆ • ————

We spent a couple of weeks each summer at our grandmother's home in New Rochelle. Grandmother's home had an elevator of which I was terrified, because I had once gotten stuck in it. The metal car had stopped, the steel door opened, and exposed a gap. The elevator had stopped between floors! I was powerless to convince it to resume travel as my little fingers anxiously pushed the buttons to go up or down. Even ringing the faded, red emergency button did not bring an immediate response. I was eventually rescued, but I could never completely trust that monster again.

Nana Ingram was so well loved and respected in the community that *we* became special just because we were her grandchildren. Nana and her sister, Aunt Burt, were twin pillars of strength and inspiration in the black community. They were the worker bees in their church. The Boys Club and Women's Club were also the beneficiaries of their talents and energy.

Many people remembered my mother, Liz, and her brother, Buddy, for their accomplishments in local activities as well. Some even remembered me as a baby. They all smiled and marveled at the resemblance among us. Members asked how ma was, or where we lived now. I felt strangely special somehow.

Throughout the apartment, only one photo was displayed of Nana's husband, our grandfather. Willie Ingram's picture stood near the telephone, which rested on a desk in the narrow hallway. Grandfather looked handsome, but stiff and uncomfortable in his suit as he posed for the photo. In the faded, black-and-white image, he was sitting in a straight-back chair with no scenery. In the frame, a small inset photo of Grandpa Willie was featured; he was wearing his World War I army uniform with his rifle beside him. Nana still had his World War I rifle behind the door in her bedroom. Sometimes, I'd sneak in there and look at it.

Those years were rough for "colored" men. Limited opportunities and low expectations restricted most men to service sectors in the growing economy. Grandpa Willie worked as a chauffeur for many of those years and performed other jobs to provide for his family. He suffered with a physical weakness that manifested as tuberculosis. The TB kept him away from his family for stretches of time that were lost forever. Alcohol eased his pains. Grandfather wrote plays to express and inspire him during those difficult times. This writing made him a hero to his daughter.

My mother was definitely daddy's little girl. The few times she'd speak of her father, the stories were always ones with pride and sadness. Ma was bitter that grandfather had left them prematurely, although she didn't comprehend her feelings at the time. Her young life started to unravel after he died, and it was hard for her to forgive him for that. Suddenly, after not coming home from the last sanatorium visit, she was alone with her mother and younger brother. While they were disciplined and focused, she was the dreamer who had lost her soul mate.

Her father had died and left her. Her brother was succeeding where she hadn't. Her youthful lover had used and abandoned her with a bastard child. Her husband was a disappointment. Consequently, I became a living reminder of her disillusionment with life.

I learned that adults live in worlds of lies and secrets. The first violation children experience occurs when parents force them to doubt what they actually see in adult behavior. Children want to be open and honest about their lives and the events that surround them. Adults curb and stifle their impulses to seek truth when it conflicts with the images they wish to project.

When my brother, Jasper, was getting close to school age, one of my friends asked me why my brother was called Junior instead of me, as I was the oldest. Being the firstborn, my pal explained, meant that I should have been Jasper Jr. I had already reasoned that out. With innocent candor, I told my friend that I honestly believed that my brother was nicknamed Junior, because he looked more like daddy than I did. I wanted desperately to believe my twisted, childish logic.

The lengthening shadow of doubt that Jasper Rose was my father darkened my thoughts. The question my friend asked out loud was one I dared not verbalize. Then, one day, I discovered a laminated newspaper clipping on our piano. It was the announcement of my mother's wedding to Jasper Rose in New Rochelle in 1952. By that time, as a seven- or eight-year-old, I could read and do the math. I was born in February 1949. The wedding announcement was September 1952. Things weren't adding up right. Why had the clipping suddenly appeared for me to see when I came home from school?

"Could a woman have a baby without being married?" I wondered. "Who was I? If daddy wasn't my father; then, who was?"

I didn't know anything about the proverbial "birds and the bees" or where babies really came from. With a better than two-year gap between my birth and their marriage, I strongly suspected that daddy wasn't my father. Had mother left out the article on purpose for me to see? Was it her way of confirming my growing suspicions without saying anything?

William Rose was just a name. Who was I really? Secrets and lies surrounded me. I kept my questions to myself. I intuitively knew that I wasn't to speak of this. It was best to just go on pretending I didn't care and not ask any embarrassing questions. "You are who we say you are" was implied.

———— • ◆ • ————

The outside world continued piercing my consciousness. Civil Rights marches were going on in the Southern states. Articles in *Jet Magazine* and other black publications featured important stories about events that were happening in the civil rights movement. The movement was being led by the NAACP and the SCLC as they fought for equality for "colored" people in the former slave states of the South.

That grown-ups weren't all equal was still an abstract concept to me. Cruel names were used to put down people, often behind their backs. Occasional racial tension was felt among individuals in Charter Oak Terrace. However, the battle rarely became one group versus another until we reached the teenage years.

We heard words like nigger, spic, Guinea, mick, Jew, and dago spat with venom during an argument or confrontation, but it wouldn't destroy a relationship. The name calling was usually the last resort of a feeble mind to express itself forcefully. It was worse to be called a cry baby or a sissy.

I wasn't a Goody Two-shoes, but I did avoid calling people names. I knew the pain of name calling and those names were not heard at home. Our mother, to her credit, referred to other neighbors either by name or as the Jewish lady, the Italian gentleman, the Greek family, or the Puerto Rican family. Her references were respectful and accurate. What she may have said about individual people or families could be judgmental and mean, but she didn't use race or ethnicity as indictments against them.

At that time, like most "colored" people, our world was basically divided into "colored" and Everybody Else. The Everybody Else was mostly white people. "Colored" people (including the descendants of black African slaves), Native Americans, and any obvious mixture of these groups were considered second-class citizens by circumstance and practice.

The highest compliment one black person could give another, after being shown a new item they purchased, was to hear: "It's just like what white people have!" In the North, it was easier to display such material equality without being beaten or lynched. In Hartford, if a black man was overly ostentatious in his attire, or loud and ignorant in his behavior, other blacks tried to correct him. Even black people who were secretly admired for being outrageously bold and incredibly successful were accepted, as long as they didn't forget their "roots."

"Roots" was the code word for the "blackness," or the unique, shared experience that bonded different clans and tribes from black Africa to what was beginning to be called Afro-Americans. "Stay Black" was the phrase used to remind black people—who were successful in the white world—that they were still "colored." In other words, the expression warned not to use acceptance in the white world to feel superior to your people. At that time, subtleties of race and culture were fluid and under increasing pressure to change from all directions. During these years, I had no idea how explosive and volatile my future as a black man would be.

My kid brother, Emmanuel, was born that summer on July 10, 1959. Daddy was proud as a peacock when he brought ma and the new baby home to show us. "He looks like Khrushchev," daddy joked, referring to his bald head, which resembled that of the Russian premier. We all agreed. Along with Junior and Dorcas, I watched young Duncan and tried to make things a little easier on our mother. I sensed that she was beginning to feel overwhelmed.

The illusion of living a Christian life and raising a Christian family was in tatters by the time I was ten-years-old. The strain of maintaining a routine of Sunday school and church attendance was wearing down my mother. With the birth of Manny, she had five children that she was practically raising as a single parent. She struggled to feed us and maintain a household amidst the ruins of her shattered dreams.

Her body was breaking down, and her failing health eased her into the miracle world of pharmaceuticals. By better living through chemistry, modern drug therapy promised to heal and cure the battered and broken; drugs became the salvation for many people who were feeling overwhelmed by the pressures of life.

My mother didn't intentionally abuse drugs, but she began to use prescription medications to help her cope on several levels. She had legitimate physical problems in the beginning, but those ailments morphed into a shield to discourage attacks and elicit sympathy. How could you not feel sorry for anyone valiantly struggling with potentially life-threatening diseases? These aids in her struggles were right there in our kitchen, on top of the refrigerator, and out of the sight and reach of the little kids.

If we came home from school and she was trying to rest, we tried to keep quiet as we played or watched TV. We didn't want our mother to have to "go away." "Go away" meant "they" might send ma to a place in Newtown, Connecticut, where they put mothers whose kids drove them "crazy." I was led to believe that it was a "nervous" hospital for mothers with nerves that were shot. These moms were distraught souls with kids who had pushed them over the edge.

In his own way, daddy was proud of his family and his accomplishments. He raised himself up from the life of a struggling boy on a Caribbean island to a naturalized American citizen. He had an attractive, feisty, and intelligent wife; five healthy and robust children; a decent paying job; and fraternal friendships that held him in esteem. Jasper Rose Sr. was a typical male head of the household who liked things neat, clean, and orderly at home. As is often the case, he had married his opposite.

Although it may be unfair to say that she was his opposite, our mother wasn't a neat freak. Like so many people with artistic temperament, she was not determined to keep an orderly household. Moreover, this would have been virtually impossible with four rambunctious kids and a new baby in the summer of 1959.

What she tried to do, on her better days, was make life at home fun and funny. She laughed at our silly stories or jokes, and she liked to sing songs with us. In addition, ma made cooking dinner a family project. When the house was straightened up, so daddy could see it neat and clean, it didn't take long before toys and furniture were relocated.

In those days, all neighborhoods were fertile grounds for vendors and door-to-door salesmen. Most mothers were home with younger children, completing chores, while school-age kids and dads were away. After school hours and during summer months, the ice-cream vendors paid regular visits to streets where kids excitedly waited, clutching money in their small hands. More women were learning to drive, but most families only had one automobile. Moms were weekend drivers, going to the market for groceries or running other errands that had been put off until Saturday.

Salesmen made their way through Charter Oak Terrace and the surrounding community. Some sold sets of encyclopedias, Bibles, or children's books. Vacuum-cleaner salesmen visited often, as did hawkers of household implements designed to make life easier. American consumerism was growing. Folks exhibited new and growing impulses to buy and own things. Whether it was "keeping up with the Joneses" or keeping up with the times, the door-to-door traveling salesmen were experts at making everything seem affordable. After a small deposit, the people from Fuller Brush came by each week to collect a few more dollars for their sold articles. The pay-as-you-go plan worked fine as long as you didn't buy more than your budget allowed.

———— • ◆ • ————

Nana came to visit us every Thanksgiving. It was a tradition by the time I was ten. She spent Thanksgiving with us in Hartford and Christmas with our uncle Buddy, in Westbury, New York. We looked forward to nana's visit. When she was with us, it truly seemed like a time of plenty. Nana brought each of us a big chocolate turkey and a Thanksgiving card with a couple of crisp dollar bills. The chocolate turkey arrived just in time, because our Halloween candy would be exhausted.

Our parents looked forward to nana's visits, too. She sent money before her visit, so that ma could stock up on everything we needed. Daddy enjoyed her visits, because her financial contribution took the pressure off him a bit. Also, his wife tended to behave differently when her mother was there.

Actually, we all did. Nana somehow made us want to act better than usual. She wanted to see our school work and projects as she spent time with each of us, going over drawings, homework assignments, and test papers. A good report card elicited praise. Daddy seemed to spend a little more time at home when nana was present, and he and ma called a truce to their running feud and power struggle. When dad was completely out of the doghouse, ma found time to make his favorite coconut cake as one of our Thanksgiving desserts.

At Thanksgiving, so much more food was in the refrigerator and cupboards that stolen slices of meat or handfuls of cookies went unnoticed. I overindulged at every opportunity. I took pieces of candy from our mother's big box of Fanny Farmer chocolates. Each time I had a chance, I ate something whether I was hungry or not. It was my silent revenge for the many times I went hungry and felt helpless and frustrated.

Nana rejoiced at her opportunity to go to church with us. Reverend Moody and the congregation at Shiloh Baptist enjoyed her visits. They respected her faith and dedication to the church. In addition, they appreciated nana's daughter's contribution to their church services and her growing Christian family.

Our Christmas lists were short. At that time, companies did not aggressively market to children as they do now. Our wants were fairly simple. We knew moms and dads were determined to see that kids had the necessary things like underwear, socks, dresses, sweaters, and other practical stuff. We wrote thank-you notes to each relative or family friend that sent a set of pajamas, slippers, or a clip-on tie. (Admittedly, we were less than thrilled about such practical gifts.) We were grateful though, because we knew sensible presents from relatives or friends took pressure off our parents.

When visiting Santa Claus, my familiar sense of dread emerged as we made our way to the elevators. The crowds jostled and pressed until each car was full. The elevator car would rise smoothly and rapidly as the operator maneuvered a lever that controlled the direction and speed of the car.

Rather than take the elevator to a lower floor after meeting Santa Claus, nana agreed to take the escalator at my urging. We stopped on the mezzanine level for lunch; nana treated us to hotdogs at an inexpensive snack bar. After our meal, nana gathered her many packages and herded all three of us onto the escalator for our final descent to the first floor. That's when the accident occurred.

During our ride down the moving stairway, nana lost her balance. Whether one of us jostled her or otherwise caused her to fall, I don't remember. In a flash, nana was lying at the bottom of the escalator! Her body was twisted unnaturally, and she cried out in pain. Her packages were scattered, and we stood around her crying, as strangers hurried to assist her.

I clung tightly to my brother and sister as the ambulance attendants made their way into the store; they eased her onto a stretcher, and ushered us into the back of the rescue vehicle with her. Traffic parted, and buildings passed in a blur. The siren screamed and attendants worked at comforting nana and easing our fears.

Nana's leg was broken. She stayed in Hartford Hospital for a while, and eventually, she was released to us for her convalescence. Nana would spend Christmas with us that year. She was stuck in Hartford!

The cards, letters, and phone calls started coming before she got home from the hospital; she was missed by many people in New Rochelle. Nana worked for the Coleman family several days a week and maintained a busy schedule of church and community activities that would tire out much younger people. And she made time to spend with her two sets of grandkids during the year.

Some relatives made the trip to Hartford to see nana. Uncle Buddy visited, of course, because he and Aunt Burt handled nana's affairs in New Rochelle. Her extended stay with the Rose family through Christmas and beyond exposed the fading illusion of a happy family. By spring, nana was back in New Rochelle, and we were back to hard times.

By now, daddy was always gone except to sleep and change clothes. Ma was becoming more stressed and seeking relief through medication. The money was tighter than ever, and ma had to make it go further. Any money nana sent was always needed. The good news was that summer offered a more reliable source of money for kids. Discovering empty soda and beer bottles, with a few cents deposit on each, was like panning for gold. Each week we'd take a wagon and troll through the neighborhood's backyards. Sometimes, we knocked on doors and asked for empties. People who weren't keeping them for themselves were glad to give their bottles to us.

———— • ◆ • ————

During those months, I was growing in two directions at once. Sometimes I'd feel dark moods come over me, and though I tried to conceal them, my thoughts were altered and I became manipulative and selfish. I stayed alone as much as possible during those times.

I didn't like movies or stories about children longing to find their fathers. A rage welled up inside me. I experienced internal dialogues regarding how foolish I was. What difference did it make who my father was? My destiny was in my own hands! No unknown or absent father could influence me! I knew I wasn't adopted. There was no doubt that Mary Rose was my biological mother. I was a reflection of her looks and emotions. The biological father was just a sperm donor—a drone bee.

———— • ◆ • ————

During a summer's stay at nana's in New Rochelle, I discovered an old clarinet that my uncle had played. Since I had a good ear for music, evidenced by my constant whistling of popular tunes, nana said I could take the instrument home. Once the school year began, I signed up for music class and band.

I was the only boy in the clarinet section and the only brown face in the band. The music director devoted some extra time to me, because I was one of the few kids who didn't take private lessons. Walking to school with my books and instrument case gave me a distinction I hadn't experienced before. I was a musician! I drank in the notoriety.

My interest in Cub Scouts was fading at the same time we were preparing to become Boy Scouts. The advancement to Boy Scouts was more expensive, and I'd have to travel farther to join a troop. The upgrade did not appeal to me. A pattern was beginning to repeat itself in my young life—fear and failure.

Instead of moving up to the Boy Scouts, my interests took a turn in a new direction. I responded to an advertisement I saw frequently in magazines; it was an invitation to sell a weekly tabloid-sized newspaper called *Grit*. This newspaper contained features about country and farm life as well as articles of general interest. I eagerly sent my application with a deposit for the first few shipments. At twelve-years-old, I saw this opportunity as a way to earn regular income. Hartford produced two large daily newspapers: *Hartford Courant* and *Hartford Times*. Both papers competed for readers and advertisers and were delivered by paper boys with large canvas bags. These young men rode their bikes every day throughout the neighborhoods of the south end, delivering Hartford's daily news. I envied the paper boys and their entrepreneurial spirits; I looked forward to establishing my own territory.

Soon, a roll of about a dozen papers arrived. I was in business. All I had to do was sell my papers each week, send in the required payment, and keep the profits. I even envisioned an army of sub-agents selling papers for me all over Hartford.

I started with my immediate neighbors. Some residents bought papers to help me out and to see if the paper interested them. Many budgets were too tight to spare even a few cents toward the purchase of my paper. People were nice, but most said no to regular subscriptions. After the first burst of enthusiasm, I was losing my drive. I'd need to expand my territory to find people interested in such a different type of newspaper.

I became disheartened as my fears grew at the thought of trolling for subscriptions. This selling was not like going door-to-door on Halloween. Peddling papers meant facing possible rejection. More importantly, my new enterprise required self-discipline and follow through, neither of which I possessed.

After a few weeks, my orders of papers began to accumulate. I never said a word as a new roll of papers arrived each week. I wouldn't even open the bundle; I tossed them into the living room closet and wished they would disappear. I was ashamed of myself for giving up so quickly. The notices demanding payment went unopened. Soon the publishers of *Grit* stopped sending their newspapers and requests for overdue payments.

———— • ◆ • ————

Aunt Bertha came to visit us that summer of 1959. She drove by herself from Trenton, New Jersey, to see her favorite niece and family. Aunt Bertha seemed the opposite of nana. An earthy woman who smoked and drank, she did not judge others' behavior. We loved her for that.

The day after Aunt Bertha arrived, I was playing touch football. It was one of those sweltering hot afternoons that forced even diehard athletic kids to play in slow motion. The game came to an abrupt end when I went out for a long pass. I slipped, tripped, and slid onto the sidewalk. My left arm was caught under my body as I braced my right hand for the fall. I was a mess of skinned knees, arms, hands, and elbows when my comrades helped me home. Ma and Aunt Bertha cleaned me up and treated my wounds. In a short time, I was back outside with the guys.

Later that evening, I was asleep in the top bunk when I was shaken awake. I assumed it was time for me to go fishing with Charlie and Paul, as we had planned. However, it was Aunt Bertha who had awakened me. I had been moaning loudly. She asked me what was the matter, and I instinctively cradled my left arm and blinked when she turned on the light. My left arm was swollen twice its usual size and throbbed with pain. As my eyes became accustomed to the light, I saw how plump and fat my hand and fingers were.

Daddy was home that morning, and he offered to drive me to the hospital emergency room. He used Aunt Bertha's black and yellow car to take me to St. Francis Hospital, where he had worked for a time. Later that day, I returned home with my sprained arm wrapped in an ACE bandage and supported by a sling. I was the talk of my little group of friends.

———— • ◆ • ————

On September 28, 1961, our baby sister was born. That made six kids in our home. Our world began to disintegrate. Our parents were testing a trial separation. It wasn't as if they were a loving couple who sought to restore the passion and commitment of their marriage. They were more like a couple that wanted to be rid of each other, but didn't know how to go about it.

Divorce was rare, and poor people seldom considered it. Society frowned on divorce when children were involved. It seemed like a sign of failure when two adults put their own selfish needs ahead of the well-being of the children. An alternative to divorce was voluntary separation for a couple when—for whatever reasons—they just couldn't live together any longer.

Daddy was gone. I felt the tension in the house subside, although our world had dissolved into the unknown. The "ties that bind" disconnected, and we were adrift. A frustrated and frantic woman with six confused and wounded children laid a course for survival. Ma was determined to keep her children together, no matter what.

———— • ◆ • ————

I was losing my shyness and becoming more comfortable around people. I was learning to put people at ease, and they felt comfortable around me. I discovered my own sense of humor and that I could make people laugh. I even found confidence to regularly talk to girls. I teased the girls in the band a little, and I listened patiently when they needed to talk. The neighborhood girls in Charter Oak Terrace were more often like pals, than girlfriends. I took girls seriously when they talked, and they respected and trusted me because of that.

I was becoming a "Mr. Congeniality" type. I was shy, yet friendly, clever, funny, and interesting. I had a curiosity about people that was genuine, and a thirst for knowledge that was growing. I was welcomed in various groups of students. The smart kids thought I was smart, or at least smart enough to appreciate their brains. The jock kids were comfortable with me because of my knowledge of sports and admiration of their skills. The girls saw me as a friendly, sympathetic listener with good advice, and their boyfriends saw me as non-threatening. I was projecting the perfect persona, which evolved out of my need to survive.

My teachers weren't as easily swayed by my winning personality. They wanted results. My report cards during most of my primary school years recorded the same observations: "William has the ability to perform well when he applies himself." Standard teacher talk noting that I usually only did enough work to get by. These educators saw my lack of interest as a rejection of my potential.

We weren't color-blind in sixth grade, but we weren't color obsessed either. With barely a handful of blacks at Batchelder School, race did not make a major impact, one way or the other. At least at school, we all seemed to be equal.

I knew that the church had to be a part of our lives, because of my grandmother. Ma felt the same way, but was weakening. She was becoming worldlier in her behavior and more tolerant of my reluctance to travel to the other side of Hartford to go to Shiloh Baptist. When school chums and church outreach people from Christ Methodist Church invited me to attend, I jumped at the chance. This church was directly up the hill from our neighborhood, and just like nearby Batchelder School, was considered lily-white.

I attended Sunday school there and felt welcome. I really loved getting out of church, rushing home to change clothes, and playing outside. I didn't know anything about religious denominations at that time, but I learned that Methodists practiced sprinkling rather than full immersion for baptism. That difference in methods convinced me that I made the right choice.

Nana wasn't sure how to take the news that I was going to a Methodist church. Not only was it a Methodist congregation, but it was also all white. On a theoretical level, that was not a problem for nana, because she truly respected all people. However, it was never a part of *her* life experience to worship with anyone other than her own people.

At that time, due to the segregation of churches, Sunday became the most segregated day in America. Nana appreciated this fact. Hence, she wanted me to invite her to Christ Methodist Church at a future date. That was typical nana. She was happy that I was going to church somewhere—even with an all-white congregation—rather than not going at all. Inviting her to attend church with me wasn't in my plans, but I promised to look for an opportunity for her to join me during one of her visits.

Our Sunday school teacher was a man. I don't remember if he was an associate pastor or not, but I'll call him Pastor Bob. He knew he had a class of fidgety young boys who wanted to be almost any-where but there on a Sunday morning. Pastor Bob knew how to get our attention, because he started off talking about things that were of interest to us.

Pastor Bob asked us if we noticed that our willingness to use curse words around our friends and in the street suddenly disap-peared once inside our homes—or more specifically, in front of our mothers. We all laughed nervously. That question was truly thought-provoking! I had come a long way in recent years with my ability to use profanity. All the boys were becoming fairly comfortable with cursing, and it had become a rite of passage into manhood. After all, the most accomplished users of profanity that we knew were often our fathers or other grown men.

Pastor Bob embellished on his theme and challenged us to note how our language automatically changed when our mothers, or someone else we respected, were in earshot. His observation was true, and I was mystified by the mechanisms in our brains that ignited the change. How did this happen without conscious effort? I knew that in some homes, profanity was used liberally by both parents and other adults, whether kids were around or not. However, there were not any swear words being thrown around the Rose household, unless daddy swore about something or at mommy.

Pastor Bob wove our boyhood experiences into our Sunday school lessons. He showed us that our minds operated on two different levels at the same time. We each had two faces and two personas. I knew this pronouncement was true, because I could see it in my own life. I was actually glad that I had a public persona that was less shy and awkward than the real me. Did Pastor Bob mean that we were all busily deceiving ourselves and each other about who we were?

In order to make church school enlightening and engaging, Pastor Bob transformed ancient characters with strange-sounding names into real people with problems we could relate to. He evolved the Sunday school's simple lessons about history into insightful stories about genuine folks.

Pastor Bob taught my confirmation class. I had to pass a written exam to be confirmed as a member of the Methodist Church, and of the body of Christ. I enjoyed the illusion of accomplishment far more than the actual work required to succeed. I was intellectually lazy, and wouldn't put forth the effort required to really absorb my studies. I never saw this shortcoming as a big problem, because I was constantly distracting myself. With confirmation class, it should have been different. Pastor Bob gave all of us the gift of insight into ourselves. I did not appreciate this gift. My time of reckoning arrived during the written final exam for confirmation.

The test wasn't supposed to be difficult, because it was basically a review of our Sunday school classes. However, I didn't prepare, and it showed. I struggled with some answers and guessed at many of the multiple-choice questions. I was stumped by a question and did the unpardonable thing. I glanced at the fellow's exam next to me for a clue to the answer.

I passed the test and was scheduled to be confirmed over the Easter holiday. I tried not to think about how I'd done it. I'd gotten by again, but I knew I really didn't deserve to be confirmed. I cheated, and I was ashamed of myself, again.

I was nervous on the morning of confirmation. It was a magnificent spring day. Pastor Bob gave each of us in his class a small book, which he said he hoped we'd read and enjoy. The book was a small volume by C.S. Lewis entitled *The Screwtape Letters*.

I read *The Screwtape Letters*. It was fascinating to read. That little book gave my thirteen-year-old mind a vital insight into the battles that were often being waged subconsciously. The ugly side of human nature seemed to dominate our potential goodness every-where I looked. Why was it so hard to be good?

———————•◆•———————

Bill collectors began coming to the house regularly, looking for a few dollars to apply to the "balance due" amounts until the next week or month. They pleaded for "just a little something" to avoid reclaim-ing merchandise. The items could be anything from household appli-ances to a set of World Book Encyclopedias—usually sold by persuasive door-to-door salesmen. It was easier for mother to say yes, and promise to pay a small sum regularly, than to say no. Her pride refused to admit to some stranger that she couldn't afford a few dol-lars a week to aid her kids' education or that she didn't deserve the latest gadget or labor-saving device that other women found indis-pensable. Ma could not concede to how far we had fallen.

The shades would be drawn and the doors closed as soon as a bill collector's car was spotted in the neighborhood. If one happened to elude detection and knocked insistently at our door, it usually fell to me to tell the lie: "My mother's not home." The collection agent would ask when my mother was expected, and angrily state that I was to tell her he had come by. I promised I would. I hated those times. The disconnected phone remained silent, the small grocery owner gave us bones for the dog that would be boiled for soup, and the anx-iety-riddled watch for bill collectors continued.

After the mailman came on the first of the month with a check from the State of Connecticut, sometimes a few dollars were leftover to pay a patient peddler. Happy days were here again! The refrigera-tor held food, and the phone had a dial tone. For a couple of weeks, we felt like everybody else.

———————•◆•———————

The atmosphere was electric on the first day of seventh grade. With anticipation, we learned which students were condemned to Miss Motto's classroom. It was a reunion for some of us who hadn't seen each other all summer. We nodded and spoke quietly as we chose desks. As usual, the rambunctious, the shy, and the lazy students gravitated to the back of the classroom. The smart and ambitious kids took seats in the front. In my typical fashion, I sat in the middle and closest to the door. I hoped to be barely noticed when I left the classroom for band practice and safety-patrol duties.

We went silent when the "Dragon Lady" strode into the room. Miss Motto was impeccably dressed with sensible shoes. Her hair was pulled into a tight bun of silver fibers which made her pleasant features seem a little severe. After taking attendance, she introduced herself and relayed her philosophy of junior high school. Miss Motto said that as seventh graders, we were actually junior high students. She spoke animatedly about how we were big fish at Batchelder School, a little pond. She added that when we graduated junior high school, we would be little fish in a big pond, high school. She expected our best efforts at all times, and indeed, wouldn't settle for anything less! We would attend at least one math class with her, and she warned that it would be tough. The math class would be tough, but we could do the work; she wanted to give us a good foundation in order to excel in high school.

Far from inspiring, her little talk was depressing! Not only did my decorum need to change in homeroom, but I also had to excel at math. I couldn't believe my misfortune. All of my dread over the summer seemed justified. Miss Motto's classroom was going to be hell!

I added another extracurricular activity to my schedule at the beginning of the school year. I tried out for our school's barbershop quartet. I was selected to join out of about twenty boys who auditioned. I never thought of myself as a singer, but I had a good ear for harmony and a decent voice. I was classified as second tenor. Barbershop singing was a completely different form of music than I had ever experienced. I loved it instantly! The four-part harmony was intricate and challenging.

With safety patrol, the school band, and the barbershop quartet, I required a lot of time to leave classes early or arrive late. Each student carried an activities schedule, but for the most part, we were on the honor system. Students were expected to be truthful about practices and keep up with missed classes, tests, and homework. Miss

Motto prepared a workbook that she called Supplemental Math for her students to use during the school year. It featured formulas of algebra, geometry, and trigonometry that scientists at MIT were teaching! This woman was frightening.

I did not let Miss Motto impact my success in junior high school. I was a prince on the school campus that year! It was the high point of my young life. I was successful at juggling classes and activities. I had the respect of most of my peers, teachers, and adult acquaintances in the neighborhood.

CHAPTER 4

ALTERED STATE

I was comfortable in my skin, and my public persona reflected this confidence. However, my darker, private side used food to sedate my self-loathing. My body began to disappoint me. I became fascinated by the possibility of changing from a wimp to a winner, and sent for the muscle-building program by Charles Atlas. For my fourteenth birthday, I finally got a set of barbells to transform myself into a powerhouse. I craved the respect that came with a good build and strong physical presence over the esteem that came from good character or self-discipline. I coveted form over substance.

My name was William to my family and in the neighborhood. I liked the name William. Its origin came from a word meaning "guardian' or "protector." I liked that concept. Among my schoolmates, I became Bill. I liked that, too! I was both William and Bill.

William had been the bedwetting stutterer, liar, and thief—a cowardly bastard with a loser self-image! Bill was the upwardly mobile musician, singer, and future writer. Bill was Mr. Congeniality!

The idea of becoming a writer was planted by my mother. She insisted it was in our genes from her father. Ma obsessed over her own self-expression through writing. She wrote her own poetry in the wee hours of most mornings. I adopted the idea of becoming a writer! I worked to strengthen my vocabulary and spelling ability. I paid a little extra attention in English class to sentence structure and punctuation. I was becoming a serious reader of everything.

Mary Rose wanted to be the ideal American mother, who sewed her family's clothes, prepared sumptuous meals from scratch with enough for leftovers, washed and ironed mounds of laundry each week, and presented a clean and welcoming home. That was not her reality. Ma sewed and mended from necessity. She cooked what she could afford, and tried different ways to prepare the same fare. The house was seldom presentable, and we rarely had our school friends or neighborhood kids over when ma was home.

Because of her early hours of writing each morning, ma needed to rest by afternoon. She retreated to her room and napped or rested before fixing supper. Her daily afternoon break left me in charge of my siblings. I issued discipline, and controlled what we watched on TV after school. I tried to be a benevolent dictator when I was in charge.

———————•◆•———————

Our mother searched for a way to rebel over her life as wife and mother. She had a few girlfriends who supported her declaration of independence from daddy. Now, they were showing her worldly vices to soothe her inner conflicts. We got a kick out of our mother's new antics. Seeing our strict and saintly grandmother's daughter smoking and drinking was comical! Even ma saw the obvious humor in it. She was also determined to express her independence from other people's expectations.

———————•◆•———————

I had completed seventh grade and survived my first year with Miss Motto as homeroom and math teacher. I did better than expected with a little extra effort. Over the summer, as a fourteen-year-old, I could work picking tobacco like some of the older neighborhood boys. I was old enough to do farm work, which paid pretty good money for a young teen at eighty-five cents an hour. The money could help my mother financially, and make the expenses of the coming school year easier to pay.

I was afraid to pick tobacco on a farm without a companion, although I didn't admit this fear to myself. Unfortunately, my pal, Charlie, was a year younger, and at thirteen couldn't sign up for farm work. Because of my anxiety of working without support, I acted as if the opportunity didn't exist. In addition, I was frightened by the thought of performing what we all heard was hot, dusty, smelly, and back-breaking work.

I signed up to be a junior counselor with the summer Christian day camp for a few weeks. Once again, I sought the path of least resistance. The Christian day camp position was honorary—no money was involved. Because my counseling position did not pay, I still had to collect discarded soda and beer bottles for pocket change.

With some of my bottle-collecting money, I bought my first baseball glove that summer. I lovingly broke it in—the way young boys are taught by their dads or others—until it was flexible and comfortable. By September, I was ready to go back to school. I was anxious for my friends at school to admire it.

I picked up where I left off with band, the barbershop quartet, and safety patrol as my extra-curricular activities. Mr. Green, the band director, had an ambitious program planned for us that fall, so rehearsals were intense. I was chosen to play a difficult solo at a critical part of the concert. My alto-clarinet part consisted of about nine mournful notes, bridging two movements of "The Battle Hymn of the Republic." I was terrified at the thought of performing this solo.

———— •◆•————

On November 22, I stayed home for a rest. I wasn't deathly ill, but I had a cold. My attendance had been good, and I convinced myself that I needed time off. I was still in my pajamas and robe when I heard a knock at the back door. It was a minister from Shiloh Baptist Church. He had come to give my mother a "love offering" of money for playing the piano for choir rehearsal.

My mother struggled to maintain some semblance of emotional and mental equilibrium. She was in deep pain, and all her medications couldn't touch it. She hadn't gotten out of bed much during that week, and I think some of her friends were concerned about her. The reverend had come by to counsel and pray for her, if she would speak with him.

Ma pulled herself together, and soon she and the reverend were having a cup of tea in the kitchen. I could faintly hear their voices as I sipped my tea and watched television in the living room. All three channels were covering the president's visit to Dallas, Texas. President John F. Kennedy was on a tour of the Southern states for the Democratic party to shore up support for his reelection run. Along with the president in Dallas was Vice President Lyndon Johnson—a native son of Texas and a long-time Democratic power broker.

President Kennedy was a relatively young man. He and his lovely wife, Jacqueline, worked hard to win the respect and admiration of most Americans and others around the world. His run for the nomination and presidency against Richard Nixon was the first political campaign that I had any interest in. The drama of the scion from a New England family was captivating; he was a war hero, married to an elegant, lovely lady. When the subtle bigotry against Catholicism was factored (which made Kennedy an underdog), the stage was set for a nail-biting election.

The leader of the free world and his lovely wife rode in an open limousine; they acknowledged adoring citizens and spectators that lined their journey. Suddenly, the presidential motorcade sped up and left the plaza in confusion and disarray.

"The president has been shot!" the correspondent exclaimed. Few generations had ever heard these words in their lifetimes.

Then, almost as if to confirm his own disbelief, the reporter announced the news grievously: "President Kennedy has been shot."

I echoed his words loudly and without thinking. "The President's been shot!"

Ma and the reverend stopped their conversation in the kitchen and hovered by the stairs at the edge of the living room. We watched silently as Walter Cronkite and others recounted the events of the past few minutes. It was a surreal experience that I knew millions of others were experiencing simultaneously. My mother cried softly, and the reverend dabbed at his eyes; he kept saying, "I can't believe it," as he shook his head.

Soon, the reverend departed, and ma returned to the dark comfort of her room. I continued to watch the black-and-white images on the TV screen, mesmerized by the events of living history parading before me. Before long came the famous moment when Walter

Cronkite removed his eyeglasses and stated, as calmly and professionally as possible, that President Kennedy was dead.

Like the rest of the nation and the world, I watched the events of the next few days unfold and spill into our lives via TV and radio. I followed every twist and turn as authorities and reporters worked tirelessly to piece together fragments of clues into a picture that we tried to make sense of.

Lee Harvey Oswald was captured, and his wife and mother were interviewed. Then, Jack Ruby thrust himself into the national nightmare as we anxiously watched the president's alleged killer being transported from the Dallas jailhouse to his arraignment. Clearly visible to all viewers, Jack Ruby pumped bullets into the body of Oswald! Oswald died, and Ruby was jailed. The conspiracy theories evolved exponentially— like germs—dividing and subdividing as soon as they were born.

Other images swirled around in the vortex of that terrible time: the swearing in of Vice President Johnson as President of the United States; the former first lady, Mrs. Kennedy, in her still blood-splattered dress at the hurried induction; and later, Mrs. Kennedy, in dignified elegance with her children by her side, viewing the passing casket of the nation's president before a still-stunned world.

———— • ◆ • ————

Life and time moved on. We performed our band concert before a full auditorium before the Christmas holiday break. With the pall that hung over the nation, "The Battle Hymn of the Republic" seemed appropriate and maybe even hopeful. The song reminded us that we had survived worse as a people, and we would endure in spite of our current pain.

I sat with my bandmates under the stage lights, nervously following along with the sheet music as the hymn progressed to my solo. My alto clarinet hung by my side, and I prayed for the ability to remain calm and not mess up. Mr. Green pointed his baton toward me, and I played my nine notes. When my part was over, I breathed a sigh of relief. From that moment on, my life should have been a success. Instead, I began my meltdown.

———— ◆ ————

There was a growing disquieting agitation in my mind that I couldn't turn off or escape for long. This disturbance impacted my performance at school. At fifteen-years-old, I was a good speller. I worked to master spelling in school and on my own. Learning words and their root derivations dovetailed nicely with my love of history and geography. Although I had an appreciation for spelling, I was unprepared for an upcoming test. That dilemma was in and of itself not a big problem, because even without studying, I always did well on spelling tests. This exam, however, was different; it was pass or fail, and one wrong answer meant you scored zero.

I was stuck. I could not recall the spelling of one word on the test, and I couldn't come up with an excuse to leave class. I got a classmate's attention, and he moved his test paper into my view. I leaned slightly in his direction and stole a glance at his paper. We both got zero. Our English teacher noted that we both misspelled the exact same word. In addition, she noticed my sneaking a peek. I was mortified. I got caught taking the easy way out of an easy exam, and I destroyed the trust with this teacher I worked hard to develop.

My English teacher's disappointment in me was painful. I made every effort possible to be a model student after that time. I didn't like that teacher. The students made fun of her. Her classroom demeanor was just as dry and shapeless as she was. However, I was still addicted to being liked by my teachers, so I really wanted to win her over again.

Miss Motto's tough-minded, no-nonsense homeroom and math classes gave me some self-discipline I needed. She was demanding, but fair and personable. In spite of my reservations, I came to respect and like her a lot. But as an eighth grader, with only three months until graduation, I began to feel empowered and rebellious.

After a period of good behavior, I decided to blow off English class one afternoon. Another test I didn't want to take was scheduled. I lied about having band practice for the spring concert and was excused from class. I'd take the test another time. Only a couple of places were available to hide or hang out during classes. I chose the boys' lavatory.

I was hardly in there ten minutes before the door opened and a couple of guys came in. After hearing the normal toilet sounds, I began to smell cigarette smoke. The fellas had lit up next to the opened window. Another couple of minutes passed before I left my stall and went to the sink to wash my hands. Just then, the door to the restroom opened again.

Junior, my brother, walked in. We rarely saw each other at school, so we laughed at the coincidence. We joked and talked with the other two guys; they were fanning the smoke out the window. Suddenly, the door burst open again. This time, it was my English teacher! She stormed into the boys' restroom and caught us goofing off. I was busted!

I stood outside Miss Motto's classroom, wishing I were anywhere else. I was totally humiliated. I wanted to blame my brother or bad circumstances, but honestly, I was angry at myself. I had ensnared myself in a web of lies.

Miss Motto entered the hall, and I followed her to the principal's office. The one teacher I truly admired and respected would see me as a fraud—the liar and cheat that I was at my core! I fought to hold back tears.

A hurried conference took place between the teachers and the principal. Justice was swift, and without appeal. I received the equivalent to the death penalty. I was stripped of all my extracurricular activities! I was granted the last quarter of the school year to concentrate on my studies and contemplate the error of my ways.

The pain of those days was a wake-up call for me. I still had a chance to seriously buckle down and really begin to grow into the person I was pretending to be. I wanted to convince Miss Motto and the other faculty that I suffered a temporary lapse of judgment that caused me to deceive them.

Soon, the school year was over. During the graduation ceremony, my former bandmates played "Pomp and Circumstance." After the commemoration, I took my mother to meet Miss Motto. In spite of my difficulties, she still believed I had the goods to succeed in life; I just needed to put forth the required effort. Miss Motto did her best to prepare our graduating class for high school. I loved her calm dignity and demanding spirit. I would never forget her.

————— • ◆ • —————

That summer I knew I could not limit myself to babysitting on weekends or collecting bottles to earn the money I wanted. With high school financial demands approaching, I needed serious money. My closest friend, Charlie, was picking tobacco that summer, and I signed up to work the farms as well. As young teens, we would make eighty-five cents an hour doing farm labor—that sounded pretty good to us. We knew it would be back-breaking, hot, dusty work with long hours, but we encouraged each other by sharing thoughts of what we could do with our money.

I needed to obtain my first Social Security card in order to sign up for work with COLBRO, the shade tobacco growers in Windsor, Connecticut. A birth certificate was required to get a Social Security number—the necessary number allowed me to join the legions of dark young boys entering the working world.

A few days after applying for my card, I walked into the living room to find my mother sitting there. I knew something was wrong. I don't recall seeing ma sitting and staring in this manner before. Something was terribly wrong. Her left hand laying limply on her lap. She looked up at me, and past me. Her hand clutched a yellow document. She'd been crying.

"I thought they changed this," she said with tears in her voice. "I thought…I told," she started and stopped. Mother wasn't making any sense, and she knew it. She pushed the yellow paper at me.

"CERTIFICATE OF BIRTH—CITY OF NEW ROCHELLE, NEW YORK—WILLIAM LLOYD INGRAM—FEBRUARY 21, 1949—MOTHER: MARY ELIZABETH INGRAM—FATHER: UNKNOWN."

There it was—my worst fear! "FATHER: UNKNOWN" was official now, complete with a registrar's stamped seal embossed over a couple of signatures. Although I lived with the near certainty that Jasper Rose wasn't my biological father, I never suspected that I had a different name from his or the rest of my family. My mother tried to explain.

"Your father's name was John, John Withers, a boy I knew from church in New Rochelle. He played the saxophone. He was quiet and moody," she went on softly, reflectively, as she gazed past me.

I stood in stunned silence, but my mind raged! John Withers? Who the hell was John Withers? What was she talking about? Mother searched my face for a reaction.

"He died from a drug overdose," she said with a shrug and a sigh. "He got into drugs before you were born. He didn't want anything to do with you...." Her voice trailed off. I wondered if she considered that she had said too much.

"He was handsome, and I loved him," she whispered as her head fell back onto the chair. "I thought they changed the name on this," she said, motioning towards the birth certificate.

All the blood drained from my head. What could I say? She was in agony! Had she deluded herself into believing that these documents magically changed after she was legally married?

I was flesh of her flesh, and I felt her pain. The only way I could alleviate her agony was to avoid asking questions. Mixed feelings started swirling around inside me. I felt no impulse to touch or hold her. I wanted to relieve her anguish; it distressed me to see her suffer, but I didn't want to release her from her guilt.

I went to my room with the yellow piece of paper. I couldn't bring myself to look at it again, but I didn't have to. The words were emblazoned in my mind. "WILLIAM LLOYD INGRAM—FATHER: UNKNOWN." Who the hell was I? I surely wasn't this William Ingram. I was William Rose. This secret had been buried for fifteen years, and it would have to stay buried.

I placed the birth certificate with my old school papers and report cards. Then, I noticed my baptismal certificate—a clean and official-looking white card with gold-embossed lettering and my name in script: William Lloyd Rose. I thanked God. A baptismal certificate could be used for identification—as well as a birth certificate—when applying for a Social Security card. When signed up for summer work, I took out the freshly minted Social Security card of "WILLIAM L. ROSE." My secret was safe.

Picking tobacco was the only legitimate work for fourteen- and fifteen-year olds. Making eighty-five cents an hour seemed like a huge sum. We awakened before the crack of dawn and boarded the blue school bus as it made its stops around the Charter Oak Terrace and Rice Heights projects of the south end of Hartford. As the morning mist rose off the warming glades and meadows, our bus approached the fields of white muslin cloth as far as the eye could see. Beneath the white canopies were the young tobacco plants. The shade of the muslin cloth protected and nurtured them. Dirt roads divided the muslin fields and large sheds, barely seen in the distance. The fields were already alive with workers as we parked beside other long blue school buses with the name COLBRO on the sides.

Many of the Jamaicans and other West Indians came to the region specifically to work the tobacco fields. Laborers with particular skills and experience had nearly year-round employment in the industry. Charlie and I were summer help, a necessary evil. The "clipboard guy," who put us to work, had no respect for us or in our ability to perform. His job was to weed out the useless employees as soon as possible.

This clipboard-clasping supervisor had the calm arrogance of a benevolent dictator who knows he holds your fate in his hands. He was probably a college freshman or sophomore. With the aid of one of the veteran workers, he offered a quick primer on "suckering" tobacco plants. After the demonstration, he assigned rows to each of us and put us to work. We were given old potato sacks to set on the ground beneath our butts.

I tied my burlap sack around my waist. The dirt was smooth and cool as I slid along, rapidly picking off the small "sucker" leaves that were growing on the tobacco stalks. The "clipboard guy" watched and evaluated each of us in our rows. He waited at the other end of what had seemed like an endless row of plants, and quickly directed us to another row. Then, he wrote something on the clipboard.

The new boys learned quickly not to wipe the sweat from their brows with their bare hands, because the tobacco juice could mercilessly burn their eyes. Handkerchiefs and large bandanas were utilized to avoid that painful feeling. Exhausted after a long-day of toiling, our spirits buoyed as the bus cruised over the roads and highways to the south end of Hartford.

Finally home, I happily washed the dried sweat and caked dust from my tired body, ate heartily, and slept soundly. The alarm woke me the next morning in the pre-dawn darkness, and it was time to do it all over again. So this was the real world.

My first paycheck came the following week. It was a thrill to see my name typed on a COLBRO check. At eighty-five cents an hour, the pay wasn't enormous, but it seemed like a small fortune to me. I deposited most of my earnings in my passbook account. I proudly gave my mother some money and kept a bit for pocket change.

I didn't like the tobacco fields—the long, hot, merciless sun—or the bone-tiring work. This aversion should have inspired me to seek a higher education as an alternative to hard manual labor. Nevertheless, my plan was to look for a different way out.

————— • ◆ • —————

During this time, we were on public assistance and always waited anxiously for the first of each month to receive a welfare check in the mail. The few dollars I offered now and then paid a bill or bought groceries. We depended upon welfare assistance, a public program, but a personal shame to the growing number of families who needed it. A generation of people—who had endured the Great Depression and experienced war rationing—were among the groups seeking subsistence assistance from the state. They were proud and independent. On days when the mailman didn't deliver the check, we were completely crestfallen. We suffered humiliation when asking for an extension of credit at the grocery store where ma ran a tab. And it was demeaning—after filling a shopping cart with groceries—to hand the cashier a welfare check with identification.

I focused my smoldering resentment of our circumstances on my mother. In the good times, she overindulged us and herself without much discipline. Lean weeks would follow. During those lean weeks, she would often be at her best—creating meals from small bits of food and making a fun game of naming the new concoction.

Sometimes, she would be at her worst—hiding in her room and living on tea and medication. Her behavior was distressing, but her rationing meant we would have something to eat. When that welfare check finally arrived, we gleefully walked home from the First National Supermarket, laden with bags of staples and goodies. Let the good times roll.

——— • ◆ • ———

My grandmother was pleased and proud that I graduated from junior high school. During our summer visit, she made a special point of explaining to me the importance of a good education. She saw no reason why I wouldn't succeed in high school and go on to college like my Uncle Buddy. Grandmother chose this time to tell me that she started a college fund for me after my birth. She had no knowledge of my fall from grace during my final semester at Batchelder School. (I followed the family tradition of not sharing bad news.) I put that episode behind me and looked forward to starting fresh in high school.

——— • ◆ • ———

My transition to high school was not smooth. I didn't like anything about it. I felt forlorn and awkward as I wandered the wide corridors and busy classrooms. I signed up for the band with the hope that it would give me something familiar to restore my identity. I had become that small fish in this big pond!

Academically, my first semester performance was terrible. I was suffocating inside. I couldn't find my "oxygen level" at school or at home. My entire persona—that I had crafted and projected during my Batchelder School days—had been shattered. I didn't like recognizing myself as a lazy, lying cheater. I didn't know what to do with that awareness. I began to convince myself that I was different, that I was changing my life.

My failure to thrive showed in my grades; they were barely good enough to allow me to remain with the concert and marching bands. My first semester grades reflected my frustration with adjusting to high school. I only had the band as a distraction from my academics, so I couldn't blame poor grades on too many extracurricular activities.

Few of my Batchelder School bandmates, or even school acquaintances, attended Bulkeley. Absorbed into the high school student body, my old classmates and I no longer felt any special connection. Yet, the marching band offered a challenging and fun opportunity to perform at the school's football games. It afforded me a chance to connect with other students as well. However, if I did not bring up my grades, I could get booted out of the band. The band director made it clear that my weak grades could jeopardize my band eligibility.

As my first high school year progressed, a new magazine caught my attention: *Dog World*. I subscribed to the publication and received a large poster of all the AKC (American Kennel Club) recognized breeds. I hung the poster on my bedroom wall. Now, my aim was clear. I decided to become a veterinarian and write stories featuring animals (à la Jack London). I refocused my attention on learning in order to achieve this goal.

My grades began to show a marked improvement. In addition, I was included on a list of freshmen who showed the most academic progress since the first semester. My position in the band was assured. And I thought of upgrading from general studies classes to college preparatory courses. Attending Penn State University and its veterinary medicine school became my objective as an eventual destination.

———— • ◆ • ————

As the sixties magnified race relations in America, our situation in New England was under scrutiny as well. Black and white critics pointed to the North's de facto segregation in neighborhoods and school systems. The South's racism was more obvious because of Jim Crow laws and voter registration tests. But the Northeast's class consciousness overlaid its racism because it wasn't codified to exclude Negroes. Thus de facto segregation was only acknowledged because a light shined on it.

————•◆•————

"The NAACP Sucks" was written in black letters over the side entrance at Bulkeley High School. The message appeared after the first days of school, and it was removed after a short time.

————•◆•————

Sonny Liston had become the heavyweight boxing champion of the world by twice destroying Floyd Patterson in the ring—both triumphs in the first round! Sonny was a master intimidator and a brute who was reputed to have organized-crime ties. Unlike Floyd Patterson, Liston wasn't loved or respected by some American spectators. However, some fans viewed him as an American hero; they trusted in his potential ability to annihilate a brash young fighter from Louisville, Kentucky, who was hounding him for a title fight.

Cassius Clay ("The Louisville Lip") was everything many Americans—black and white—hated about the new generation of black youth. ("They don't know their place!") The young people were considered loud and irritating, too. In many ways, the loud-mouthed boxer and Olympic champion was a throwback to the first black heavyweight championship match with Jack Johnson.

Cassius Clay had the body of a great, well-muscled athlete, and the handsome good looks of a matinee idol. He was supremely confident in his boxing skills and his ability to outthink his opponent. This mix of self-assurance and brashness was dangerous for a Southern black man to brag about in the sixties. Clay was artful at boasting to the media and taunting Sonny Liston for a chance to take away his championship belt.

Cassius Clay versus Sonny Liston was more than just a "mating dance" between boxing promoters with the goal to stage a fight with huge box-office grosses. The match said a lot about race relations in America. One's philosophy on race was exposed by one's attitude toward either fighter. The Liston supporters liked his workman-like manner of climbing into the ring, staring down his opponents, and destroying them like an irresistible force of nature. Clay supporters liked his style and flash, both inside and outside the boxing ring; he never seemed to shut up. Clay's quick wit was something boxing fans and sports writers weren't accustomed to hearing from a pugilist. He projected an air of good-natured arrogance that emanated from fearlessness. Arguments bubbled up everywhere.

"I'd like to see that Clay get put in his place! I hope Liston shuts him up!"

"I want Cassius Clay to teach that old thug Liston a lesson."

I marveled at Clay's public persona, but felt that he had talked himself into an impossible dream. Despite his clever poetry of "float like a butterfly, sting like a bee," he was outgunned by "The Bear." (Liston was affectionately called this nickname by those who compared his embrace to that of an angry grizzly.)

I stayed up that night, listening to the fight on the radio; it took place in Miami, Florida. I wasn't a boxing fan, per se, but had watched some bouts on *Fight of the Week*; I was familiar with the general terminology and scoring of professional boxing. The tension building up to the match was like nothing I'd experienced. The fight announcers brought the blow-by-blow and color commentary into our imagination, so we could visualize the brutality and feel the tension. When the fight was over, Cassius Marcellus Clay was the new heavyweight champion of the world. The world was stunned. The new champion acknowledged that he had "shook up the world!" And indeed, he had.

Daddy visited at irregular intervals. He came by to see the kids, especially the youngest two (Manny and Sylvia). Sometimes, he gave mother a few dollars. Seeing the children was about all he did. He liked the contact with us, but wasn't very good at interaction. He viewed more things to criticize than to praise. Often, his visits were awkward and unsatisfying for all.

We were barely surviving financially. As a result, we looked forward to his visits on Saturday afternoons or school days, because he would reluctantly hand ma a few dollars. The welfare system of child support at its best barely met the basic needs of families, and the program was always resented by fathers for its intrusion into their financial lives. The regular withdrawals from their paychecks made it easier for them to appear to be diligent. However, the process tended to violate their manhood and fed a smoldering resentment toward the grasping hands of ex-wives and children.

———————•◆•———————

I started smoking a pipe. During walks with my dog, Princess, I felt the hunger for a new persona—an older, more mature character. As a future writer, I believed in my mind that pipe smoking symbolized this maturity.

My mother didn't understand my pipe smoking. Daddy had smoked a pipe for years, and now Charlie and I would smoke a pipe full of Cherry Blend tobacco as we watched our fishing lines dangle in the water or walked around the block with Princess.

Ma discovered a half pack of cigarettes I had purchased the year before. I was embarrassed by her discovery until the image of a deep-thinking writer, smoking a pipe full of a fragrant tobacco, seized my imagination. She didn't attempt to confront me over her discovery. As she only saw me with my pipe on rare occasions, she hoped the fascination would fade. The gulf between my mother and me was widening, and my new habit was a declaration of independence by me.

———————•◆•———————

I didn't respect any man enough to emulate or use as a positive role model. I evolved my own composite of the model male adult from ideals I drew from history, culture, books, and film. The Southwest Boys Club was strategically located among Rice Heights, Charter Oak Terrace, and the surrounding neighborhoods. The Boys Club felt like a home away from home. I joined while I attending Batchelder. I enjoyed hanging out and playing pool or other table games. I was intimidated by better and aggressive basketball players, so I avoided competing on the basketball court.

I joined the woodworking class at the club and impressed the instructor with my knowledge from shop class at high school. The teacher named me vice president of our woodworking class. As vice president, I was a sort-of mentor to other kids who had no shop experience. I looked forward to our classes and took pride in my role as a helper; I enjoyed the knowledge I was acquiring in class. At the end of our project season, we were awarded jackets with the Boys Club logo, and I wore mine proudly. I had started something and followed through without quitting for the first time I could remember.

————— • ◆ • —————

For my fifteenth birthday, I got a gift I didn't expect: the Visible Dog. The small-scale model of a dog featured a clear plastic body through which all of its organs could be viewed. I was delighted with it! The parts could be assembled and disassembled as a learning tool. I'm sure my mother and grandmother wanted to encourage my interest in veterinary medicine.

Aside from the thrill of receiving the Visible Dog, turning fifteen was unspectacular. If anything, I felt more burdened by turning fifteen. I believed more would be expected of me, but my fears and inner turmoil were reemerging. I spent a lot of time alone in my room, reading and listening to my transistor radio. I stopped going to Sunday school and church. I was like the rest of my friends, free to sleep late and later decide what to indulge in for the rest of the day.

————— • ◆ • —————

Before the end of the 1965 school year, I applied for a summer job; I was accepted as a student assistant with the janitorial staff. These few positions usually went to kids from poor or underprivileged families. This summer job would pay $1.25 per hour for slightly less than a forty-hour work week. I was happy about the employment, because it paid more than working tobacco. In addition, the job would be a lot cleaner and easier.

I reported for work soon after classes ended. It was a strange feeling to walk into classrooms that were completely empty with desks lining the corridors. All of the janitorial and maintenance crews moved to day shift for the summer. Some workers were assigned to supervise us. Our first jobs were mindless—removing wads of chewing gum from the undersides of desks or scraping built-up wax from classroom floors.

Eventually, I had the opportunity to use a rotary scrubber/buffer machine. This versatile piece of equipment was tricky to navigate with its side-to-side motion. Once mastered, it could be operated easily with just one hand.

The janitors and maintenance crews had the summer cleaning and restoration routines down to a science. They worked at a steady but leisurely pace, which was fine with us. I had plenty of time to socialize or daydream while performing simple tasks.

I became a cigarette smoker that summer. I liked the routine of work, coffee and cigarette breaks. A time out from work without a coffee cup or cigarette in your hand was impossible to justify in the working world. I retired my set of pipes and tobacco to my smoker's pouch and adopted cigarettes as my symbol of liberation.

That summer I read more than ever. We always had an assortment of books at home, and I also frequented the library. My great love was history, and for a time, historical novels. I devoured those books and longed desperately to escape into a dimension where I was fearless and heroic. *The Iliad*, Homer's tale of the events of the Trojan War, and *The Odyssey*, were my favorites. I read these stories in school, and did more in-depth reading of them on my own.

———— ◆ ————

The real world seemed mired in hopelessness. Wars, rumors of wars, fears, loathing, injustice, and outrage were growing everywhere. America's war efforts in Vietnam were in the news during the summer of 1965. The anxiety and outrage over an incident in the Gulf of Tonkin gave the Johnson administration the leverage it needed to strengthen our position in the theater of operations. Although the fervor over the Gulf of Tonkin Resolution ensured that the Vietnam conflict would remain above-the-fold, in all the major newspapers, the act settled into a type of low-level background noise.

The true horrors of war and depth of mans' inhumanity to man began to penetrate my boyhood delusion. I read more modern history, especially books about the hideous regime that had come to power in Germany, plunged Europe into total war, and nearly came to dominate the world! That was chilling enough, but I also read a book by a Jewish doctor who alleged he had been coerced by Nazis in a concentration camp to perform unimaginable operations and experiments on fellow Jewish prisoners! His book, among others, recounted the horrors of camp life and the systematic destruction of human beings! How could the world have come that close to total darkness?

———— ◆ ————

I could see the need for some discipline in our lives. We lived from welfare check to welfare check. The first two weeks of each new month, after the mailman delivered our check, we were in good shape. Some outstanding bills were paid, and most importantly, the refrigerator and cabinets were stocked with food. By the third week of the month, we were forced to limit our meals to a few remaining staples. By the final week, unless nana sent money or daddy came by with cash for groceries, we subsisted on extended credit.

I resented the feast or famine life we were enduring. I was ashamed of the crush of poverty on our lives. I pretended to enjoy sharing half of my pay check from my summer job. However, I was not happy to see my small amount of money come and go so quickly. I resented helping to sustain a lifestyle I was beginning to disapprove of.

I took long walks, sometimes with my dog Princess, but usually alone. I'd get a couple of hamburgers, French fries, and a shake—stuff myself—and slowly walk home. With each mouthful, my silent rage diminished as I literally ate my emotions.

Whatever ma fixed for dinner was OK with me. I could eat or not eat, because I was already satisfied. I also had potato chips and candy bars stashed in my room for my long hours of reading. If the family had pork chops, chicken, or lamb patties, I could eat a normal portion and not be seen as the glutton I secretly was. If there wasn't much on the dinner table, I simply made a baloney sandwich or heated a bowl of soup to be contented.

I felt proud when I realized that I had saved some money, in spite of helping out with groceries and indulging my cravings for junk food and comic books. I tried to ensure that we had lunch meat and bread when money was tight, because I ate these sandwiches at work. If I was disciplined at saving money—notwithstanding my excesses—why couldn't my mother manage things better? Instead of the endless feast-or-famine rollercoaster, we could avoid begging for money from nana or daddy with a little more spending discipline. And we could stop asking for credit at the small grocers.

Ma was sitting in the living room chair, where only a year before she had given me my birth certificate. She rarely sat in the living room; she was only perched there because the mail had arrived. She was jotting down a few things for the shopping list. The State of Connecticut welfare check lay on her lap. Happy days were here again!

The shopping list was just a formality. A short list of necessities she didn't want to forget. Once in the supermarket, an overwhelming array of items begged to be placed in her cart. Ma indulged herself and us with items we didn't need. After all, this abundant time was like a Holiday.

I felt a surge of power and self-control as I approached my mother. "Ma, why don't you give me some money from the check, and I'll put it in my savings account," I said conversationally. "That way, you won't get into trouble with the welfare system for saving money, and we'll have cash for the end of the month," I ended on an upbeat note.

There was silence as she continued to stare at her shopping list. I thought I was being clever by giving her a legitimate excuse for never seriously saving money before. The welfare system seemed more like a web than a net to those trapped or saved by it. Since my tiny savings account wasn't under any scrutiny, we could stash cash in it and never be destitute again, I believed.

I was encouraged by her stillness. Maybe she was giving my offer serious consideration. I rushed on. "And we can't be getting cookies and other junk food for a while, until we save some money," I said boldly.

Ma looked at me with a stare that almost stopped my heart! Her eyes were aflame with rage, and her mouth and jaw tightened. She was carefully measuring her words. "We don't get enough money to save anything," she spat. Her gaze intensified as if I were an enemy. "Don't you try to tell me how to spend money for this house," she said forcefully. "You're not grown yet!'

"I just want to help!" I shot back defensively. "Ma, you got to be tougher on the kids! You can't let them have cookies, candy, chips, and other stuff we can't afford."

"You had it, William," she said fiercely, "and they can have it, too!"

"I don't mean never," I tried to restate my assertion. "I just mean you have to manage the money better and…."

"Don't argue with me," she cut me off with a dramatic gesture. "We don't ever get enough to save," she said as she gathered her things around her and stuffed them into her handbag. "Don't think you're grown, William," she said. "Don't argue with me," she added with finality.

I replayed that scene over and over in my mind as I sat on my bed. I could feel the bite of her words as they echoed in my head. I lit a cigarette to help me calm down. I looked at my hands; they were still shaking from memory of the confrontation. I was forced by my own anger to ceaselessly replay the words we had spoken.

A frightening sense of dread enveloped me as the thought that I hated my mother fluttered through my mind. I was terrified by that thought! How could I? What kind of person would have such a thought? Wasn't it only natural to love your mother? Where did that terrifying thought come from, and why was I so suddenly tormented by it? Worse yet, what if I hated us both?

Dark Daze

I was in a bad place, in my head, for the rest of that summer. I withdrew from my family and friends even more. I spent hours alone in my room or on long walks when not working. My brother, Junior, wasn't around during this turmoil. Junior went through his own act-ing-out episodes after daddy moved out; he was more outwardly rebellious than me. Because his juvenile antics were beyond control, he was sent away to a reformatory called Junior Republic. I remember daddy taking us to visit him one summer Sunday afternoon. Junior showed us around the compound with one of his arms in a cast. It was strange visiting him there. Though he and I weren't as close as we could have been, we missed being together.

My dark moods troubled me, but I was helpless. They descended on me like fog. I could see parts of myself that were like my mother. These traits were reflected in my loquaciousness, friendly banter, and dry wit that left people surprised and laughing. Though I knew my mother's mood swings could be sudden and treacherous, I was also dealing with a part of myself that I didn't understand.

My mother said that my father was a moody loner who had died from a drug overdose. That fact was all I had. I was afraid to ask for more information. Once in a while, I'd catch myself wondering what he was like. How did he sound and move? How personable and engaging was he? Then, I'd get a chill when I thought of the demons that must have tormented him. He died of a drug overdose! Wasn't that really suicide? What if he gave in to the impulse to stop the tormenters and escape his demons with a little extra dose of whatever he was using? What if those same demons were here for me?

———— • ◆ • ————

I bought a used small black-and-white, portable TV. I put it in my bedroom, where I was spending most of my time when I was home. My mother seemed to be coping with this change. She'd send one of the younger kids upstairs to tell me when supper was ready. If it was something I wanted, I'd come down, fill a plate, and withdraw to my room. Few words were said between us since our big confrontation over who should be the head of our family.

I rejected her meals more often, and frequently, bought my own. Like an angry child, I felt that rejecting my mother's food was tantamount to rejecting her power and influence over me. I considered it liberating to spend my own money and eat in my room by the light of my little TV. I had little concern for the pain I caused her.

———— • ◆ • ————

By the middle of August, I was bored with my summer job. I yielded to my dark moods and a streak of laziness. I convinced my mother to take my siblings to our grandmother's as usual. I would stay home and continue working with Mrs. Pitt looking in on me during the week. A couple of days after the family departed, I lied to my boss at work. I said I had a scheduled family vacation to New York. The rest of that week I pretended to work while I was really just hanging out away from home.

———— • ◆ • ————

I knew I could have quit school at sixteen, but I rejected that idea. My goal of becoming a veterinarian was fading. Everything seemed to require work and a serious commitment that I didn't want to make. I was adrift, seeking the path of least resistance.

The mind-numbing routine of school drove me along. I dropped out of the school concert and marching bands, because I had no transportation to attend practices. When the clock said it was 2:10 p.m. at the conclusion of the school day, students erupted from the building and anxiously lit cigarettes. It was our declaration of independence and quest for adulthood.

———— • ◆ • ————

Daddy asked me if I'd like to make extra money picking apples that fall. He invited me to stay overnight at his place, because we would leave early. Ma agreed to the arrangement. Soon I was sitting in his kitchen eating supper. We never had time together like this before. It wasn't long before we talked about the only subject we really had in common—my mother, his wife.

He explained how he couldn't live in the chaos and turmoil that existed at our Chandler Street home. I understood and nodded in agreement. We shook our heads in disgust as we agreed ma was a hopeless mess. I still felt her outrage at my attempt to control our spending, so I was enthusiastic in condemning the way she ran the household.

I agreed that ma wasn't a good housekeeper and that the other kids were confused by her mood swings and sicknesses—both real and imagined. Daddy desired to justify his leaving the family. He wanted an ally who would validate his decision.

———————— • ◆ • ————————

Anthony was a neighborhood boy. He was about a year older than me and exuded confidence that I envied. He was friendly, good-looking, and had a pleasant personality. He needed someone to double date with him and a girl he was smitten with. The girl, Sophia, would not go out with Anthony unless her younger sister accompanied them as an escort.

Anthony had confidence that I could handle this assignment, because I had become very friendly with a former girlfriend of his. Anthony came over to our house several times to use the phone in my bedroom to call Phyllis. In his mind, he had moved beyond Phyllis. Yet, she was desperate to remain in contact with him. Once, she called our phone number looking for Anthony, and we had a conversation. We were instantly simpatico with each other. We were two lonely and confused teenagers, seeking understanding and affection. Our first talks were about Anthony. Then, we explored each other's hopes and desires; Anthony was never a topic again.

Phyllis and I spoke almost every evening, and I seriously began to doubt that she had ever been sexual with Anthony. She shared much about herself, without revealing everything. She admitted to being heavier than she wanted to be, not very pretty, and not that smart in school. We contested each other's low self opinions. I loved the sound of her voice and laughter. I was a good listener, and she liked that. My natural empathy grew as we talked, and she enjoyed my insight into some of her problems with family and friends. We were like best friends, as we shared secrets and encouraged each other's dreams.

Our contact went no further than the coiled cord of the telephone. We talked of meeting each other, and even scheduled a date, but it was postponed at the last minute by Phyllis. I was secretly relieved, because I feared her disappointment at actually seeing me. However, I was excited to meet her, and I dreamed that perhaps we were soul mates. I liked being liked by her. I wanted female validation and affection.

Anthony, on the other hand, was not pleased that Phyllis and I had become friendly—if only over the telephone. I could see our relationship upset him when I mentioned her. He was jealous that his so called cast-off might actually develop a relationship with me.

With Anthony's chances to date Sophia fading unless he could find an escort for her sister, he turned to me. Anthony didn't consider me a threat for Sophia and hoped I'd enjoy a few hours with her sister. I pumped him for information about this girl, but he proved as evasive as he had been when describing Phyllis. Still, I was thrilled and terrified by the imminent prospect of an actual date with a flesh-and-blood girl. My conversations with Phyllis emboldened me to believe that I could actually hold a girl's interest romantically and that I could be a good blind date. I made certain my mother knew that not only was I talking to Phyllis regularly on the phone, but also that I might actually be dating another girl soon.

Anthony and I took the city bus to the girls' house, a three-family wood structure on a pleasant street in Hartford. Anthony finally admitted to me that he had never met the sister, but he was sure she wasn't a "dog"—a terrible expression used by boys to describe a less-than-attractive girl.

The plan was to take the girls to a movie and a restaurant for pizza. They would be home before 9 p.m. We waited nervously on the family's porch. Promptly, the girls appeared, and the mystery was over. Cleo, the sister, was as homely as Sophia was lovely. The contrast was dramatic.

Sophia was stunning! Even without comparison to her sister, she looked like the beautiful models featured in *Jet* magazine. The girls were the same height with similar slender builds. Sophia was a beautiful young woman with milk chocolate skin and eyes and lips like a cover girl. She stood confidently on her well-turned legs.

The girls' mother appeared to look us over, and we introduced ourselves. Their mother was lovely, and there was no doubt where

Sophia had gotten her good looks. Cleo was stealing glances at us with her most appealing feature—her large, doe-like eyes.

Our date proceeded; I attempted to draw out Cleo with small talk. I was sure my conversational skills were the reason Anthony wanted me along. I was an introvert most of the time, but when my extroverted persona was on, I was "Mr. Congeniality" again. I had a knack for making people feel comfortable with me. Cleo proved extremely shy and reserved, and I wondered if any of my efforts were worth it. Sophia was relaxed and pleasant, but was sensitive to her sister's awkwardness.

After the movie, as we waited for pizza, Anthony gave into a silly mood. It was one of those moods that overcome adolescent boys when under stress. He'd been holding back his jokes since meeting Cleo. Everything seemed funny or had a double meaning, and his laughter can become infectious. Admittedly, I laughed at Anthony's one liners and craziness, but the girls were barely amused. Our awkward double date degenerated into suppressed laughter and Anthony's veiled references to my being stuck with a pork chop. (A cruel reference to a girl so ugly, that her parents must tie a pork chop around her neck so the family dog will play with her!) Our high jinx was thoughtless, mean, and truly revealed more about us.

After we took the sisters home and said our good nights, we totally gave into the laughter. I held my side as I laughed and cried. With great relief, I had survived my first date. Although, Anthony was dismayed that he had probably sabotaged any chances of seeing Sophia again.

———— •◆• ————

As winter's grip chilled Hartford in 1965, I found new depths of despair. I felt like I was suffocating and slowly being strangled by my home life and school. Public education held me like a prisoner, force-feeding me pointless lessons. Dreams of becoming an animal doctor vaporized. I saw no purpose to the struggle to become something or someone. I was too proud to ask for help. My pride hardened and poisoned my attitude toward everything.

Maybe I couldn't have been reached. Maybe I was beyond help. In either event, I turned my angry impulses upon myself. Cigarettes were my symbol of rebellion. I needed their help to cope with each day of life, in the classroom and out.

When I was summoned to the vice-principal's office at the beginning of school one day, I was caught totally off guard. I was confronted with the fact that I smoked a cigarette while on school property. This practice had become commonplace for smoking students. We began lighting up as soon as we exited the building.

The vice principal reminded us that a notice was circulated, stating that the administration was enforcing no-smoking rules on school property. I was to be among the first violators punished! We were given demerits to go into our records and a few hours of detention after school.

I chafed at this punishment. I felt like a victim of injustice as I sat with the other violators in detention until 3 p.m. I won the admiration of some classmates for having gotten into trouble; my conviction tarnished my nice-guy image. I was another boy who didn't like being pushed around by the school system. Consequently, I won the admiration of fools and troublemakers. I didn't want to believe that I belonged to either group.

Once I had a bad name, I got trapped into playing the game. I went from virtual invisibility to being a problem child with one flick of a match! My seventeenth birthday passed, and my descent into madness continued. I had little contact with family and friends as I purposely sought isolation. Even my telephone sessions with Phyllis were less frequent.

Then, in a moment of mindless stupidity, a teacher witnessed me lighting a cigarette before leaving school property. I dreaded the following day, and sure enough, the next morning I was cited: a three-day suspension. I was outraged! It hadn't been an intentional violation! It was barely a violation at all. A few more feet, and I would have crossed the street to relative safety.

There was no appeal. I was sure I was a victim of oppressive enforcement of a heavy-handed policy. I left my suspension paper on the kitchen table and sulked in my room. I was fuming with resentment at the injustice of it all! Here I was, falling from grace again, as I had in eighth grade. This time, I had the power to stop the madness. I could get out before I was squeezed by the system. I kept that thought to myself.

My mother hoped that by her *not* making a big thing out of it, I'd regain a proper perspective and return to school with a new attitude. I realized that I didn't have to go back to school—not that school or any school. The idea of quitting seemed easy, but the ability to survive in the working world appeared painful.

A truant officer dropped by the house, unannounced, when I didn't report to school. He offered a final opportunity for me to return. I refused the offer. My mother wept angrily over my decision. I remained stubborn, as they tried to change my mind. In my room, I formulated a plan in my fevered brain. I would move in with daddy and get a job. That was as far as my strategy extended, but I felt it was a beginning. I would get away from the three things that were destroying my life: high school, Charter Oak Terrace, and my mother!

————•◆•————

Anthony's visit surprised me. I was so engrossed in my meltdown that little else interested me. We talked and smoked in my room. I only half listened as he rambled about some new girlfriend. He showed me a condom, or "rubber" as he called it, and told me that he bought it because his girl insisted. He lamented that she had no faith in his strategy of premature withdrawal.

I'd heard of "rubbers," but I'd never seen one. Now I was holding the foil, wafer-like wrapper in my hands; I looked it over. Anthony said I could keep that one, and he advised me to store it in my wallet in case the need arose. The pun was intended!

I shared my plans with him regarding moving out of the house and getting a job. He was surprised to learn that I had quit school. Then, Anthony became very excited by the opportunity that presented itself. He announced that he was joining the Marine Corps. He told me that he met with a recruiter. If I joined him, we could practice the buddy system during basic training. Anthony was very enthusiastic and persuasive.

The shallowness of male relationships had kept the real Anthony undiscovered. If I delved beneath the gloss of his personality, I would have encountered a teen, similar to myself, lost in a world of confusing contradictions.

Anthony's timing was fortuitous. Recently, I finished reading a novel entitled, *Battle Cry*. The book was about a group of marines fighting in the Pacific during World War II. I was impressed by the historic aura that surrounded the image of the US Marines as a superior-fighting force. I listened attentively to Anthony's winning arguments encouraging me to join with him. He had a strong sense of urgency, because the recruitment window was closing. I would have to go downtown to the recruitment office, take a test, and sign up. Anthony assured me that I could join, despite being seventeen-years-old.

I agreed to check it out. I wasn't very enthusiastic, but Anthony had enough enthusiasm for both of us. Upon acceptance, I decided to keep silent until we were officially enlisted. I couldn't let myself think beyond that point.

The Marine Corps recruiter confirmed what Anthony told me. We would indeed be accepted on the buddy system and complete basic training together. I could get my GED (high school equivalency credential) in the Marine Corps after my high-school class graduated. We would be taught a specialty skill to be used in the service and beyond.

I was still reluctant to join. A four-year commitment to the marines required a parent's signature, because I was seventeen. That seemed like a long shot. Only my mother needed to be convinced; she was my only obstacle. My future seemed bleak no matter which direction I looked. Because of the pleas from Anthony and encouragement of the recruiter, I opted for the only path that offered potential glory.

After being accepted by the recruiter, Anthony and I were scheduled to take a general intelligence test and a basic physical exam. Depending on those results, the recruiter would visit my mother; he would obtain her signature to authorize my enlistment and secure my place in basic training before the end of May.

As rumors of an unwinnable war in Southeast Asia incited draft-card burnings, joining the mostly volunteer USMC seemed bold and patriotic. I used these arguments to convince my mother that this was what I really wanted.

Anthony and I were tested. Eagerly, we waited for our test results. We looked forward to our official swearing in and departure for Marine Corps Boot Camp.

I couldn't believe what I was hearing! Anthony was talking, but my mind had stopped listening. He said he flunked the basic IQ test for induction! What did this mean? How could he fail the aptitude test? This was all his idea! His dream! Was his dream becoming my nightmare?

"Damn it!" I cried inwardly. This couldn't be happening! I knew it was painfully real, though I searched his face for a hint that he was teasing. As we stood outside the recruiter's office, Anthony explained that he could take the test again. However, he wouldn't make this training cycle. There would be no buddy system for us. Anthony didn't appear as upset as I was.

The recruiting sergeant called me into his office. He looked sharp with a fresh crew cut, looking every inch like a recruiting poster. He repeated to me what he had told Anthony about failing the test. Confidently, he noted that I would follow through with my intentions. How did he know I felt obligated? Did he realize that I told everyone I was leaving soon for some place called Parris Island, South Carolina? He said he would come by the next day to get my mother's signature, granting her permission for me to be inducted. Then, I would attend the swearing-in ceremony with the other Connecticut recruits.

I was angry with Anthony for placing me in this position. Damn him! I didn't know what to do. I felt cornered like never before. "I'll show him," I stewed silently.

The recruiter looked out of place in our shabby apartment as he hovered over my mother when she signed the paperwork. The following day, I stood at attention before the American flag and repeated the oath of allegiance. We were given our first written orders before boarding the train for the Marine Corps Recruit Depot in Parris Island, South Carolina.

Daddy came by the house the day before my departure. I felt strange and uncomfortable, as I was carried along by events. We visited our friends, Charlie and Paul; their father invited us to step into his living room. He produced glasses and a bottle of whiskey. He poured a couple-of-fingers worth into each glass, and we held them in the air for a toast.

"Now you're a man," daddy said after fumbling for something to say. We touched glasses and I took a sip of the strong liquor that so many men craved. They laughed as I screwed my face into a pained expression at the taste of the alcohol.

It was an eerie scene as we stood there, awkwardly trying to give the moment some deep significance. The moment should have been perfect, but it was forced. Neither of the fathers had any real insight or advice about life or manhood. They were each, in his own way, concealing disappointment with life. Perhaps, it was a noble thing that they didn't want to discourage me about my life or future. Maybe it was important for them to have optimism for the young breathing life into their fading dreams. The moment passed. We said our good-byes, shook hands, and parted.

CHAPTER 5

THE ROAD RUNNER

January 1967

I wasn't dressed for travel on the highway. If the unseasonably warm January weather turned bad, I'd be in trouble. It was already late in the day to begin hitchhiking, but I was determined to put distance between me and the Washington DC bus terminal.

Short rides were all I could score from commuters and short-haul truckers. Virginia turned into West Virginia. Up and down, throughout the night, I slowly made my way across the panhandle, through the full width of the state, and toward Parkersburg. From my studies of the American Civil War, I remembered that these counties broke away from the Commonwealth of Virginia to form the State of West Virginia.

These mountainous counties were peopled by hearty folk and proud clans who determinedly scratched out a living from the land; they did this without vast plantations that required legions of slave labor. The Mason-Dixon Line was real. At one time, it was agreed upon by the nation to separate North from South—free states from slave states—by creating this line. I planned a route that avoided the Deep South where I believed I had my best chance of avoiding danger, or worse. By morning, I crossed the Parkersburg Bridge into Ohio.

While West Virginia was hilly and mountainous, Ohio was flat. Its wide, green expanses glistened in the morning dew, and made easy traversing along US 50. I was tired and sleepy, but rejuvenated by the daylight and the friendly folks. Something was happening that I had never experienced. Although we did not make eye contact, people drove by me offering simple waves of their hands. I found this gesture extraordinary, and soon was waving back.

I had crossed most of West Virginia by moonlight and didn't view the friendly "hello" gestures as I did in Ohio. However, I'm pretty sure that many of the folks were just as demonstrative to the dark figure, moving along the side of the dim-lit road.

I needed a story to tell drivers who gave me rides, so I expanded on my budding-author, fantasy persona. If they inquired about what I was up to, I said I was gathering material for a book. I had a working title of *The Road Runner*. To my seventeen-year-old mind, I felt my fantasy was plausible. I tried to make my story believable. I relayed that I was only hitchhiking to gather material. Most people seemed to take what I said in stride and were probably happy that I was friendly.

I had no ultimate plan or goal. No final destination. My short-term goal was Route 66. That fabled road became forever immortalized by the popular TV show. The alluring romance of the American Southwest was beckoning me to explore, and maybe lose myself, in that part of our country.

Cincinnati was big and noisy, after traveling through southern Ohio's small towns along Highway 50. My last ride suggested I stay at the downtown YMCA where I could get a meal and a bed for only a few dollars. I had to be careful with my money, because I had no idea how long my supply would last or I would get more when it was gone.

The Cincinnati Y was bustling with activity. I enjoyed it there, as I melded with other men of all ages and races. I gathered important bits of information from these transients. Some of these people were a semi-permanent underclass that preferred living on the margins of society.

One helpful thing I learned was that police and sheriff departments would allow a transient to sleep in an empty jail cell over night. The following morning, one would be sent on his way with no questions asked. This courtesy was perhaps left over from the days when distressed and displaced men roamed the country's highways and railroads, searching for work, a meal, or a helping hand before the next stop.

Highway 50 stretched out before me across the level flat lands of southern Indiana. Long-haul truckers and long-distance drivers became my main transportation for however long they journeyed along that road. Truck drivers became my best hope for rides, and offered a keen look into the soul of American workers. These drivers were always men and mostly white in 1966. As now, they often had their finger on the pulse of the country in ways that pundits and politicians seldom do. The highways, byways, small towns, and big cities that they drove in, around, over, and through, were where real people lived their lives. These men drove for long, lonely hours to deliver goods across the breadth of the nation. They were like river-boat captains along blacktop rivers that throbbed with America's life blood—commerce!

Truck stops were more than just a place to get a cup of coffee and a hot meal, they were also transient think tanks. Here, folks could exchange ideas and ideals about current events in friendly and lively discussions. With its ever-present country-and-western music, guys with big rigs—wearing cowboy boots and big belt buckles—would light down on stools and chairs, philosophizing about all sorts of topics.

I was usually the only black face around, but few acted as if they minded. Some of the truckers paid for my sandwiches or bowls of chili. Others helped me secure rides further along my route.

Indiana faded in the rearview mirror as I passed through small towns and open spaces. Crossing the Wabash River into Southern Illinois, I noted that the level lay of the land never changed. I was making good time, and for January, the weather was still mild. I had barely any contact with local police or state troopers, except occasionally, when I was told not to hitchhike along a certain stretch of road. I looked neat and carried myself like I knew where I was going. Most importantly, I was always respectful.

During the mid-sixties, the hippie movement came of age. Many citizens in that first wave of "baby boom" children openly rejected

American society and its values. College and university students were in the vanguard of the movement. They claimed contempt for the growing "military industrial complex" of the United States; although it gave these students all they cherished and protected them when they rebelled. Student protests against the war in Vietnam grew louder. The Midwestern states were dotted with colleges and students; hence, one "colored" boy, hitching a ride, wasn't unusual.

I boldly asked small-town police chiefs or sheriffs for permission to stay in empty cells overnight. They granted permission, if they had a bed. Most officers didn't ask questions, and I didn't answer more than asked.

I wondered, years later, if people were kind to me, because their sons or daughters were away from home. Perhaps they hoped their kindness to a needy soul might somehow ensure that their loved one's needs were being met by a helpful stranger.

———— • ◆ • ————

The St. Louis Gateway Arch dominated the skyline of the city. It was a recent addition to the St. Louis riverfront, and it had been mentioned in worldwide newscasts for its unique boldness. As I rode through the city, I stared at its graceful arc against the background of the blue sky. I was actually viewing the entryway to the West.

I rode with a young, white fellow, named John, in his pale, blue Volkswagen Beetle on Route 66. Route 66! Another landmark! That storied road of magical adventure, leisurely stretched out before us. I could almost hear strains of the popular theme music from the TV show as the VW's tires cruised over the blacktop.

John was headed to Phoenix, Arizona. I felt lucky that this young man pulled over and offered me a ride as soon as he spotted me. For the time being, Phoenix seemed as good a destination as any.

John was slightly older than me, and I gathered he was leaving school after being placed on academic probation. He departed the university in a rage and was now in jeopardy of losing his military deferment. John was going home, unannounced, and unsure what to expect.

John had a little more money than I did. He was noticeably anxious about making it home on his short funds, so we ate as cheaply as possible and slept in the car. This ride was my first time in a Volkswagen; after observing the growth in the car's popularity in the US since the early 60s, I had wanted to ride in one. Although, on the streets of Hartford, we used to gawk at them and laugh.

John thought that I could help with the driving. That sounds strange now, but at that time, there was a spirit of youthful trust. I had no driver's license and since VWs had standard transmissions, I was at a loss as to how to drive one.

We learned to stop often and unfold ourselves from the tight confines of the VW. That's when I missed the roomier cabs of the Mack's, Whites, and Peterbilts the long-haul truckers drove. The odometer turned as the miles clicked by. I looked out the window and watched America pass. What an awesome country this was!

Tulsa, Oklahoma City, and Amarillo all eventually were in the rearview mirror. There were long, lonely stretches of Route 66; it shimmered in the distance as the warm desert sun danced over the blacktop highway. "Last gas for 130 miles!" "Next gas 90 miles!" Signs screamed from the sides of the road to warn drivers.

I knew I was flat broke. I had been since Oklahoma City. I didn't know John was tapped out, too, until he stopped the car in a shabby section of Albuquerque, New Mexico. We parked in front of a blood bank, and John told me the facts of life. He had sold blood before. He insisted that it was strictly voluntary on my part. Although, if we each got five bucks for our blood, we might be able to get to Phoenix. Even he wasn't convinced, but he tried to sound upbeat.

"This is plan B," he said jokingly, as we got in line outside the building.

William or Bill was always the name I gave when asked, but I had begun experimenting with different last names. At the blood bank, I used the name I gave John: Kinkade, William Kinkade. It sounded strange to me, of course, but I made myself play the part.

I had blood drawn before and never enjoyed the experience, but we were desperate. I felt like I owed him at least the five dollars in blood money, so I agreed to help. We registered and waited to be called. The room was crowded with men who appeared to be a cross section of the region: two blacks, a few Indians, several Mexicans, and a number of white men. All had traces of desperation in their eyes, and at that early hour, the odor of alcohol.

William Kinkade was called, so I followed a nurse into a cubicle and lay on a gurney. Thankfully, she found a vein quickly, and slipped the needle under my skin. I watched as my blood slowly flowed into a plastic bag. As the bag filled, it rocked back and forth beside the gurney.

In short order, we completed our blood donating and filled up on juice and cookies. We were each given five dollars in cash. John pumped five-dollars worth of the cheapest gas (around twenty-five cents per gallon) into the VW. My five bucks would be used at our next stop, we agreed.

Our next stop came before the VW's engine warmed up. The bug suddenly lost power and John steered toward the side of the road. We sat there for a moment in silent disbelief. He tried to get the engine to spring to life, but it wouldn't respond. We got out and opened the engine compartment in the rear. Our emergency flashers warned the passing motorists that we were experiencing trouble. The smell coming from the engine revealed that our trouble might be serious. An Albuquerque police car pulled up behind us and assessed the situation. The officer said we had to move the car immediately. He radioed for a tow truck to an imported car-repair facility nearby.

We waited for almost two hours until the service manager walked over to John. The fuel pump had died, the engine was seized, and major repair work was required. Parts and repairs could take a week. He gave John an estimate for repairs and wanted to know his decision soon. John already knew what he would have to do. He walked into the manager's office and made a collect call to his parents.

I watched as John talked and nodded his head. His shoulders slumped and his face was sad. I resigned myself to the fact that our time together had come to an end. Amidst the sadness, a look of relief appeared on John's face as he handed the telephone to the service manager and walked over to me. His father gave the OK for the repairs; he was wiring enough money for the deposit on repairs and a one-way bus ticket to Phoenix. When the car was ready, they would drive to retrieve it.

John admitted to his dad that he was chastened by his experience. He promised he'd buckle down and return to school. He apologized for not being able to help me farther along. We said our good-byes and wished each other luck. I walked quickly from the repair shop to the main road.

It was early afternoon when I started walking along the highway. I caught rides going south and was soon passing through a town called Truth or Consequences. A beat-up looking pickup truck with a black man behind the wheel pulled over, and he offered me a lift. The man was going to a place called Deming. He said he was surprised to see a "colored" stranger on this road. His name was Shake, and he extended a hand in greeting. He had been to Las Cruces to get supplies for the Saturday-night party he was hosting.

Shake assured me that I was welcome to attend the party, spend the night, and leave the next morning. The thought of sleeping in a horizontal position, after being cramped in a VW bug, was irresistible. He steered his pickup onto the large dusty driveway beside a trailer home on the outskirts of Deming. There were a few other trailers along the road, but his was the largest. It featured an addition that formed the main entrance. Shake introduced me to his wife, his brother, and his cousin. With R & B music playing in the background, they were busily arranging things for the festivities.

Various sizes of tables ringed the room. A bar area was set up outside the kitchen, and a large jukebox was off to one side. In retrospect, I guess this was a juke joint, a Southern black establishment that featured informal entertainment.

Shake's brother gave me some clothes to wear and a pair of dress shoes. I even got clean underwear. With his running commentary and infectious laugh, his brother was easy to like. I gleaned from him that Shake and Gloria supplemented their income with these weekly parties. I offered to help and was put to work setting out platters of food on a long buffet table. The sun set as people arrived and paid money to Cousin George at the door. They brought brown bags with bottles of liquor or beer.

I wondered at the interesting circumstances that produced an enclave of black folks, living in the desert of the American Southwest. The American history we learned in school never talked about black cowboys or the thousands of "colored" pioneer families that left the Old South and travelled west.

After my stomach was full, I listened to the music and conversation. I fought to stay awake, but without much success. When I slipped between the cool sheets on the bed, I could still hear and feel the beat of the music as I drifted off to sleep.

The following day, I walked quickly down the dusty road toward the highway and started walking south. I was thankful no one had awakened as I washed and dressed. I didn't want to say anymore than I already had about writing a book on America as I hitchhiked. These people had been kind to me, and I didn't like deceiving them about my true circumstances.

I didn't take anything to eat or drink. I was traveling light. In short order, I was riding next to a fellow; we were heading toward a small town on the US side of the border. He dropped me off when he made his turn along the main road. I continued south along the sandy road that was warming rapidly with the morning sun. It was going to be a hot January day.

The border did not feature an outpost or guard building, as I had imagined. There wasn't a noticeable marker or sign that announced United States-Mexico division, but the road changed drastically. It suddenly became uneven and full of potholes.

"Third world" wasn't a term I was familiar with back then, but I definitely stepped into another world! The landscape began to seem more arid and dusty everywhere I looked. I decided to cut across a fenced-off area, where the enclosure was poorly maintained and had fallen. I thought I should stay off the road, but remain parallel to it. I was nervously elated. I had crossed the country to this point in the Southwest known as Old Mexico!

I slid between strands of wire fence that bordered the area and walked toward the shade. I just wanted to be out of the direct sun for a while, and I hoped there might be drinkable water available. I saw movement out of the corner of my eye only a fraction of a second before feeling the ground vibrate and seeing a puff of dust. I was startled to see a cow trotting toward me. It lowered its head, as if to charge me, and quickened its pace. I couldn't believe it! A cow was charging me, like a bull in a bullfighting ring!

I ran toward the fence where I had entered. I looked over my shoulder as I scrambled. The beast kept coming at me until I was safely on the other side of the wire fence, panting in disbelief! I didn't know whether to laugh or cry. A cow chased me? It didn't have horns, so I assumed it was a cow in my city-boy ignorance. Whatever it was, it had bad intentions toward me, and I had barely escaped!

Before long, an old car, driven by a Mexican fellow, gave me a ride to a small Mexican village. It reminded me of a Hollywood movie set with stucco and adobe buildings arranged at an intersection of four dusty roads. I saw a few old cars and trucks, several dogs, and some chickens scratching the ground, pecking in the dust.

I went into a squat, flat-roofed building that looked like a restaurant or cantina. I asked for water at the counter. I drank the first glass and a second before going back outside. With my thirst slackened, my movie-set fantasy dissolved. I felt so lost and empty with nowhere to turn. Against the building, I smoked my next to last cigarette and watched what little activity there was. I got a few curious looks, but was mostly ignored. This border town had seen the best and worst of both nations.

As I glanced around, nothing was familiar to me. The buildings, vehicles, and faces were truly alien. I was alone. I felt homesick. I wanted to get back to my country!

A young, English-speaking Mexican—in a dusty car already full of people—pulled over and asked me if I was looking for a ride to the "States." I would have understood him no matter what language he spoke. I nodded yes enthusiastically. He turned and said something in Spanish to the people in the back; suddenly, there was enough room for me to squeeze in.

The midday sun was bright and strong in the cloudless sky. I felt relieved and happy, that no matter how long we meandered along the road, I was riding again. My joy turned to terror when the car stopped behind a line of others. We were at the US border, and the border patrol officers were checking vehicles. My heart pounded like crazy!

"Oh my God," I thought to myself, "was I going to be captured by the border patrol for sneaking back into the US?" I was a US Marine gone UA (Unauthorized Absence), AWOL (Absent Without Leave), and this was not how I wanted it to end.

It was all could do to look calm, as I tried to be invisible in the back seat. The car lurched a few yards and stopped again. A border agent stuck his head in the car window and looked around. I gazed at him calmly and half smiled. I must have looked out of place.

"Where are you from?" he asked, looking directly at me.

"I'm from Connecticut," I said. The agent mumbled something to the driver; then, we were driving through the border outpost and the line of cars faded behind us.

———— • ◆ • ————

By late afternoon, I was hitchhiking and walking along the road to Albuquerque, just north of Los Cruces, New Mexico. I had no destination in mind, but wanted to seek the relative safety of Route 66.

A New Mexico highway patrol cruiser pulled off the road in front of me, in the breakdown lane of Route 25 North. My heart pounded again. Surely this moment was the end of my strange odyssey. The officer asked me for some identification and where I was headed.

"I'm going to Albuquerque," I said as casually as possible. "I was with friends in Deming," I added, hoping I could avoid closer scrutiny. I slowly searched inside my pockets for something I knew I didn't have. I told the officer my name was William Kinkade, as I withdrew my empty wallet from my pocket and began searching its compartments.

"Do you have anything with your name on it? Any ID?" the trooper impatiently asked again.

At that moment, I felt a folded piece of paper, tucked into a pocket in the wallet. I quickly unfolded it and handed it to him. It was my receipt from selling blood in Albuquerque. I pretended to be frustrated, as I continued to search my pockets for something more official. He looked over the slip of paper, ordered me to stay beside his cruiser, and radioed his dispatcher. Finally, he climbed out of his car and handed me the receipt. "Move along," he said gruffly. He got behind the wheel of his patrol car and sped off. When he dissolved from sight, I breathed a sigh of relief.

My heart raced again, as I spied in the distance, the patrol cruiser making a U-turn and speeding southward. Traffic was light, so it was only moments before he was near me again. Then, the officer made another U-turn to end up just behind me. He jumped out of his car and motioned for me to join him.

"Take off your shoes," the trooper ordered. Without hesitation, I leaned against the hood of the cruiser and removed one shoe at a time; I handed them to him. My chest ached, and I dared not speak for fear my voice would betray me. He placed the shoes on the hood and slowly examined each one—inside and out. He shook his head and handed them back to me. He got behind the wheel of his patrol car and sped off.

It was the middle of the afternoon, and the air was turning chilly. A few cars went by and none stopped as I walked beside the road near Canton, Oklahoma. Finally, a trucker stopped. I was anxious for a ride, any ride, so I climbed into the cab and we headed north.

It wasn't unusual for me to accept a ride going in the opposite direction from my destination. Sometimes, such a ride put me on a busier highway which offered better prospects for long rides. When the driver left me at a twenty-four-hours gas station in Alva, Oklahoma, we both figured it was my best chance for a ride south. The filling station snack area provided my supper break. I bought a pack of cigarettes and smoked one outside. When I came re-entered the station, the friendly manager warned me that I might have trouble getting a ride, because a storm was moving down from Kansas. Barely any traffic was on the street or at the station for the next hours. The attendant asked a couple of truckers if they could get me to Clinton, on Route 66. Alas, they were filling up and bedding down for the night.

The wind picked up, and the air was icy. The street lights swayed in the gusty winds, and I knew I'd probably be stuck there for a while. The night attendant came on duty and showed me from the beginning that he had no intention of being hospitable to me. I desperately fought to stay awake by frequently going outside, but it was difficult to escape the glare of the night attendant.

I made sure he watched as I spent the last of my money on a coffee and donut at around 2 a.m. The minutes dragged by and there was no traffic. I read everything there was of interest. I was even glad when a local cop came by and chatted with the attendant for a while. At another point, the attendant talked for a half hour on the telephone. I foolishly hoped this chat would lighten his mood.

"At first light, I want you outta here, boy," he said when I emerged from the men's room. "I don't want the boss seein' you been hangin' 'round here all night," he said sternly.

I viewed the road sign, pointing south towards Clinton, through the swirling winds. I felt angry toward the attendant for his harsh words and attitude. I was determined not to give him the satisfaction of kicking me out into the cold gales.

While the night man busied himself with duties that kept him from sitting behind the counter, I turned up the collar on my light-weight jacket and slipped out the door. I hurried from the harsh glare of the service-station lights into the gloomy dark chill of the south-bound lane.

The wind eased off, but the ever-present cold was persistent. It enveloped and tightened its icy grip around everything, as darkness descended. I was a lone, dark figure moving slowly on a stretch of lonesome country road in western Oklahoma. The entire state was in the grip of a frosty weather system that was pushing south from Kansas. I kept walking.

I saw faint lights, far off, against the darkness. They were very dim, and I directed each weary step toward their glow. It seemed like hours passed, and I wasn't any closer. Was I losing my mind? Were the lights a mirage? Could I die of exposure, my body discovered a few days after the storm was history? All I could feel was the cold. The numbing chill was my only reality.

Then, I couldn't believe my eyes. The tall box structure on the side of the road was a telephone booth! My mind was numb, and my lips were too frozen to smile at the incongruity of it. I staggered into the metal and glass box and closed the folding door. The ceiling light came on, and my eyes snapped shut from the sudden illumination. If I could have laughed, I would have, because the irony was incredible. Here I was in a telephone booth—on the edge of civilization— without a dime in my pocket!

An important fact about pay phones: Occasionally, one could find change in the coin-return receptacle. That change, often ignored or forgotten by a previous user, languished there until retrieved by someone else. Sometimes, that someone was in desperate straits. This time, that someone was me. It was almost instinctual for me to stick my frozen finger into the coin return and hope to discover a dime or two nickels. It was empty.

Good news! When my eyes adjusted to the light, I noticed these instructions beside the handset: "LIFT THE RECIEVER. DIAL YOUR PARTY'S NUMBER. DEPOSIT COINS WHEN CALL IS ANSWERED."

I lifted the receiver from its cradle and placed it beside my frozen left ear. There was a dial tone! It was incredible! There was a dial tone emanating from a phone in the middle of nowhere! I opened my mouth when I heard a voice ask clearly, "Operator, may I help you?" I tried to speak, but nothing intelligible emerged.

"May I help you?" the woman's voice asked again.

My mind was aching to get my mouth to cry for help, but only gibberish sounds came out! I slumped against the side of the booth and slid to the floor. I assumed that the operator would think I was a crank caller and end the connection. I didn't hear her voice again. Everything went dark and silent.

I heard knocking. No, banging! A policeman hammered his flashlight against the glass, trying to get my attention. I leaned slightly, and the folding doors pushed open. The ceiling light had gone out, and only the police cruiser headlights lit the area. The officer took the receiver that was dangling beside my head, and said something. He tugged me to my feet and guided me to the passenger side of the patrol car. After getting behind the wheel, he said something into the car radio's microphone. Without saying a word, he reached over and turned on the cars' heater, full blast. He drove slowly as I sat there, shivering to full consciousness.

A few minutes later, he helped me out of his cruiser and into the front door of an all-night diner. We moved toward the counter, past the eyes of a small number of late-night patrons. We sat down on padded stools. His half-finished cup of coffee was still at his place at the counter when a waitress walked over with a grin and poured another full cup.

"Coffee and a hamburger?" the officer said more than asked, as he looked me in the eye.

I nodded yes. The waitress put a mug in front of me and filled it. I warmed my hands with the heavy mug as I sipped its hot liquid.

I wasn't a coffee drinker, but I knew it would make me warm and alert.

I think every other eye was on me when she brought my hamburger with lettuce, tomato, and fries. The officer sipped his coffee as I tackled the hamburger platter. He turned on his stool to speak to some of the patrons. He acknowledged that I was the reason the dispatcher had interrupted his coffee break. That's when I learned that the operator had called police with suspicions of a person in distress in a telephone booth.

I shivered as I ate. The feeling was returning to my face and fingers. I managed to say a weak, "Thank you," to the patrolman. He raised a hand as if to say, "You're welcome," and waited patiently for me to finish my meal.

The kind officer paid for my meal, and drove me to the small, local police department; I sat in the front seat beside him. It was almost midnight when he escorted me to an empty cell where I slept for the night. He promised to wake me in a few hours so I could be on my way. I lay on the jail-cell bed and fell fast asleep.

———— • ◆ • ————

Amarillo was bustling in the early evening. I was walking beside Route 66. Rush-hour traffic passed me as I walked along city sidewalks. A late-model car stopped for the traffic light. The driver opened his door, stood outside, and looked at me over the roof of his car. He was a white man in a suit and tie.

"Do you need a ride?" he asked. I nodded yes. "Get in," he said, and got behind the wheel as the light changed. I closed the passenger door hurriedly, and we moved along with traffic. He shook my hand and introduced himself as Reverend Parker (or so I'll call him). I rattled off that I was William Kinkade, and I was returning to Albuquerque.

"I knew you weren't local," he interjected, "cause you were in the wrong part of town," he explained. "I want you to come home with me and have dinner with my family." He paused and looked at me before continuing. "I'll take you to the highway on the other side of town in the morning," he said with finality. Then, he smiled. "Okay?"

"Okay," I laughed, not quite believing my apparent good fortune.

The reverend maneuvered his car down the dark streets and around parked cars in his neighborhood. House lights gave a nice glow to the street, as we pulled into his driveway. In no time, we were walking through his kitchen door.

The reverend introduced me to his wife, son, daughter, and the family dog. All seemed genuinely happy to have me in their home. It was fried chicken night. After I washed up, I sat down with the family. The reverend joined hands with everyone around the table, and we bowed our heads when he said a short prayer, blessing our meal. I said my own silent prayer to whatever spirit of good fortune had guided me to these good people.

The reverend told the family how he spotted me walking in the wrong section of town. He had visited someone in the hospital, or wouldn't have been traveling home that way. He told them I would spend the night, and he would drive me to the highway in the morning.

I was truly thankful for this good man and his obvious courage in helping and sheltering me. The reverend didn't have to draw a picture for me to know that I was in danger in some sections of the city. I was a stranger to him, but he saw only a young, black man in need of help.

There were families where Christian love had arms and legs, and was not just paid lip service. As we talked after dinner, a warm feeling come over me. Only a few hours earlier, I thought I was dead—collapsed emotionally and physically from the bitter cold. Now, I was in the bosom of a family that loved and respected their God and tried to live their beliefs.

The reverend's soft voice and gentle touch stirred me awake before the first light of the next morning. We ate breakfast; then, he handed me a brown paper bag from the refrigerator. His wife had made a chicken sandwich for the road, he explained. As we backed onto the deserted street, I sensed I was being hustled out of the neighborhood before any of the neighbors saw me. I had no problem with that! After saying good-bye on the outskirts of town, west of Amarillo, I watched the first rays of the rising sun warm the road.

———————•◆•———————

I was just north of Lubbock when a dark-blue Jaguar swung into the breakdown lane ahead of me. I hesitated to assume it had stopped for me. The backup lights glowed as it slowly moved toward me. I hurried alongside. A handsome, older man motioned for me to open the door.

"Where you heading, son?" he asked from behind his dark sunglasses.

"Just to Amarillo; and then, Albuquerque," I added the last part quickly, not wanting to be stranded in Amarillo again.

"Get in," he said kindly.

I eased into the rich, leather upholstery of the passenger seat; it embraced me.

"My name is Harold Richards," he stated, extending his hand towards me. I took his hand, as I lied to him about who I was. I felt strength in his grip that surprised me.

"I'm going to Pampa, Texas, to bury my wife," he said softly, as he took off his dark glasses for a moment. I could see sadness in his eyes.

"I'm sorry," I said instinctively.

"Thank you," he replied, as he slipped his glasses on. "She passed away recently, and the family is gathering in Pampa to bury her," he explained. He turned his luxury automobile, shifted into gear, and merged into traffic.

Mr. Richards was tanned with wavy, white hair. I guessed that he was in his sixties, which seemed ancient to me. A dress shirt, slacks, and tan loafers made for a picture-perfect image of casual elegance. A sport jacket hung behind the driver's seat next to a garment bag.

"I'm coming from Los Angeles, California, and I'm behind schedule," he said after we traveled a few minutes in silence. "I can take you to Amarillo, but Pampa is northeast of there," he added, almost apologetically.

Mr. Richards gestured towards a brown bag between us. "Have you ever eaten pheasant?" he asked with a smile.

I said, "No."

"You're welcome to try some. If you like it, finish it. I've eaten all I care to."

I looked into the bag and saw chunks of meat. I took a bite and tasted its sweet, roasted flavor. The pheasant was tender and delicious. There was a cloth napkin beneath the bag. I spread it on my lap and slowly finished the tasty meal.

We chatted as we rode along. Mr. Richards said his wife had died after a long illness. He told me he was a painter in Los Angeles and gave me one of his business cards.

"If you ever get out to LA, look me up," he said, as he pulled off the road. "I have a lot of work sometimes and trouble getting help."

He was letting me out, west of Amarillo along Route 66. I appreciated the timing of this moment, because there was still plenty of light and it was a pleasant day.

"I've thoroughly enjoyed our time together," he said enthusiastically, as I stepped out of the car.

He reached toward me. "Good luck to you," he said, as he handed me a folded bill.

"Thank you so much," I said, genuinely grateful for his kindness. I watched as another of my road angels drove off, leaving me better than they'd found me. I unfolded the ten-dollar bill he gave me. Except for the money and his business card, I could have dreamed I rode in a Jaguar and ate pheasant!

I had no intention of ever going to Los Angeles. The Watts riots were very recent history. The situation scarred the image of "La-la land" in my mind. I never thought I would see Mr. Richards again. Nor could I have known that this brief encounter would eventually have the most significant impact on my entire life's journey.

———— • ◆ • ————

Route 66—from Tulsa, Oklahoma to Gallup, New Mexico— was familiar to me. Then, Arizona beckoned. Arizona didn't really beckon, but a friendly driver was going to a place called Snowflake. This fellow claimed that Snowflake was the home to a large Mormon enclave. I only associated Mormons with the state of Utah. Their distinguishing belief in multiple marriages led some smaller groups to break away from its large governing body, renouncing the practice of Polygamy. He said that Snowflake was established by such a faction.

My new driver said he wasn't a member of the Mormon faith, but had first-hand knowledge of it. He assured me that I would be welcomed as a visitor to the town. This time, I rejected the idea of another detour. We parted company near Holbrook, Arizona, and in short order, I had a ride heading west to a city called Flagstaff. The big-rig driver said there was a large, truck stop on the outskirt of the city. I'd probably have a good chance of catching another ride there. I hadn't decided on another destination, yet. I was avoiding making a decision. My personal rage and pain had faded, but my confused thought patterns still dominated my thinking.

———————— • ◆ • ————————

Flagstaff, a high-altitude city, was subject to dramatic and sudden changes in weather. With night approaching and a bad weather system threatening, I welcomed the bright lights of the truck stop.

My chances for getting a ride out of town were shrinking. The harsh, cold front whistled through the truck stop. I was so hungry that my stomach growling. With my last bit of change, I bought a hot cup of coffee. I had to nurse it until morning, so I retreated to a small table in a distant corner.

The truck stop was slow. With a storm approaching, it became a déjà vu, all over again! It was eerily reminiscent of events leading up to my recent near-death experience in Oklahoma. I must have looked like a pathetic figure, as I stared into the darkness.

"Here you go, honey," the voice said sweetly, breaking my spell. The waitress set a hot bowl of soup before me. From her apron pocket, she took a couple of packs of crackers, napkins, and a spoon. I thanked her for her kindness. She returned immediately, and refilled my coffee cup with a friendly smile.

The hours slowly crept by, as I sat awkwardly fighting off sleep. I was desperate for sleep. Reluctantly, I left the diner for the restroom. I chose a stall at the end, sat on the toilet seat, and slumped against the wall.

I awoke feeling sick to my stomach! I tried to stand, but was too weak. I rested my head on my knees and breathed slowly as I tried to gather my wits. I panicked as I fully awoke and felt my head pounding. My neck and back were aching. I had to get the hell out of there!

I struggled to my feet, unlocked the stall door, and staggered toward the door. I burst through the truck-stop entrance and gasped for air. The frigid mountain air filled my lungs. The strong odor of diesel fuel and the warm restroom had made me sick.

I leaned against the wall, as cramps gripped my stomach and forced fluid up and out. The chilling cold felt good and helped to keep me conscious. I felt my head slowly clear, and the intense pains subside.

Directly, my breathing became more regular, and the cold began to feel uncomfortable. I forced myself to stay outside longer to ensure that I was really better. My intense headache faded, as well as my neck and back pain.

I walked into the diner and asked for a glass of water. I sipped from my second glass, as I watched the first light of dawn illuminate the nearby roadway. Route 66 was my way out. I needed to get moving to escape the storm that threatened to settle over the area.

Snow flurries began to fall as I walked along the highway. I knew it was the beginning of February, but this was Arizona! I didn't realize that it snowed in Arizona. Sure enough, the white flakes swirled madly around me.

Everywhere I looked was covered in white. Here I was again at the mercy of the elements! I was in a quandary as to what to do. I could return to the truck stop or hope to be rescued by a brave driver.

The police car pulled up quietly behind me, rolling along until he was sure I noticed him. He turned on his emergency lights and signaled for me to get into the back seat of the cruiser. I wasn't actively hitchhiking, so I thought he wanted to check me out.

The warmth of the cruiser was a welcomed break from the worsening weather. I immediately told the officer I was going to Phoenix. I was in a caged compartment where the rear doors had no handles. The office secured the rear door; then, he got into the driver's seat. I reached into my pocket for my ID, as the patrolman reported over the car radio that he was bringing in a vagrant.

I was shocked! Before I could protest and show him my receipt from the Albuquerque blood bank, he looked at me—over his right shoulder—and said he was taking me in for vagrancy. He barked, "Anything else you have to say, tell to the judge."

My weird, rebellious, wrong-headed odyssey was certainly over. I was sure of that, as I sat in the holding cell of the Flagstaff, Arizona jail. Directly, my shameful behavior would be revealed, and USMC or Navy MPs would return me to Camp Lejeune, in chains!

The large, holding cell was filling rapidly with a wide assortment of characters. We were the residue of Flagstaff's streets, roadways, and bars. One of the talkative jailbirds in the holding cell was very familiar with the routine. As other "guests" were ushered into the cell, we got weather updates. In the couple of hours since I'd been hauled in, the storm intensified. Nearly a foot of snow was predicted to accumulate. It was a small blessing that I had been picked up and incarcerated. I would reserve judgment until after I found out what I had to do to survive.

I readied my mind to defend myself if threatened. I was determined not to reveal any weaknesses, so I sat there trying to look formidable and dangerous. I avoided direct eye contact with anyone.

I listened as the chatty fellow babbled on. He was a wealth of information. He asked a passing deputy who the judge would be that morning. He recognized the name and announced that those of us who were picked up for vagrancy would be held in jail for a few days. He explained that the city of Flagstaff received a certain sum of money from the state of Arizona for every vagrant it brought in and housed for a certain number of days. His revelation sounded dubious, but no one argued with him. I figured I was down for the count no matter what. In a short time, I would be in the Marine Corps brig, dealing with the realities of a life I tried to evade.

"William Kinkade," the court bailiff shouted.

"Here, sir," I said. I rose from the wooden bench.

"Come forward," he ordered. I made my way to the front of the packed hearing room and beside the five fellows that formed a line in front of the judge's bench.

The judge announced that we were all charged with vagrancy, having been found within the city of Flagstaff without any local address or visible means of support. We were ordered to pay a fine or serve a week in jail. No one was able to pay the fine.

The jail door closed behind me, as I was placed into a four-bunk cell with three other guys. As far as I could tell, I was the only black guy in the entire jail house. All three cellmates were older. The men were friendly towards me right away. I made a fourth for card games, and that was an important activity to pass the time in the cell block.

The oldest cellmate made a point of showing me the ropes. He was on good terms with the trustees and had probably been one himself. This friendship was important, because the trustees could make ones stay more comfortable. The trustees were prisoners, who were "trusted" with a certain amount of freedom within the cell block. They received more privileges for good behavior.

The old timer's chief concern was the food. He assured me that I was fortunate, because the Chinaman was back in the kitchen as principle cook. He and another fellow withdrew sandwiches from hiding places and sat at the wooden picnic table in the center of the cell. They offered me and the other new inmate part of their fried egg sandwich, but we both declined.

They explained that no lunch was served, so one was smart to make a sandwich with a portion of breakfast for later on. This time was when a friendly trustee was appreciated, because he could secure you seconds on breakfast. In addition, a trustee could provide bread wrappers for wrapping sandwiches or other items, like hard-boiled eggs and toast.

I had hunger pangs, but wanted to tough it out; I was assured of having something to eat later. Word circulated that the Chinaman was preparing his premier dish of fried rice.

Newspapers and magazines were available to read, and naps could be taken any time. After a few hours of card playing, I was ready for a nap. However, my hunger pangs wouldn't let me doze for long. Finally, the food cart made the rounds. I took my pie tin of fried rice and two slices of white bread and joined the others at the picnic table. I gobbled down my food, because I was told the trustee would be back with more. Sure enough, the trustee returned with more servings and empty bread wrappers. I made a fried rice sandwich for later, and put it under my pillow.

The old timer confirmed the story of Flagstaff receiving some type of reimbursement for housing vagrants and transients. He said that we were worth twenty-five dollars per head, per day, and that a week was the usual sentence.

My time was taken up with card playing, reading, naps, and long stretches of boredom. I wasn't as bored as the others were, because every time the entry door to the cell block swung open, I feared it was someone coming for me! I tried to act unfazed by any activity or loud voices that came from the sheriff's booking area.

The week of incarceration ended a day early. I was ordered to the front desk immediately after breakfast. The clerk returned the plain brown envelope I had placed my wallet, comb, and cigarette lighter in during booking. I was free to go.

Outside the station building, I felt the warmth of the morning sun on my face. The bad weather was gone without a trace! A mid-February warm spell descended over northern Arizona.

I withdrew the receipt from the Albuquerque blood bank from my wallet. It was my only form of identification. As I put it back in my wallet, I noticed the business card from Mr. Richards. I rubbed my fingers over the embossed lettering:

"HAROLD RICHARDS   DESIGNER / PAINTER

GRAMERCY PLACE   LOS ANGELES, CALIFORNIA"

I heard his words again: "If you're ever in LA, look me up. I might have some work for you." I slipped the card back into my wallet and decided to trek to Los Angeles, California.

Part II:
BRIGHT PASSAGE

CHAPTER 6

LOST IN PARADISE

Josh looked like a beach boy with his shaggy blonde hair, deep tan, and a bright smile. He was antsy to get home, a place called Long Beach, California. I told him that I was going to LA, and he said that Long Beach would put me very close. He was disappointed I couldn't help with the drive, but he vowed to keep driving straight through until we got there.

The border crossing at Needles, California surprised me. Cars were stopped, as uniformed personnel approached and asked questions. Josh explained that they were state inspectors, checking vehicles for produce with insect infestation or disease that might enter California under quarantine.

Josh's hand excitedly shook me awake as we neared Long Beach. It was a warm and humid night and only an hour before dawn. He stopped beside the curb of a well-lit intersection. The streets were empty with only the intersecting roadways as witness to the changing traffic light. The warm wind swirled around us as we said our good-byes. Josh pointed me north and assured me that I would reach Los Angeles soon.

The early morning's muggy air slightly stirred the palm leaves as the breeze changed directions. The city was alive with activity, and the noise level was elevated. I was definitely in a city! The houses were nice, and the streets were clean, but somehow it wasn't as I had envisioned. I thought that the address of Harold Richards perhaps occupied a gated mansion or mini-estate, like many of California's celebrities.This neighborhood looked like many others with well-maintained and neat-looking homes on moderate-sized lots. An assortment of trees, fences, street lamps, and mailboxes bordered the sidewalks.

It was early afternoon when I approached the house. I was nervous. I probably looked like hell, but I was there by invitation. A large, late-model station wagon was parked in the driveway beside the house; it had a wooden extension ladder secured to its roof rack. The rear window of the tail gate was down, and I could see drop cloths, various sized paint containers, brushes, and rollers. Wallpaper rolls and a stack of sample books laid across the rear seat.

Farther down the driveway, I could see a garage with an opened, swing-type garage door. There rested the Jaguar I rode in Texas. It wasn't a dream. I felt buoyed and confident as I approached the ornate, front entrance and rang the bell.

I could hear voices inside the house. A woman's voice was loudest. A figure approached; the figure was Mr. Richards. He peered through the screen door as he dabbed at his mouth with a napkin. He recognized me before I had a chance to speak. In the direction of the woman's voice, he said, "I'll be right back." Then, he opened the screen door and stepped outside. Mr. Richards nervously glanced over his shoulder as he emerged. I took a step back. I got the immediate impression that he didn't want the "woman's voice" to see us talking.

"Hi, Mr. Richards, I'm William Kinkade," I said gleefully, hoping he'd be as happy to see me as I was to see him!

"Yes, yes," he said distractedly. He shook my outstretched hand. "I remember you."

He was taller than I remembered. His silver hair was disheveled; he was wearing white, paint-splattered coveralls and tennis shoes.

"My daughter's here now," he said nervously with another backward glance. "This isn't a good time. I don't have any work for you now," he said softly.

He directed us toward the sidewalk as he continued to talk, anticipating my thoughts.

"Business is slow now. Things should pick up within a month or so."

I noticed another car parked on the street in front of the house. It was probably his daughter's.

"I'm sorry I can't do more right now," he said apologetically, as he pressed a few dollars into my hand. "Good-bye," he said with finality. Then, Mr. Richards hurried back inside the house and closed the door.

My mood was totally deflated! I had been given the bum's rush as I hustled away from someplace I was not wanted! I walked away quickly, not wanting to cause Mr. Richards any embarrassment or problems with his daughter. They were evidently in the midst of a tense situation.

I counted the three dollar bills he gave me. I had absolutely no idea where to go next. Eventually, I walked down dirty streets, littered with debris and wandering people. Grocery store carts—filled with clanging glass bottles and tethered, large, plastic bags—were pushed along by living ghosts.

I'd never seen such an urban wasteland as the skid row of Los Angeles! This time was long before the generic term, "homeless people" was used. Predominantly, men of different ethnic and racial backgrounds dwelled in this depressed part of town—those who had slipped, fallen, or been pushed into the margins of existence.

My stomach was as empty as my pockets when I walked to the door of the blood bank. The few dollars Mr. Richards gave me were spent on food and cigarettes. I was flat broke again. Selling blood would be a temporary fix.

"They're closed," a voice said from behind me. "They closed at three o'clock today," the voice added.

I turned around to see a short, black man with sad eyes and a friendly smile.

"They won't open again till tomorrow, seven o'clock," he added before I asked. "You sellin' blood or plasma?" he inquired.

"Blood," I answered. I didn't want to be friendly, just factual.

"If you sell blood you can't do it again for a month you know," he stated. "Plasma, you can sell twice a week. They pay four dollars each time for plasma, eight dollars a week," he rushed on, ignoring my nods of understanding.

"I know," I said sharply. "I just need a few bucks to get outta here." I wanted to appear firm and in control to hide my frustration. I needed to be left alone so I could think what to do next.

"My name's Luther," he said, extending a dark-skinned hand.

"William," I said as we shook. His firm grip broke my resistance to contact. I felt a twinge of guilt for being so brusque toward him.

"You from back East?" he asked. I nodded yes. He wasn't going to just shut-up and go away.

"You shouldn't be sellin' your blood like these winos," he said with genuine concern in his voice.

We leaned against the cinder-block building along with a few other men who were standing or sitting beside the structure to avoid the sun's heat.

I offered Luther a cigarette. He accepted it, and we lit up and smoked in the shade.

"You could get some good money doin' day labor," he said, breaking the silence," if you're not afraid to work."

I looked interested, so he continued. "Different guys come down along Nickel Avenue, Fifth Street, looking for help, early in the mornin'. It could be anything from loadin' or unloadin' trucks, cleaning up at a construction site, or boxin' stuff up at a factory. They all pay at the end of each day in cash. They don't ask any questions. If you show them you can work, they'll pick you every day they need help!" He paused to let that sink in.

"Sometimes they only take two or three guys out of twenty," he continued, "but if you're not an "alchy" or a "druggy," you could get regular work. A young guy like you should get picked right off! These other fools only get enough money to buy a bottle of Santa Fe wine, or some reefer, and won't work steady!"

"I'm not afraid of work," I said defensively. The idea of anonymous work for a few days was appealing. I was won over by this little, brown man. He was genuinely trying to help me!

I needed help. This megalopolis—called Los Angeles—was immense. It seemed huge and unending, as one area merged into the next. The sprawling city featured blacktop roads as connective tissue, and streams of traffic everywhere, constantly! But I felt like I couldn't find a way out, yet. Maybe Luther was showing me the way.

"You can come over and stay at my place," Luther was saying when I started listening again. "It's not far from here, near where they get workers in the morning." He motioned his head toward the side and started walking. I followed. We walked along concrete streets past nondescript buildings and vacant storefronts. The sidewalks were littered with men in various stages of lifelessness. Some were barely more animated than the wind-blown debris they existed in.

It was a sad view, as we walked in the warmth of the mid-afternoon sun, past storefront Churches, religious rescue missions, and flop houses. The unpleasant stench of unwashed bodies, fermenting garbage, and stale wine mingled with LA's ever-present smog.

Luther told me that the missions served "soup and salvation" around six o'clock each evening, and some offered a place to sleep for the night. We passed the Midnight Mission, the Los Angeles Rescue Mission, and a large building that dominated the corner of Fifth Street called the Fifth Street mission.

A few blocks away was Luther's room in one of those nondescript buildings with rooms for rent by the day, week, or longer. I followed him up one flight of stairs into a wide hallway. His door opened into a room with a bed, chair, and a large window that overlooked the street.

"Come on in an' make yourself comfortable," he said, as he walked to the window and lowered the shades to break the intense intrusion of sunlight.

I sat in the well-worn, upholstered chair. The bed was pulled together with a dingy-looking sheet and spread gathered below two pillows. The room smelled familiar, like the street below.

"You wait here," Luther said. "I'll be right back. I'm gonna get a few things at the store. What do you smoke?" he asked, as he stepped into the hall.

"I'm quitting," I lied, "right after I finish this pack," I said emphatically, as I patted my breast pocket.

He shrugged and was gone. Why had I lied to him? The thought of quitting smoking hadn't crossed my mind before. Why didn't I want him to buy me a pack of Camel Filters? I didn't know why, but for some reason I suddenly felt uncomfortable. I spotted a floor-stand ashtray alongside the bed. I leaned over to reach it and pulled it beside the chair. I lit one of my last three cigarettes.

A weird thought flickered across my mind. I might need that tall ashtray as a weapon! Where did that thought come from? Why was I sitting there with this uneasy feeling growing inside me? Should I just leave and wait out in the heat until I could get a bowl of soup and a bed for the night?

Soon Luther was back with a plain, brown paper bag. He set the bag on the bed. Then, he tore it open to display its contents. He withdrew a bottle of wine, a package of lunch meat, a box of saltine crackers, and a pack of cigarettes. "Help yourself," he said casually, as he reached for the wine bottle.

"You want a little wine?" he asked. Luther unscrewed the cap and poured some into a paper cup.

"No, thanks," I said politely. I had never had wine, but my thoughts flashed back to the stories the Pitt brothers used to tell me about winos in the north end of Hartford, drunk on "Sneaky Pete" wine. (It was called "Sneaky Pete" because it went down easy, but would "sneak up" on you and make you drunk.) I smiled inwardly at the memory.

"Help yourself," he urged again, as he stuffed a cracker sandwich into his mouth. I wanted to reach over and take a few saltines and a slice of baloney, but I couldn't move.

"Not right now," I said weakly, and lit another cigarette.

"You smoke reefer? I got some reefer," he said excitedly, and he reached between the mattresses to withdraw a hand-rolled cigarette that must have been the marijuana. I'd heard of it, but had no desire to try it.

"No, I'm fine," I said with a little forced laugh.

Luther ate a few more of his snacks and, dispensing with the pretense of drinking from a cup, he took a couple of big swigs from his wine bottle. Next, he cleared the items from the bed, placed them in a paper bag "hammock," and set it on the floor. After a yawn, Luther stretched on the edge of the bed and slowly removed his shoes. Then, he lifted both legs and swung them around until he was lying prone. He adjusted the dingy-looking pillow beneath his head.

"You could stretch out here for a while," he invited, as he closed his eyes and patted the space beside him.

That caught me off guard! Wow! What was going on in his mind? Damn, would I have to fight my way out of the place? I inched the ashtray stand a little closer.

"No," I declined. "I've gotta get going," I added determinedly.

"You don't have to lie down," he said hurriedly. "You could just stay here for awhile," he lightly pleaded in a nervous voice.

Could he feel me slipping from his web? This was why I had felt uncomfortable! Was he some kind of pint-sized chicken hawk, looking for ignorant losers to seduce? Did he think I was queer? I stood up and stretched, trying to conceal my nervousness. I had to take control of the situation! I was younger, bigger, and probably stronger than him, but I was on his turf—in his web.

I took a couple of short steps toward the door. Luther didn't move; he just stared at the ceiling. His eyes were sad as he felt the soft oblivion of the wine embrace his mind and soften his pains. I unbolted the door, said a hurried good-bye, rushed down the stairs and out of the building.

———————◆•———————

I smoked my last cigarette as I stood in line outside the Fifth Street mission's side entrance. I was still nervous and upset about my encounter with Luther, and hoped I wouldn't see him again. That entire incident, added to everything else since arriving in LA, made me believe I truly hit bottom!

The line to the mission stretched around the corner onto Fifth Street. The heaviness in the air lightened; it was more comfortable in the early evening, when the doors to the mission opened and the folks in line began to shuffle in.

A tall, slender, black man with very close cropped hair and a friendly smile greeted the arrivals inside the chapel. He nodded to some familiar faces, and he made eye contact and shook hands with a few others. He called himself Brother Johnson.

We settled into folding chairs which faced a stage and pulpit. The room quickly filled to near capacity. Hymnals were passed out. Brother Johnson led the singing. Many folks sang the words without looking at their hymnals. Some sang enthusiastically; others never opened the book or pretended to care about anything other than the meal to follow.

I sang. The hymns were familiar to me. A wave of nostalgia washed over me as I thought of my mother and grandmother. I was so far from where they tried to lead me. Why had I rejected God and expunged the church from my life? I was so lost that I felt virtually hopeless. I had betrayed family, God, and country! Could I ever be forgiven for these actions?

Brother Johnson said a prayer before introducing the speaker that evening. Martin Brett, the director of the mission, gave the message from the pulpit; he was in his late fifties with thinning gray hair atop a large face that was lined with experience. Brett was a solid–built, rather heavy-set, white man. His dominant physical characteristic was the absence of his left arm. His suit jacket's left sleeve was tucked into his left jacket pocket.

Martin Brett spoke calmly, but passionately, as he recounted his own experiences of trying to "lose himself in the bottle." He testified how the grace of God offered him a second chance at life and blessed him beyond his wildest dreams with family, good health, and a purpose. Brett knew his audience well and kept his statements simple and sincere. He had a lively delivery and yet, he didn't come across like a typical preacher. I had mixed emotions. I was genuinely moved by his testimony, and my personal nostalgic moments reminded me of my lost yearning for God.

My palms sweat and my heart was pounded as "that" moment approached. "That" moment was the one that I heard some men speaking of, as the best chance to score a cot for the night. I had to answer the "altar call."

The "altar call" was a ritual in evangelical worship services. At the close of the speaker's message, the repentant sinners are called forward to make a public acknowledgment of their desires to "get right with the Lord" and turn their lives around. The wonderful hymn "Just as I Am" was sung by some attendees while others hummed along. ("Just as I am, without one plea, but that thy blood was shed for me.")

A few men slowly walked down the center aisle to the front of the chapel. Some men openly cried as they shook the hands of Brother Johnson and Martin Brett; then, they stood with heads bowed as others joined them. I felt myself moving forward. I looked Brother Johnson in the eye. Martin Brett stepped from the platform and embraced me with his one arm.

When no others joined the group of ten or so, we prayed for our souls to be healed. Afterward, each man was given a pamphlet with details on what actions to take to be saved. We were urged to seek counseling with Brother Johnson or Brother Brett after the meal. Then, those men with legitimate needs—who weren't drunk or high on drugs—might get to sleep in the dormitory for the night.

The bowl of hot soup and few slices of white bread tasted like a gourmet feast to me. Most of the diners exited the soup kitchen onto Fifth Street, but I returned to the chapel to converse with the brothers. Brother Johnson was talking to someone. Brother Brett motioned me to an empty chair opposite him; he looked me over carefully. I expected questions regarding my presence on skid row.

Martin Brett asked if I was sincere in my desire to give my life to Christ. I assured him honestly, that I was. I embellished my answers with phrases I learned from many years of interacting with church people. He was impressed and asked if I'd like to help them at the mission. It was a ministry of the Reverend Fred Jordan, a well-known television pastor on a weekly program called *Church in the Home*. I agreed to consider his offer overnight, which assured me of a place to sleep.

I woke up early the next morning. I lay quietly, remembering where I was. I felt troubled by what I had done with my life up to this point. I silently wondered if indeed the hand of God might actually be guiding me, saving me from myself. I prayed for guidance. I was a fugitive. All I had to do was turn myself in to make things right. But I was a troubled and confused young man who needed some time and a place to sort things out. Was this the place?

At 8 a.m., the six men who slept there were summoned to morning devotions in the chapel with the limited mission staff. Arranged in a small circle, we listened as Brother Johnson read a bible passage and explained what it meant to him. Other staff did the same, and we all recited the Lord's Prayer. I delivered it forcefully and fervently. I wanted to find the God of the Lord's Prayer and get to know him. I wanted to change my life!

After devotions, we ate breakfast. Brother Johnson asked if I'd thought about Brother Brett's offer. He seemed pleasantly surprised when I said that I wanted to stay and help the ministry for a while. Brother Brett joined us, and they welcomed me.

I was introduced to Emil, the cook, who put me right to work. Martin Brett said that I would be paid a stipend of two dollars per week. I noted the date of the morning newspaper on the counter: February 21, 1967. It was my birthday. I was eighteen-years-old.

CHAPTER 7

TO SERVE WITHOUT HONOR

May 1966

The bus lurched forward into the darkness. It was a school bus with firm vinyl seats and a narrow aisle down the center. It reminded me of the Sunday school bus. The train ride down had been the luxurious part of our journey. I, and the other Hartford area recruits, bunked in sleeper cars for the long trip to Parris Island, South Carolina.

Having boarded the train in the late afternoon of the previous day, more than twenty-four hours had passed. We were treated like welcomed guests. After we enjoyed our meal in the dining car of the train, most of us were ready to climb into bed. The bus jerked and bounced, but did little to stop me from dozing off whenever we traveled on smooth pavement for a while.

The bus stopped suddenly; then, slowly and steadily it turned toward an area bathed in bright lights. Every eye was opened now, and we could see other buses parked nearby. After parking, the driver opened the folding doors. A gruff-looking, white man in a Marine Corps uniform stepped aboard the bus. He looked quite impressive in his Smokey Bear-type hat that nearly brushed the ceiling. He was in a khaki uniform with stripes and ribbons on his chest. He looked a bit intimidating as he put his hands on his hips and peered toward the rear of the vehicle.

"Get off this bus, quickly and orderly, and line up on the yellow footprints on the blacktop!" he shouted. "Now move!!" he ordered. Then, he pivoted just enough to allow us to pass him.

"Move, move, move, you maggots! Get off this bus!" he screamed. We pushed and scrambled to disembark and run to the big, yellow footprints painted on the blacktop. Other marines shouted as we exited the bus, ordering us to line up and shut up! The entire area, bright with day light, was bombarded with screams and shouts from all directions as all the buses emptied.

"Welcome to the Marine Corps Recruit Depot at Parris Island!" the sergeant shouted so he could be heard by all the silent and traumatized recruits. "You will do everything you are told to do without hesitation! Is that clear?"

"Yes," some shouted back. Others nodded, hoping their willingness to cooperate would help him calm down.

"I…can't…hear…you!" he bellowed.

"Say sir, yes sir!" the other marines ordered.

"Sir, yes sir!" we yelled.

"I still can't hear you," the sergeant barked.

"Sir, yes sir," we screamed back in surprising unison! Alert now, the desire for sleep fled our tired bodies.

If you've seen a Hollywood movie about fresh recruits entering a military boot camp, you have a pretty accurate idea of my experience; it is meant to be an intense shock treatment. And it is. The Marine Corps is especially noted for making boot camp an indelible stamp on one's mind! By the wee hours, hundreds of raw recruits had been processed through the receiving area. Each was given enough gear to fill his sea bag, and regulation hair cuts were completed by a squad of barbers. Our civilian clothes and personal items were packaged for shipment home.

Some of the same NCOs that yelled and screamed at us stayed with us for the duration of boot camp. They were our drill instructors. The senior DI was a solidly built black man with a chiseled face, fiery eyes, and a piercing stare. Staff Sergeant "Lockjaw" talked through clinched teeth, but always had perfect enunciation and managed to be understood.

Sergeant "Lockjaw" walked up and down the center of the squad bay with a disgusted look on his face. "You ladies are the saddest looking pukes I've ever seen enter my Marine Corps!" he spat through his clenched teeth. "I can't believe you think any of your sorry asses are going to get to be a marine! You are maggots! Do you hear me?"

"Sir, yes sir!" we screamed.

If a recruit thought his first meal would be a chance to eat a good breakfast and calmly reflect on his first hour's experiences, he was mistaken. During what passed for personal time, we were ordered to write a letter home to put the concerns of anxious relatives at ease. Our Marine Corps manual was our constant companion. Kept in a rear or breast pocket, it would be consulted countless times during boot camp.

After our wake-up call, inspections, and punishments, we lined up for "head call." The "head" in marine terminology is the toilet and shower facilities. The squad bay had designations like a ship, so there was a port side and a starboard side. Port was right; starboard was left.

"Shit, shower, and shave!" was the call. Like everything else in boot camp, these tasks must be completed rapidly and efficiently. The toilets were in a row with no dividers or stalls. With one recruit on a toilet, one or two other recruits would face him, as they waited their turn.

"Let's go, ladies! Move it, move it, move it!"

We piled into the "head" with our shower shoes, shaving kits, and a bar of soap as our only companions. Every shower faucet forcefully aimed the water at our heads, and clouds of steam crept along the ceiling. With white towels around our waists, we made our way to the sinks and mirrors with our shaving kits in hand. Everyone had to shave! We formed a line behind the fellow in front of us at each sink, and after wiping the steamy fog from the mirror, we lathered up and scraped the peach fuzz from our baby faces.

After morning "head call" and before chow, we were inspected again as we stood on line in front of our bunks. The DIs walked slowly down the row and checked our appearances. Our utility trousers were to be neatly bloused above our highly polished boots. Our brass belt buckles must gleam in the morning light and be aligned with our zippers and shirt-button plackets. If we wore white tee shirts, they must be neatly tucked. Our shaving jobs were inspected with a flashlight; we held our chins high in the air, and the DIs ensured our peach fuzz was scraped. Anyone's shaving job found suspect was ordered to dry shave right there under close scrutiny. Now, we were ready for drill or PT (physical training).

Hurry up and wait! It was a universal reality that we were hustled from sleep to chow, class, PT, chow, class, PT, class, chow, class, and bed—all at a double-time pace. And then, stand in line and wait!

"School circle," the drill instructor barely whispered, but the word spread among us like a raging fire through dry brush.

"School circle!" we'd repeated loudly, as we immediately stopped whatever we were doing and hurriedly gathered around the DI.

In the evening after chow, most of us were busy with personal tasks, making our next day as problem free as possible. Boots were spit-shined, brass was polished, hats ("covers" in the marines) were starched and shaped, footlockers were organized, letters were written, and the Marine Corps manual was studied. Small snatches of conversations occurred during these times, and friendships began to form. This time was the closest we got to a break. When "school circle" was whispered, we rushed to the DI like chicks to a momma hen!

DIs gathered us around them during "school circles; they taught us everything we needed to know—from the Marine Corps Manual to the Manual of Arms. They talked to us almost as if we were human beings. Even Staff Sergeant "Lockjaw" dialed down his disgust at our presence in "his" Marine Corps and taught us with enthusiasm and some humor.

We learned the history of the US Marines during these sessions, including the proud traditions and high standards set by those who had served before us. From the halls of Montezuma to the shores of Tripoli, Guadalcanal, Tarawa, Iwo Jima, and the Chosin Reservoir where others had served with honor and many had fallen.

And we learned the "Marines Hymn." One night as we lay in our racks, waiting for lights out, the on-duty drill instructor began singing the hymn softly. "From the Halls of Montezuma, to the

Shores of Tripoli...." Without prompting, we all joined him in whispering tones as he flicked off the lights. We continued in the darkness and ended with that soul-stirring finale, "We are proud to claim the title of United States Marine."

The moment was perfect, as we drifted to sleep with thoughts about our experiences up to this point in the corps. That first week had been the most terrible week of my life, but now, lying in the darkened squad bay with the final strains of the hymn echoing in my mind, I felt a sense of accomplishment. I had survived!

———— • ◆ • ————

A few of the first recruits were gone already. Quiet rumors swirled: one had punched a drill instructor; another one was caught sleeping during his "fire watch" for the second time (He was sent to a unit called "motivation" platoon.); and a third recruit (frequently picked on by the DIs) pulled some strings to get himself processed out of the corps. (His parents were "connected" was the rumor.)

Ten years earlier, a huge scandal occurred during boot camp at Parris Island. The troubling event ended with a congressional investigation into Marine Corps Basic Training practices. The story we heard: A drill instructor marched his platoon into a Parris Island swamp at night, and some of the recruits drowned. The lid blew off the Marines Corps pressure cooker at Parris Island. Outraged citizens demanded that congress investigate, punish, and reform the basic-training program!

Stories of physical abuse and excessive cruelty were uncovered. Proud and decent marines were disgusted. New training procedures were put into place. Drill instructors were closely monitored to ensure that they didn't snap under the pressure of transforming platoons of raw, unsure mama's boys into marines. This was the new and improved Marine Corps. The DIs scrupulously avoided touching recruits in any manner—usually.

———— • ◆ • ————

A feeling of sickness suddenly washed over me. I felt like I was going to pass out. I was dizzy and confused as I listened to the instructor in the front of the classroom. A short time later, we were dismissed and ordered to assemble outside. The room spun around me as I wobbled to my feet and moved slowly toward the door.

"Come here, boy!" Sergeant "Lockjaw" called me over to him. "What's wrong with you?" he asked gruffly, through clenched teeth. I stared blankly at his chest and tried to focus my mind. He looked directly into my eyes. Then, he placed his hand on my shoulder and pulled me closer to him. He felt my abdomen with his other hand. "Have you moved your bowels, son?" he asked with a tinge of concern—almost fatherly. It disarmed me.

"No sir," I managed to say. I was ashamed and embarrassed to admit that I couldn't "go" during all of the high energy and emotional tension of that first week. Hunger, and that same tension, kept me eating. Now, I was hopelessly bound up with constipation!

Staff Sergeant "Lockjaw" had seen this before and wasted no time in getting me over to sick bay. There, I was given an enema. A corpsman from the dispensary's medical team hung a large water bottle of warm water over my head in the toilet stall. The warm fluid flowed down the rubber tube into my impacted bowel until I felt like I would burst!

I felt ten pounds lighter when I was ready to return to my platoon. I was grateful to Sergeant "Lockjaw" for not making a big deal of my situation. I resolved to try extra hard to earn the kindness he showed me.

Then, my past reappeared to haunt me and ruin my resolve during the second week of basic training. After we returned from our morning run with Sergeant "Lockjaw," I saw the contents of my footlocker dumped on my rack. This regular occurrence was a common sight when we returned from an activity or class, but this was the first time it happened to me.

As soon as I saw my shower shoes on the floor under my rack, right where I left them, I knew I was in trouble. The rest of the platoon was dismissed to the showers. A sergeant said something to Sergeant "Lockjaw," and both pairs of eyes looked directly at me. They nodded. Was it my imagination? What had I done to deserve special scrutiny?

The shiny silver bars of our first lieutenant joined the discussion with the DIs. Sergeant "Lockjaw" called me over to the meeting. He looked sad.

Is this your wallet, Rose?" he asked, as he thrust the object in front of my face.

"Sir, yes sir!" I answered, as my heart sank. I hadn't opened my wallet in almost two weeks, although it seemed like a year. I suddenly remembered what was in it. Along with a few dollars were one filter cigarette and a condom in its silver package.

"You're goin' to hell!" a DI said gleefully. "Your ass is going to hell!"

"This is contraband, boy," Sergeant "Lockjaw" stated. "What are you doin' with this contraband?" he demanded.

"I forgot, sir," I said weakly. It was a lie. Although I hadn't thought of it for weeks, I kept the condom given to me by Anthony long ago to show other guys. The cigarette was the tangible symbol of my rebellion. I had the opportunity to discard both items when we first arrived at Parris Island. During our initial processing, we were ordered to include such items in the contents of the package that was shipped home. Why had I clung to these two items?

The Lieutenant said, "I'm sending you to "motivation." He turned to Sergeant "Lockjaw" and said, "I'll get the paperwork ready. Get him outta here!"

Motivation

Each day of basic training was vital to the development of a marine. If more than a couple of days were missed, a recruit would be dropped by his platoon. "Motivation" was punishment for misdeeds. It was an intense psychological and physical proving ground. The hell of "motivation" was supposed to make basic training almost heavenly.

I stood at attention as the "motivation" DI looked over my paperwork. One DI strode over to me, put his nose next to mine, and asked forcefully, "Do you resent authority, boy?"

"Sir, no sir," I responded. I'd never really heard that before. *Did* I resent authority? Did I not like being told what to do? Did I hate the hard-assed, in-your-face, arrogant, rage-filled, ball-busting drill instructors?

If PT was used to build stamina or correct and punish us, "motivation" was designed to take us to the edge of tolerance and sanity, and push us over! The DIs wanted to see what we turned into when pushed! Their mandate was to break you and remake you, to help you "get your mind right."

I channeled my anger and frustration into my efforts to succeed. I took their bait and played their game. They didn't think I could survive, so I'd show them! I would give it my all! While part of me wanted to break down, another part was determined not to give them that satisfaction. My first couple of days at "motivation" were days of mutual discovery. The drill instructors saw me showing a desire to succeed, and I saw myself discovering my ball of determination. I would avoid failure.

Because "motivation" disciplined recruits at different levels of basic training, there were some activities that I hadn't seen yet. The confidence course was a series of obstacles—logs, fences, water hazards, and ropes—laid out in a linear arrangement. The confidence course was intimidating, and I had no illusions about successfully conquering it. However, I was going to give it my best effort—even if it killed me. If I progressed over the obstacles, I ended up high above the ground with a thick, long, braided jute rope as my only way down.

While the DIs screamed at them, I viewed draftees walking the log bridge to reach the summit; leaping onto the fat, dangling ropes; and hurriedly descending to the ground. Most recruits managed the slick ropes. Others barely descended before jumping or falling to the sand pit below.

Although my arm strength was weak and my palms were sweaty, I leapt onto the rope and wrapped my dangling legs around the thick jute. I plummeted down, clinging to the rope as if it were a life line! The DIs were yelling at me to let go! I couldn't let go, because its fibers scorched the palms of my hands! I rode that rope all the way down to the sandpit; then, I lay there in agony with my palms on fire!

The drill instructors stopped screaming and hustled me to the infirmary. My hands had swollen, and huge blisters formed on my fingers and palms from the rope burn. The pain was excruciating! I fought back tears while the corpsman worked on my hands. After cleaning and disinfecting where he could, he applied salve to both hands and wrapped them in gauze bandages. I looked as helpless and pathetic as I felt.

My "motivation" experience had ended. I was stuck in the infirmary for a few days until my hands healed. For a short time, boot camp was suspended, and I was just a patient. In addition to my rope burns, I came down with the mumps during my sick-bay stay. I had avoided this disease during childhood.

Ten days later, I was released from the infirmary, processed out of "motivation," and placed in a training platoon that was about two weeks behind my original unit. Needless to say, I wasn't greeted warmly by my new drill instructors. I must have seemed like a total screwup. But they were professionals, and determined to transform me into a marine.

The few letters I wrote home were vague about boot-camp life. I made no mention of the difficulty I was experiencing or the trouble that placed me in "motivation" platoon. I offered that my case of the mumps was the primary reason for my original graduation date being pushed two weeks.

———————•◆•———————

The drill instructors' breakdown in my new unit was similar to the other units: one black and three white NCOs. All the officers I reported to were white. In theory, we were all shades of marine green, but in the 1960s' corps, one noticed race.

Since marine recruits were almost all volunteers, as opposed to army draftees, we nurtured a sense of superiority. Our DIs encouraged such notions to bond us and form the marines' fabled esprit de corps.

Our DIs fought our natural tendencies toward racial segregation by ordering us to "checkerboard" whenever a cluster of blacks formed amidst a group of whites. Whenever we congregated for classes or exams we'd hear the sergeant's southern drawl; he commanded the "colored" recruits to "checkerboard." "Spread out y'all," he'd say to the few blacks in his unit. "Checkerboard, checkerboard!" Even the NCOs and officers who were resentful of integration of the corps followed orders and encouraged recruits to mix.

Parris Island was in the grip of a hot South Carolina summer in 1966. The heat felt merciless to us Northern boys. We were given salt tablets every day to help us retain sufficient body fluids. We lost tremendous amounts of fluid in the sweltering heat before, during, and after PT or drills. We regularly drank vast quantities of water.

We drilled constantly, learning to move as one unit with one will—that of our duty drill instructor. Each DI's marching song differed, but the cadence was the same. We studied marching formations and commands in our handbooks, and we practiced marching everywhere we went. We began to see the fruits of our practices as we improved and learned to incorporate the *Manual of Arms* into our routines. The *Manual of Arms* offered the proper handling and maneuvering of our rifles, by command, from one required position to another.

Each command was seared into our brains with constant drilling. Each time we drilled, we competed against our last performance and some idea of perfection. Sometimes, we observed a unit that was close to graduating, and we openly marveled at their deft moves and precise execution. Eventually, we competed against platoons that were on our same training level.

———— • ◆ • ————

The pecking order in every unit becomes clear after a short time together. The self-disciplined, clear-thinking, organized minds have the least problems. These top men strive for excellence and stand out as hard workers and motivators; they seldom get picked on by DIs or fellow recruits. Not always are these individuals good people, necessarily, but they do possess the tools to succeed, and they know it.

Then, there's the middle tier. The bulk of recruits fall into this group. Good at some things and passable at others. These men are anxious to achieve success and join the elite tier.

Next, there is the bottom tier. It's the most fluid group, because many of those near the bottom realize they have nowhere to go but up—or out. They don't like being considered non-hackers and screwups. These recruits usually endeavor to join the middle tier.

A teachable recruit in the military meritocracy is rewarded more often than a civilian willing to learn in the outside world. A hunger to be taught counts in basic training, whereupon, connections may carry more weight in the civilian world. The bottom-tier guys were often the butt of jokes. Men like me, who took things rather good naturedly, were generally liked and guided through some rough spots by fellow recruits.

As "Mr. Congeniality," I didn't suffer the verbal abuse others did. I was soft and flabby, but never so fat as to be designated a "fat body" by our drill instructors. Those poor souls were restricted to eating a "fat body" diet at chow. I was weak and slow, but there were those worse at PT than me. My efforts and determination counted for much among my peers, and I kept my personal anger or frustrations internalized.

I wasn't very smart or clever in most areas, but I still performed well enough to languish at the top of the underachievers. This position allowed me to remain below the radar of the super-achieving, dominant males in our platoon.

My friendly character was my best defense from the super gung-ho recruits. Gung-ho guys were the opposite of the slackers. They were always ready to perform and they inspired their fellow recruits. Many of these fellas were natural leaders who led by inspiration and example. Others relied on intimidation to "inspire" greater efforts from the lesser among us.

The Physical Readiness Test, or PRT, was the pinnacle of boot-camp performance. This test, near the end of training, pitted each platoon against the others that were in the same training arc. The test was the justification for extra training and drilling. The entire two-day challenge concluded with a long run, during part of which we carried the extra weight of a full field pack and rifle.

At times the brutally hot South Carolina summer limited our outdoor activities. The entire base operated under a system of flags, which alerted company commanders of weather restrictions on training. A red flag limited outdoor PT and drill. A black flag meant we weren't to march or drill.

I was friendly with a white fellow who was my bunkmate. I had the upper bunk and Arnie, the lower one. He was from New York State. We were both in that subgroup of recruits who struggled to sustain our mediocrity. Then, there was recruit Bangston, a dark Negro with an intense attitude; he was of average height and build with chiseled features beneath his taut black skin. His piercing dark eyes were full of intimidating rage.

Bangston had natural abilities and self-discipline, so he was never far from the top of the rankings in physical training or the classroom. Yet, his own achievements weren't enough for him. He took joy in belittling those who exceeded him, and treated with disgust those who struggled beneath him. With his scowling countenance, he easily could have been voted "least likely recruit to be messed with."

Recruit Bangston was a reminder of all the intimidators in my life. I had never come up with a real answer for them other than avoidance or fearful confrontation. Mostly Bangston just looked at me with disgust.

About half-way through boot camp, the "smoking lamp" was lit. This term was used by the Marine Corps to designate a time and place for smokers to light up. All smoking recruits had suffered mandatory withdrawal for weeks.

We were allowed to buy smokes and other comfort items during visits to the post exchange store (PX). Finally, we indulged when the duty DI said, "The smoking lamp is lit. Smoke 'em if you got 'em." The sad irony of lighting up and smoking a cigarette, after having suffered pain and humiliation for hiding one, wasn't lost on me. I started smoking again for the same reasons I started in the first place—to soothe my emotions.

I failed at the rifle range. Many of us had never fired anything other than a BB gun. Some of us flinched in anticipation of the rifle kickback. Others couldn't break the habit of jerking the trigger, instead of squeezing it, for accurate shooting. Many recruits never learned to breathe correctly, or properly adjust the sights on the weapon. Still others, simply had poor eyesight, poor coordination, or were poor students. Whatever the reasons or excuses, we went UNQ (unqualified) on the rifle range. All those who qualified would be awarded a Marksman, Sharpshooter, or Expert Medal to wear proudly on their uniforms.

A number of us went UNQ, including my bunkmate, Arnie. Such a large number of unqualifieds prevented our platoon from winning a streamer—a specific-colored ribbon added to our platoon standard and carried by our guide when we marched.

Other platoons regarded us as losers when they marched past us with their rifle-range streamers flying from their standards. None of our DIs was happy with our poor performance, because it reflected on them. The elite riflemen, and those who just squeaked by, were disgusted with us, because we cost our unit a streamer. Recruit Bangston was very upset and glared at us more than usual.

The smell of chlorine was strong as we shuffled from the changing room to the pool area. We gathered along one side of the Olympic-sized pool. The swim instructors weren't there to teach swimming; they were lifeguards that day. They stood around the pool and joked with our drill instructors.

We formed a line alongside the pool's edge. Each group poised silently before the glistening water. When the whistle blew, you were to plunge in immediately. If you could swim, you were to make your way to the opposite side and climb out. If you couldn't swim, you were left to flail about helplessly until one of the swim instructors reached you with a long pole and pulled you from the water.

I walked to the edge of the pool. I was terrified. Maybe I would be able to swim. The whistles pierced the air, and without hesitation, I plunged in with the others. I wasn't going to give anyone the chance to say I was too afraid to jump in—even if I drowned!

I flailed about, poorly imitating what others were doing. I was more beneath the water than above it when I awkwardly moved my body toward the pool's edge. I swallowed water in desperate gulps, endeavoring to breathe while struggling to stay above the chilly waves. "Where was that pole?" I thought to myself. Each time I opened my eyes, I could just see it within my grasp. Then, it was gone. The instructor was playing with me, as I watched him cruelly play with others.

Finally, I felt the pole thrusted at me, and I quickly seized it with both hands. I clung to it desperately, until I was pulled to the side of the pool and out of the water. I coughed, choked, and spewed water from my nose and mouth! My eyes burned from the chlorine. While shivering with my ears draining pool water, I could hear the laughter I knew would be there.

Once again our platoon came up short. We had too many non-swimmers. Therefore, we didn't qualify for another streamer for our still-naked platoon standard.

———— • ◆ • ————

The PRT obstacle course was different from the one at "motivation." The major distinction was the rope climb. The thick jute ropes were knotted at regular intervals, all the way up. One had to utilize arm strength and leg coordination to pull oneself from knot to knot.

The day of the PRT finally arrived, and it was hot and muggy. The rope climb and long run were my two weakest events, and I didn't sleep well. The image of the rope hung in my imagination like a hangman's noose. A handful of us could cause our platoon to fail the test—and we knew who we were.

By the time we got to the rope climb, it was early afternoon. We were hot, dusty, and tired. I approached my dangling rope with a group of others, and waited in the sand for the starter's whistle to blow. When the whistle blew, we leapt from the sand pit onto the lowest knot of our ropes and began the climb, racing against each other and the clock. I climbed, jumped, and pulled my way up until I reached the top! I grasped the large metal turnbuckle and peered at the starter, waiting for the signal to descend.

The starter signaled me to come down. I was jubilant! I had done it. I accomplished the rope climb! I received congratulations and cheers from my platoon mates, and my chest swelled with pride. I sought Arnie and offered him some advice as his group formed a line: "Jump and pull yourself up at the same time!"

When it came Arnie's turn to climb, I caught sight of his anxiety. The whistle blew and the groups attacked their ropes; Arnie trailed from the start. He flailed about with his legs so much that he tired himself out! He barely clung to the rope after only a few knots. I stood helplessly in the distance, attempting to will him up the rope! Before he could get beyond the half-way point, the climb was over. Arnie had run out of time.

———— • ◆ • ————

The run in the Physical Readiness Test started in the heat of the afternoon sun. Clouds of dust rose and swirled around the elliptical track. Three platoons of our company double-timed around. No singing or cadence call aided us as we ran. In short order, the formations broke down as strong runners passed the slower ones. Only recruits were running this time.

Coming as the last event of a grueling day, it quickly felt like a marathon run. The sweat poured from me as I jogged around the dusty track. Each recruit had to find his own rhythm to maintain his pace. The pride I felt after my successful rope climb melted away; I feared dropping out of the run. I had to keep sprinting in spite of the pain or fatigue. I had to reach beyond my endurance to prove to these bastards that I belonged!

I was barely shuffling when I crossed the finish line under the time limit. All my aches and pains disappeared for a moment as I basked in the glow of that accomplishment. It was over. The dreaded PRT was finally history, and I had survived it!

Arnie, and some others, dropped out of the run. I witnessed Arnie stumbling to the side of the track and collapsing onto his back. He lay there with his chest heaving as he coughed and gasped for air. One of our DIs stood over Arnie, yelling and attempting to ridicule him back onto the track. Arnie didn't respond.

I made my way over to Arnie; he was laying on his side with his head propped up on one bent elbow. I sat on the ground near him without saying a word. My heart ached for his disappointment.

The whistles sounded the end of the run. The clock beat a few die-hard stragglers, sluggishly jogging around the track; they garnered more admiration from their fellow recruits and DIs than those who gave up. The day was over. Once again, we had failed to win a streamer. We failed at our last chance to add a pennant to our platoon standard before graduation.

The steaming hot showers washed away the dirt and grime from our aching bodies. While we dressed for evening chow, joy and anger mingled uneasily in the atmosphere of our squad bay. We were almost US Marines! We were different recruits from the time when we arrived; our drill instructors shaped and molded us into stronger men. That was their job.

I accomplished what I didn't think I could. In doing so, I surprised my fellow recruits and DIs. I discovered what the Marine Corps wanted me to discover—a will deep within me from which I could draw strength.

Later, we recounted the day's events with our DIs. One said he was pleased with our efforts, but it was regrettable that a few non-hackers cost the platoon a streamer from the PRT. "Back in my day, if somebody cost us that streamer, we'd have a blanket party for the son of a bitch! I have no use for quitters in my Marine Corps," he said forcefully.

———•◆•———

The night air was thick and warm. We heard the trucks outside, maneuvering around the complex of buildings and spraying pesticide to kill mosquitoes. "Lights out in one minute, ladies," the DIs announced. "Lights out," was the command before the fire-watch recruit plunged the squad bay into darkness.

I wished to fall asleep, but I heard subtle movements and whispering. I lay perfectly still, straining to listen and hoping for sleep at the same time. Suddenly, they were there in the darkness! Like phantoms, I felt their presence on both sides of our bunk!

There were at least four, and Bangston was the leader. I detected his tense whisper; he barked instructions to his henchmen! Without opening my eyes, I sensed what was happening. This team of shadow avengers seized Arnie in his bunk, pronounced sentence on him for being a quitter and non-hacker, and executed punishment!

They held Arnie tightly, as he struggled to escape. I heard the punishment squad pummeling him with their fists! The bunk rocked, as they wailed away angrily! Then, it was over—at least for Arnie. The phantom squad moved onto other bunks; the muffled sounds of punishment could be heard by all. One of the targets tried to hide in the "head," but the fire watch alerted the goon squad to his presence. He was dragged back, without protest, and beaten.

I felt heavy-hearted for my friend Arnie, and yet, I felt lucky that I wasn't a victim. I couldn't cry for him or the others, but I came close. I buried my face in my pillow and listened to the sounds of silence, yearning to escape into sleep. The world was suddenly uglier.

By graduation, Arnie's face lost most of its puffiness and discoloration. He began to look like his old self again, but he didn't act like it. He remained quiet and withdrawn, even from me. I knew our relationship was altered and probably over. Friendship bonds that were formed under pressures were ending—a unique circumstance to that time and place.

In short order, we polished our brass, shined our shoes, and posed for graduation photos. We wore "mock" dress blue uniforms in the snapshots. We were ready to leave Parris Island and progress to more specialized training in our MOS (Military Occupational Specialty).

Graduation fell on a bright, sunny day on August 3, 1966. I didn't invite any family members to the ceremony, although I finally finished something I started. I was still ashamed of what I deemed as my dark side. That dark side put me into the "motivation" platoon. I deserved all of my pain. Yet, I longed to find a way to transform my fears and loathing into a positive and reshape my weak character.

————•◆•————

Camp Geiger was a bus ride form Parris Island. Every marine is proud to announce that the first MOS is rifleman. Whether or not they qualified on the rifle range in basic training, each marine is expected to become an expert in knowledge and handling of his rifle. Aside from that tradition, however, there is very little glamour to being a grunt. A grunt is a basic Marine Corps rifleman. His job entails advancing through contested ground, finding the enemy, and killing or capturing him!

The aptitude test that I took in basic training indicated that my MOS would be rifleman. I was disappointed. I knew I wasn't highly intelligent—which would have put me on track for a more challenging MOS—but evidently, I had a higher opinion of my talents than the Marine Corps. The reality was that as the Vietnam War escalated, the rifleman (the actual backbone of all ground forces) was doing the heavy lifting. I was a seventeen-year-old high-school dropout. What else was I suited for?

Things were a little more relaxed at Camp Geiger. We were US Marines now, although we were at the very bottom of the food chain. Very few of the graduating platoons ended up in the same training company or specialty schools at the camp. Some went to artillery or radio school. Others were chosen to become super-grunts and trained to join the marines elite fighting force called Force Recon.

In the August heat of North Carolina, we were introduced to weapons and tactics. We performed maneuvers in mock war games, using maps and compasses. We became intimately acquainted with the backbone of the Marine Corps infantry, the M14 rifle. In addition, we were acquainted with C Rations, the source of sustenance for troops in the field.

I applied myself to the challenges at Camp Geiger and tried to come to terms with my personal demons and the difficult time I had at Parris Island. I stayed out of trouble, and at the end of my time at Camp Geiger, I was promoted to PFC, Private First Class.

I looked forward to returning home on leave. It was more than four months since I'd left the world of Charter Oak Terrace, my family, and friends. All my old feelings diminished. Though, I had one thing I had craved—a new persona. I was a United States Marine!

The homecoming was great! There were hugs, kisses, hand-shakes, and back slaps. We took photos and made phone calls to relatives. I slept in my old room. My brother Jasper was still away, and I missed talking to him.

————— • ◆ • —————

I reported to my new unit in the Eighth Marines of the First Marine Division, Fleet Marine Force (FMF), Camp Lejeune, North Carolina, as a Private First Class. The marine base sprawled over coastal North Carolina, adjacent to Jacksonville. If Parris Island and Camp Geiger were like towns, Camp Lejeune was the big city. This was the real Marine Corps. Constantly, traffic flowed in and out of the guarded main gate onto wide boulevards, past manicured lawns, and around large barracks and office buildings.

Garrison duty—life on the base was becoming a negative, draining experience for me. With a 0311 MOS, that of a rifleman, my only required expertise was to be combat. The training was challenging, but not very interesting. Forced marches and mock war games were an unsatisfying alternative to hours of cleaning and prepping for inspections. GI cleaning in the military is the universal religion. When we had a field day, it was a cleaning and organizing spree that involved everyone.

Liberty was the carrot; the reward was dangled in front of each unit for enduring hours of drills and passing various inspections. If your unit failed inspection, you were denied any weekend passes. It was time to "turn to" and start cleaning all over again. That was the stick! The carrot and stick always worked as a motivator. Liberty passes from the base could be for twenty-four, forty-eight, or seventy-two hours! The seventy-two hours, three-day passes were the most prized and the most difficult to obtain.

Jacksonville ("J-ville") was the lure for many of those with a one- or two-day pass. Like any military circus town, it had the amusements required to entertain a large and transient community of marines and their dependants. A lot of the guys roamed the landscape, searching for watering holes where they could indulge in adult beverages and enjoy female companionship. Female companionship ranged from a few hours at a no-tell motel to romance and marriage in some cases. When the weekend liberties ended, fellas returned to their units with tales of drunken lunacy and sexual exploits!

On weekends, when most of the unit earned passes, I stayed on the base. I tried to fit in where I could, but I was too much of a loner. I did what I'd always done, stayed friendly with all (as "Mr. Congeniality") and withdrew deeper inside myself. Soon, I was more isolated than ever. Slowly, I began repeating my old patterns.

There were times when I was tempted to hang out with some other horny guys, go to a local fun spot, meet some girls, and maybe "get lucky." But I held back, stayed on base, and read or went to the movies instead.

My desires never said no, so I slipped back into the loving embrace of food for comfort. I ate my meals in the chow hall and ate after evening chow from the "bogey bait" trucks; they travelled around the base selling food items and snacks. I was putting on the pounds, becoming a "fat body" and hating myself for it! What I ate in private showed in public, and the seams on my uniforms were stretched to their limits.

I smoked to curb my appetite, but was only successful during duty hours. Come evening, I yearned for my comforters of food and cigarettes. Each day's boredom or bedlam demanded to be ended with my self-destructive indulgences. I was out of control and out of shape in short order. I was a stranger in a strange place. Once the oppressive discipline of boot camp was over, I had trouble dealing with the freedom of garrison duty.

The good news is that there was no temptation in the field, and we were in the field a lot. We were trained and prepared for possible deployment anywhere in the world. We practiced helicopter landings and amphibious landings. We performed a large field exercise during a cold and wet week in the boondocks in mid-November. The exercise was miserable with sand and mud everywhere, and everything rain soaked. Units were confused and lost. Our company commanders ensured us that we got a good taste of what real combat conditions could be like. We learned to depend on each other and keep our heads.

The cold and dampness permeated everything, and by the second night, I couldn't get warm or stop shivering. Directly, I was taken from the field with some others who succumbed to the elements. Again, I was a non-hacker! A day later, the remaining unit returned, and we scrubbed and cleaned for an inspection, taking place prior to the Thanksgiving holiday.

I spent that Thanksgiving on the base. It was like a ghost town. The mess halls offered foods to comfort those like me who sought familiar Thanksgiving flavors. However, I was determined to get into better shape and lose the extra pounds I put on since leaving Parris Island. I bought a vinyl sweat suit to wear while jogging and exercising.

I skipped evening chow. My brilliant strategy was to sweat off excess pounds and sleep through the pain of hunger. I jogged around the nearby field in the early evening. As the sweat poured from my body, I nurtured the image of a slender body for Christmas leave. I went to bed with a terrible fear and realization inside me. I couldn't do four years in the Marine Corps in my present state of mind! I was beginning to unravel. I was becoming a danger to myself.

———— •◆• ————

I was given Christmas leave, and along with another marine, hitched rides from Camp Lejeune to Hartford. It was a long way to go for only a few days, but a plan was forming in my fevered brain. My scheme gave me a new sense of purpose and more importantly, hope. I would escape my military obligation and return to my life before Anthony convinced me to join the Marine Corps on the buddy system!

The Christmas holiday came and went. The old, sentimental emotionalism wasn't there for me any longer, but I played along. I found the key to my plan: my birth certificate.

Back at Camp Lejeune, I was upbeat as I waited to talk to the company commander. (I requested the appointment as soon as I returned from leave.) I offered no indication as to why I urgently needed to see the captain. My only claim was that it was a personal matter.

When I was finally standing at ease before his desk, I handed him my birth certificate. My hand shook slightly as I said, "Sir, I respectfully request to be discharged from the Marine Corps on the grounds of fraudulent enlistment." The captain looked quizzically at me and the paper I handed him. "I enlisted as William Rose, sir, but that is not my legal name. My real name is William Ingram," I added. I didn't want to appear too excited. I wanted him to regard it as an unfortunate dilemma for me.

Somehow those words—fraudulent enlistment—had entered my frenzied thoughts. Had they come from the first recruitment talk? Eventually, they reappeared in my tormented mind like a door marked "EXIT." I was fearful at first that I might indeed be in serious trouble for enlisting as Rose, so I did as I'd done throughout my school years: I kept it my secret. Now, in my twisted desire to escape yet another commitment I made, I thought I could use the secret as my way out.

"I don't think this is going to be that big of a problem," the captain said, as he began writing something on note paper. "My understanding of fraudulent enlistment is that it pertains to individuals who use false identities to conceal criminal pasts. They attempt to evade legal authorities by enlisting in the military under assumed names. I don't think you fit in that category," he concluded. He finished writing and clipped the note paper to the birth certificate. My heart sank.

"I knew I was Ingram when I signed up and was sworn in, but I lied and didn't say anything," I said.

"Private, the Marine Corps is not going to discharge you for something like this," he said, as he looked me in the eye. He had my records on his desk. He saw through me and determined I was looking for an easy way out. "I don't believe you have to worry about any punishment," he continued thoughtfully. "This appears to have been an error in judgment. I'll send it up the chain of command and to legal. I think it'll come down to you picking the name you want to use, and your records will reflect that," he added matter of factly. He wanted to be sure that I was under no illusions that the Unites States Marine Corps was letting me go so easily. I thanked him for his time and left the office empty handed and despondent.

————•◆•————

We were shipping out to Cuba. Some of the guys in our unit thought the move to "Gitmo" was a prelude to being dispatched to that place called Vietnam. The war was getting louder and uglier. It penetrated the minds of many young men who were eager for a chance to prove their mettle in real combat. At that time, I considered a real war preferable to six more months of tedious training as a grunt.

After my disappointing confession to my company commander, I was in the doldrums. My mood spiraled lower when I was assigned to kitchen duty. Everything was going against me, my victim-obsessed mind told me. Therefore, I was really surprised when I was given a four-day leave the week after New Year's. I quickly hitched a ride back to Hartford.

I had never been this low before. I was out of options. I smoked cigarettes, ate junk food, and furiously searched my imagination for an escape from the mess I had made of my life. Was I now my father, the man I never knew? Were we both here now—my father, injecting a needle in his arm, and me, looking for a path out of this life?

My Marine Corps boot camp graduation photo Aug. 3rd 1966. I am 3rd row from top & center

Left - right : Jasper,Dorcas,William holding baby brother Duncan

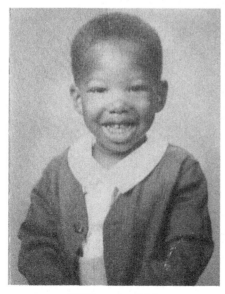

William as a child

William as a youngster

Willam's junior high graduation photo (1963)
I'm 2nd row center

This was a collage of photos assembled of all 6 kids
The center photo of me in uniform with baby sister Edith Sylvia

My brother Jasper

My brother Duncan

My brother Emmanuel (Manny)

My sister Dorcas

Our grandmother, Blossie (Nana to us) spent Christmas with us while healing from a
broken leg. She's holding baby brother Emannuel (1959)
L - R: Duncan, William, Dorcas, Nana, and Jasper

My sister Edith
Sylvia

My mother Mary Elizabeth and
I after I had returned home.

My Uncle William (Buddy) and his wife Aunt Evor, flanking Aunt Bertha

A family Thanksgiving gathering after my return home

All 6 siblings at a 2005 gathering in Hartford.
L-R: Dorcas, Jasper, Duncan, William (author)
Emmanuel (Manny), Edith Sylvia

The author, William L. Ingram.

CHAPTER 8

ALMOST HEAVEN

Morning devotions were held in the mission's chapel. Brother Johnson was there—neat and clean shaven. He led the group. We each chose a bible verse to quote before Brother Johnson said a prayer to begin our day. Only a few of us were in the chapel most mornings. Emil, the large, stocky, white-haired cook; Brother Donavan, a huge black man with tufts of hair sprouting from his otherwise smooth, round face; old Irish Bill, a wizened and wrinkled troll-looking character; Brother Johnson with his big eyes and Cheshire cat grin; and me. (Whenever Martin Brett, the mission director, attended morning devotions, Brother Johnson dutifully sat with us in the circle so Brother Brett could lead the session.)

I fit in right away. I was a young pair of hands and legs that Brothers Brett and Johnson prayed for. The mission was my temporary refuge from my world of confusion and fear. I knew I was a fugitive, and I feared each day that my whereabouts would be discovered. Everyone would consider me an unpatriotic liar and coward! But I suppressed my fears, and devoted myself to being helpful and eventually, indispensible.

Emil took me under his wing immediately. He was delighted to have an eager apprentice with a hungry mind. He needed help preparing the evening soup, because all he got from his usual volunteers was a full helping of complaining. "You're a good boy. You don't complain about working in the kitchen. The others only want to fill their bellies and not do much work," he said almost every day of the first week since I joined the mission.

Emil was German and Swedish stock. He had well-muscled, white arms covered with the same white hair as on his head and eyebrows. I concluded that he had been a nice-looking man in his earlier years, before drink took its toll. After years of wear and tear—beneath his big, bushy, eyebrows and jowly cheeks—was a kindly expression that made me feel comfortable.

He showed me how to peel vegetables for his soup, and open number-ten ("10") cans of vegetables, if we didn't have enough fresh produce. Emil was a real chef for most of his adult life, I learned. Although he wasn't one to sit around and talk about himself, I gleaned a lot of information from him during the course of a normal day.

In fact, I learned more from the workers at the mission than from all the people I'd known in the past. These men taught me about the fragility of human beings. They were not like those I knew who tried desperately to conceal weaknesses beneath bluff and bravado.

The mission workers were all broken vessels, people who were damaged during their journeys. Then, they found themselves at one of society's waste dumps. They were the reason I felt so at home. I finally found a place where I didn't have to fit in, because fitting in wasn't required on skid row. I learned to keep my mouth shut and listen. I communicated with my ears and eyes, because facial expressions reveal volumes about us.

Peeling vegetables in the mission kitchen became therapeutic for me. I peeled veggies into a garbage pail alongside a large pot of cold water. Potatoes, carrots, purple-top turnips, onions, rutabagas, and parsnips were among the produce I came to know intimately. I handled these vegetables with respect. It was a small, yet significant awakening, a spiritual connection. I had not known this feeling before. The irony of drawing such satisfaction from peeling vegetables wasn't lost on me. As a fugitive, I joyfully performed tasks that I had resisted during my last acts of defiance at Camp Lejeune.

The Marine Corps had tried to become the father that I never had. Yet, I chafed at the authority it exercised over me. I ran from the corps, as I ran from home. Now, I was cutting the skins off potatoes and carrots in a skid-row kitchen, three-thousand miles away. I was happily and dutifully performing tasks that I could have completed on base with the same attitude. "You resent authority!" The words echoed from my boot-camp days. It was painful, but true. Was my emotional fog clearing?

———•◆•———

The soup was the life blood of the rescue mission. It's what got the derelicts, winos, and other transients to seek sustenance at a place that also offered salvation. Soup and salvation was a sweet and sour combination. The incentive of serving soup so that the brothers could also serve salvation was as old as calling Los Angeles, "Lost Angels." Our mission, like the other missions on skid row, was to extend a ministering arm of an evangelical organization. Donations to the missions went to buy food and supplies to keep the kitchens well stocked. Our fresh vegetables were almost exclusively supplied by a local fellow who was one of the oddest characters I would ever meet.

Brother Bedrose was the Fifth Street missions' angel of mercy. And like most angels, you never knew when he would appear. His name could have been a shortened version of Bedrosian, which may have made him Armenian. His ethnicity appeared to be Middle Eastern. One noticeable characteristic about him was indisputable size. Brother Bedrose was huge! He was built like a lumberjack or a pro wrestler.

He had a swarthy, olive complexion of someone from the Mediterranean and a prominent nose! His cheeks were pock-marked; his large eyes were shaded by big, bushy eyebrows that appeared alive and friendly. Bedrose had a full, though graying, head of hair and large hands with thick fingers that appeared well acquainted with hard work.

I first met Brother Bedrose after a couple of nights at the mission. The staff retired to their rooms for the night after cleaning up from the evening service and soup meal. My room was on the second floor with the others, in the rear of the building overlooking an alley. It was after 9:00 p.m., and I was reading my bible before going to bed.

I could hear a distant, muffled sound of someone banging on a door. I strained to hear as my pulse quickened and a terrible fear seized me. I heard more voices and sounds of movement; then, there was a knock on my door. It was old Bill; he came to ensure that I didn't get out of unloading the vegetables. I joined the others in the kitchen and dining room.

Outside the open, double doors of the dining hall was parked a station wagon. In the dim outside light, I saw a giant, six-feet-five man, perhaps in his late fifties or early sixties, unloading various containers of produce from his car and placing them on the sidewalk.

"Praise the Lord! Praise the Lord!" he repeated sporadically, whether someone echoed him or not. "Praise God!" he exclaimed. When our eyes met, he handed me a crate of veggies.

I watched the others for a clue as to what to do. Brother Donavan, who was always praising God in barely intelligible mutterings, was the only one who seemed to match Brother Bedrose's enthusiasm. Emil was in charge of our small work detail, and he directed the placement of the boxes and crates. I could see he wasn't happy about the produce. "Half this shit is rotten!" Emil said to no one in particular. Directly, he heated leftover soup over a high flame on the kitchen stove.

Old Bill didn't hide his disgust with our night angel. He left as soon as the station wagon's contents were unloaded. Brother Bedrose, perched at one of the long tables, intently watched the door to the kitchen. He spouted "Praise the Lord," occasionally. Emil sent me to his table; I carried a saucer with half a loaf of bread and a tub of butter. In short order, Emil appeared with a large bowl of steaming vegetable soup and placed it in front of eager Brother Bedrose. "Praise the Lord," he exclaimed, as he grasped the soup spoon, blew on the hot liquid, and sipped his soup.

Brother Bedrose looked like the Aladdin's lamp genie come to life, especially with the steam from the broth rising before him. "Praise the Lord," he mumbled through mouthfuls of food. "Praise God."

Emil called me into the kitchen and ladled a second bowl of soup. I placed it beside Brother Bedrose's nearly empty first bowl. "Praise the Lord," he exclaimed, sliding the full bowl in front of him. Emil and I contemplated our guest while he devoured his meal in the dimly lit kitchen. "He's a crazy, old bastard," the cook said matter of factly. "He goes around to supermarkets, collects their old produce, and brings it here. But you never know what time of night he'll show up," Emil complained with a helpless gesture.

After a while, Brother Bedrose stood to his full height and bellowed toward us near the kitchen door. "Thank you, brothers. Praise the Lord." Within an hour of his arrival, he left in his beat-up, empty station wagon.

---•◆•---

When I came down to the kitchen the next morning, Emil had selected many of the items to be thrown out. "Eighty-six that shit stuff," the cook growled. I knew the military term for getting rid of something was to eighty-six it, so without question, I tossed the rotting produce into the garbage. "That crazy coot," Emil continued, shaking his head. "Some of this isn't even fit for the soup pot!"

Brother Johnson was glad to see that the vegetables arrived. He occupied a room in the mission. Yet, usually after services, he secured the building and left. He walked wherever he went. I assumed he stayed in a nearby room some nights.

Brother Johnson was slightly taller than me, which put him over six feet. He had no clear accent that I could detect, but occasionally he spoke of Philadelphia as if it were home. Johnson was soft spoken with large, expressive eyes and a ready grin. Many of his gestures and mannerisms were strongly feminine without hinting at homosexuality. It was like seeing a man during his formative years who greatly resembled a powerful female presence.

Brother Johnson was friendly and likeable without being close to anyone. Though he wore a bow tie at times, he preferred a buttoned collar with no neck wear. He dressed neatly and understated. Instead of a suit jacket or sport coat, Johnson wore a lightweight jacket with a zipper front. The jacket was always dark brown to match his trousers.

Brother Johnson was at the mission much of the time. During most days, he disappeared for an hour or so. He usually carried his bible. Sometimes I observed him when he left the building. With a half grin on his face, he strode down the street purposefully, taking long steps as he leaned forward, as though walking against a stiff wind. I wondered where he went on his mysterious outings. I didn't wonder out loud though. We were a quirky bunch; we gave each other space to heal the wounds that brought us to skid row in the first place.

Brother Donavan obviously had mental and emotional issues beyond those of the other staff. Everyone ignored him generally, and he seemed to return the favor. This relationship was like one between a big, slow-moving dog and a family that steps over the animal or only speaks to it when necessary. Obediently, the dog does as it's told—moves, eats, and seeks an out-of-the-way resting place; the pup remains there until its world is disturbed again.

Like the family dog, Brother Donavan was definitely in his own world. He could be found sitting on one of the stairs—rocking rhythmically back and forth—while muttering barely intelligible phrases to himself. His murmurs contained praises to God, but these utterances were never as clear as Brother Bedrose's "Praise the Lord" exclamations.

Brother Donavan was a huge black man who weighed close to four-hundred pounds! He stood no taller than five feet six; he sported a large, round head with smooth facial features broken by a scraggily crop of whiskers. His whiskers were not cut or combed, but were curled together in random patches around his chin and cheeks. I guessed him to be in his late thirties. Donavan's short-cropped hair was called nappy by black people. His big, brown eyes avoided direct eye contact.

Brother Donavan was out of place at the mission, because he barely communicated on any level. Sometimes he would just sit in his room, rocking and mumbling, without eating or taking part in morning devotions or evening services. Considering his gentle and harmless demeanor, who was I to question his presence? Perhaps he was cared for because of who he had been, like a family member whose personality died before his or her body.

I thought of primitive cultures where such people were considered "touched by God," and not touched in the head. I hid my own demons, and all of us were damaged in visible and invisible ways. So, Brother Donavan was treated like a mascot who wasn't required to do anything.

————— • ◆ • —————

Old Irish Bill was a short, wizened, ugly, bitter, and little white man. He was a busybody troll whose nose was in everyone's business. Not being familiar with trolls, except in fairy tales, I didn't realize that they had two faces. At least Old Bill did! Like many visitors at the mission, Old Bill was a recovering alcoholic. (Back then, he was called an "alchy" or a wino.) Supposedly, Bill had dried out and been saved.

Old Bill had all the telltale signs of a hard drinker; he looked old beyond his maybe fifty-or-so years. His weary eyes, red-veined nose, and craggy-lined face told the story of the gutters he crawled through. No taller than five feet, he exhibited the slight and wiry build of an ex-wino. At one time, Bill drank, rather than ate.

And Old Bill could turn on his Irish charm. He could lay on the blarney thick as you please when he talked to strangers who visited the mission. The other face of Old Bill was saved for the derelicts and lost souls who dined on soup every night. He barely concealed his contempt for them, although they were now where he had been. I didn't understand the tendencies of many who changed to look down on those who struggled.

Old Bill didn't think much of his co-workers at the mission, but he charmed them to their faces; then, he belittled them behind their backs. I thought I was the only one who saw that this angry, little person took no joy from helping his fellow man; someone, who despite his testimony, never seemed changed by Jesus. I tried my usual approaches to befriend Old Bill when I first joined the mission staff, but I could sense his resentment. I suspected that he saw through my hypocrisy of being saved, and he was judging me for that. Soon, I understood that he was one of those mean-spirited and hateful people. Old Bill dominated our relationship through intimidation. I couldn't do anything to please him. He nitpicked and criticized me whenever he could. It wasn't long before we were enemies. I hated Old Bill, but I felt so guilty for hating him. I denied my feelings and tried even harder to please him, or I avoided him—neither approach worked.

———————— ◆ • ————————

Martin Brett and Brother Johnson liked me immediately, and Reverend Jordan took to me when we met as well. Emil, Brother Donavan—and others who volunteered or left donations at the mission—enjoyed talking to me. I was "Mr. Congeniality" again. My warm personality was more sincere than ever. I aspired to reignite a loving, Christian approach to all contacts now. I endeavored to become a real Christian and live the life I rejected soon after my Methodist confirmation vows.

This attitude made me eager to help with tasks around the mission. Cooking with Emil, cleaning floors, vacuuming, folding laundry, or stacking chairs were some of the chores I performed in order to maintain the large building.

I was young, teachable, and willing to help. Everyone, except Old Bill, welcomed my attitude. I was a dramatic contrast to the typical, crusty, dried-out wino that stayed at the mission (These men were sober until the lure of the bottle was too great to resist). I was a fugitive with terrible guilt over a secret I feared would be revealed any day. Could I become a born-again Christian, based on a foundation of lies? Perhaps, a forgiving God's help could guide me to some clues to the answers I needed.

William Kinkade was my new name, and I wanted desperately to build a new persona around that name. Whether I was Brother William, Brother Bill, or Brother Kinkade, I relished the chance at a new start in life.

A few weeks after I was comfortable in the mission, I played around on the organ and piano. I told people that my mother played the piano and taught lessons, but that I had no real skill myself. Everyone seemed impressed when I practiced each morning on the organ after chores. I knew how to read music, and the mission stocked music books. I loved the organ, because it made me sound more musically talented than I was.

Only when Reverend Jordan invited a keyboardist to the mission did the piano or organ get played. Singing during services was usually a cappella. Evening services attracted a motley group of street people. No matter what the gathering, most visitors enjoyed the singing. The worship songs were Christian standards that many learned in former lives and better times. Now, these melodies soothed their aches and pains.

The hymnals were placed on the chairs before we opened the doors. The only song that was always sung, played, or hummed was "Just as I Am." This song was a fundamental component of Evangelistic revival services for years. Presently, this hymn played at the end of service during "alter call." It was the same song that played when I walked to the altar weeks before.

When I opened the chapel doors into the dining hall, the line of men shuffled past the steam table that exhibited Emil's large pot of hot stew and stacks of white bread. Emil ladled the savory broth, with chunks of meat and vegetables, donning his ever-present white apron. I kept the reserve soup hot, made sure the bread stacks were plentiful, and dispensed the coffee.

Guest preachers usually enjoyed having soup with the men. This connection made it important that the soup we served was the best. We never ran out of soup, but it was a guessing game as to how much would be required. We came dangerously close to running out a few times, but Emil pulled out the old "soup stretchers" by adding more water, seasoning, and a few vegetables.

After the meal, Old Bill, Brother Donavan, and others on staff washed dishes and wiped tables. This time would have been the best for Brother Bedrose to pull up in his station wagon and exclaim, "Praise the Lord!" It seldom worked out that way.

As the warm winds of spring1967 swirled around Los Angeles, I found myself in a quandary. I was genuinely sorry for my misdeeds, but still too proud and foolish to turn myself in. I knew my day of reckoning would come, but I wanted it on my terms. In the meantime, I took advantage of my self-imposed exile by transforming myself.

The mission boasted an extensive and varied collection of books that had been donated over the years. I studied several books at once. I intended to strengthen my vocabulary, so I learned several new words a day. I dedicated myself to learning more than ever before! In all my years of public schooling, I never considered education as a pathway to becoming a better person. Now, I was determined to make that transition. With the help of God, I resolved to vanquish my inferiority complexes. The Lord would guide me to become a Renaissance Christian. I would study his word and show myself approved.

In addition to morning devotions, I read the bible voraciously. I stored several versions in my room along with a bible concordance and a Greek lexicon to further illuminate the large amounts of text that I was reading. As I dedicated myself to the new direction in my life, I found few allies and little encouragement among my housemates. Brother Johnson and Martin Brett didn't encourage extensive discussion or questioning about confusing passages or apparent contradictions in the bible.

"That's interesting, Brother Kinkade," Brother Johnson might say, responding to a point I was expounding on. "All you need to know is that you are saved by the blood of Jesus," he would add with finality.

The enthusiasm and energy of my youth was probably entertaining to them. I believed that serious and profound truth, beyond human wisdom in the bible, was meant to be discovered. Why weren't we going deeper into the meaning and mystery *behind* the scriptures during morning devotions? I wished to do more than read a verse or passage and let it stand on its own. I endeavored to explain what I understood and what I questioned. Eyes rolled and long audible sighs were emitted when I spoke for a minute or two longer than our allotted time.

My mind awakened to my human thoughts and interactions with a divine being beyond my understanding, but not beyond my reach. The bible reflected that other minds sought insights concerning this being, too. Creature was seeking his creator. My main solace became the radio. Turning the dial a few degrees, especially on Sundays, I could get a better-than-average college course in Comparative Religion.

Long before I arrived in the City of Angles, the region was called the "land of fruits and nuts." A few of the "nuts" were thought to be religious groups and churches that proliferated over Southern California. Radio was the principal outlet for these various groups, after they grew beyond their humble beginnings on street corners and behind storefronts. Radio gave them legitimacy through exposure and access to potential new followers; it also offered financial support.

LA witnessed generations of the saw-dust trail Evangelists that preached salvation gospel in tent revival meetings from the desert to the seashore. Many now-established organizations were forced to compete with upstart groups over the radio airwaves. Wall-to-wall religions expressed views, ranging from fifteen-minute bible-study classes to short sermons.

Our mission's patron, Reverend Fred Jordan, progressed his ministry from humble beginnings. Reportedly, he emerged as a "hitch-hiking evangelist" who accepted rides from strangers and talked to them about Jesus and God's plan for man's salvation. His ministry transitioned to radio broadcasting when he established his *Church in the Home* program. This show was designed especially for believers who were shut-ins or otherwise unable to make it to services. Its popularity grew so much that it shifted to television as well; it was broadcasted on TV every Sunday morning. It was required viewing for us.

On Sundays, after participating in morning devotions and watching the *Church in the Home* broadcasts, I listened to Christian radio programs and read in my room. Some of the tracts and articles contradicted what I believed, but I read them with an open mind. And I prayed. I prayed as I was taught as a child, and as I witnessed others pray from pulpits and in prayer meetings. I prayed fervently for the wisdom of Solomon and the patience of Job.

———— ◆ ————

I started exercising again. The pounds had piled on me, and I was forced to find bigger clothes among the donated items. I utilized an empty room next to the library to work out. I performed the PT calisthenics I learned at boot camp. In the beginning, I exercised as religiously as I read the scriptures, determined to shed the excess pounds. By the third week, I was working out sporadically. My familiar life pattern was repeating itself.

The daily tensions of living as a fugitive gnawed at my resolve. I sought comfort in the arms of my beloved. "She" never said no! Food was always ready to "embrace" me and comfort my feelings of pain. "She" called to me from the kitchen, where I indulged myself in blissful secrecy. The power of past patterns dominated me as I resorted to sneaking sandwiches to my room; I devoured these delights in secret. I ached inwardly, as I surrendered to the sin (as it's known in the Bible) of gluttony. I prayed for deliverance during the daytime, but sought food for its comforting "embrace" at night.

I let my mustache grow in an attempt to look older. Although I was eighteen-years-old, I looked younger. Some assumed that I was Brother Johnson's younger brother or son. Although I never left the shadow of the building, I sought a hiding place within myself. Psychologically, I hid behind my facial hair and layers of fat. These traits insulated me from the pains of inner conflict.

I settled into a routine by that summer. I awoke early and prayed. "This is the day that the Lord has made. Let us rejoice, and be glad in it. Amen." Emil would be in the kitchen, preparing for breakfast. I assisted him or finished sorting vegetables from Brother Bedrose's produce delivery. Brother Johnson would call us to the chapel for devotions; then, we ate breakfast. My chore was to clean up after the meal while others completed general cleaning and tasks.

After lunchtime, some staff members witnessed on the street with Brother Johnson. With bibles and pamphlets in hand, they prowled the streets around the mission. They were keen to give their testimony and witness to anyone who listened to their story of God's ability to change lives. Some residents, who claimed that they were saved a night or two before, never came back. I never ventured beyond the sidewalk where Brother Bedrose parked his car. With my duties in the kitchen demanding much of my attention, I was excused from witnessing on the streets.

I played the organ before services, as the early birds drifted in. While Brother Johnson and Brother Brett beckoned to the people passing, they loved hearing the music fill the mission. By 4:30 p.m., I opened the chapels' side entrance. It was the same door I entered for the first time only a few months before. I placed the large, A-frame, sandwich sign on the sidewalk. The sign announced the hours for services. I greeted the regulars and newcomers, as Brother Johnson did on my first day. Old Bill and Brother Donavan set up chairs. Brother Johnson would relieve me at the entrance, so I could play the organ. I managed to create my own world where I was respected and appreciated.

Once I was behind the organ, it was like being on stage. I played a few secular tunes that I liked, such as "Somewhere over the Rainbow" and "You'll Never Walk Alone." Then, I performed the gospel songs most loved to hear, like "The Old Rugged Cross" and "Onward Christian Soldiers." I refused to be considered an accompanist, because I had no real talent. I avoided playing musical interludes during services, especially when we had a guest speaker. Occasionally, I played the song, "Just as I Am" for the "altar call."

We were each called upon to give our personal testimony at one time or another. This event usually took place before services began. Sometimes, it *was* the service. Staff and visitors stood; then, they spoke whatever was in their hearts. With few in attendance or a packed house, Brother Johnson or Martin Brett gave their stories of how they came to know the Lord.

I rehearsed my story, so that when that moment arrived, I would be prepared and less terrified. I hurriedly stepped to the pulpit from the organ. I spoke nervously, but sincerely. I relayed my story of a boy from back East who rejected old-time religion in his youth. I spoke of searching for answers and thanked God for guiding me to the Fifth Street mission, Reverend Fred Jordan, Brothers Brett and Johnson, and my Lord and Savior, Jesus Christ.

My testimony went over well. My relative youth made it easy to accept the fact that I wasn't a longtime wino who found his way back to God. My story offered some praise to the ministry of Reverend Jordan, but extended the glory to God. My prodigal-son testimony echoed a favorite Christian story of redemption. Most hearers related to the consequences of making poor choices, and almost everyone liked the happy ending.

Only Old Bill resented me. I became more comfortable with public speaking, and I was popular among the attendees. Consequently, Old Bill had difficulty thinly concealing his contempt for me. He considered me an upstart and phony. I hated him, for hating me.

————— • ◆ • —————

Martin Brett was a nice man. His large physical presence and missing arm drew one's attention immediately. Whether the arm was lost in World War II, Korea, or some other tragic event, I don't recall. His real life wounds cost him his family, and nearly his existence, when he resorted to alcohol for solace.

As a born-again Christian, Brett had no shame in recounting the folly of his ways. He had hit bottom before joining Reverend Fred Jordan's ministry on skid row. He gladly admitted that Jordan helped him turn his life around. He conveyed his personal salvation story frequently on his Sunday broadcast of *Church in the Home*. He also relayed it to attendants at the mission.

Brother Brett came by the mission regularly, but he never interfered with its daily functions. During one of his visits, he approached individual staff members and gave each a small cash stipend. He valued the mission experience and believed that the work was good for men struggling to recover their dignity. He also wanted to reward those same men for their efforts and give them hope of brighter futures. At first his gift was only two dollars. (He understood that this amount was a mere pittance to most men. Some of the members had made and lost fortunes during their lifetimes!) The two dollars was a blessing, but it also posed an unbearable temptation to some to buy cheap wine and reward themselves for a week of sobriety.

When Martin Brett increased my stipend to five dollars a week, it was like he was saying that he appreciated the role I played at the mission in helping Emil and Brother Johnson. Unlike the others, there was no obvious reason for a young man like myself to be nurtured back to health at the mission. In theory, after I developed a relationship with the Lord, I could have reentered the big world and become a productive member of society. But I had dark secrets that kept me in place. They were happy to have me work there for as long as I wanted to stay.

My weekly five-dollar bill went where my two dollars had gone—into a hidden envelope in my room. Since I never went out, I didn't need any walking-around money for Life Savers, chewing gum, etc. All my needs were met. Food, shelter, clothing, and personal-care items were plentiful. Books, magazines, and the daily papers were available. I had a radio in my room. More importantly than the few extra dollars from Martin Brett was his permission to take a donated TV and record player to my room as well.

Reverend Fred Jordan was slightly taller than six feet. I never saw him dressed in any clothing other than a tailored suit and tie. With his lovely wife on his arm, they were a couple that attracted attention in any setting. The story of Reverend Jordan's humble hitchhiking ministry fit right in with the lore of other religious pioneers of Southern California.

The Dust Bowl refugees brought their Bible-Belt love for fundamental preaching along with their search for better lives. Simple folks wanted simple faith—a deep and abiding faith that represented a caring God with a plan for their lives. God, family, and country were the patriotic trinity they embraced. That was the generation of post World War II America. Throngs of bible-thumping evangelists found their brand of gospel welcomed in LA among the Baptists, Catholics, Mormons, Spiritualists, Pagans, and opportunists.

The fruits of prosperity often left a bitter taste of hypocrisy in the hearts and minds of the post-war generation. Their baby-boom offspring were also affected. Those youthful "rebels without a cause" folks of the 1950s were now hippies, peaceniks, and black-power groups (among others) that rejected segments of society. This generation fiercely created its own subcultures.

The civil rights movement, the sexual revolution, the military-industrial complex, and the black power movement (among other machinations of the cultural revolution) left broken individuals in the margins of life. Thus, winos; druggies; and mental, emotional, and spiritual cripples were pushed aside by these subcultures that sought to create society in their images. We were together now—at the bottom.

Reverend Jordan's ministry was developed for many of LA's lost sheep. His weekly broadcast gave his television congregation a chance to aid their fellow men by donating to his skid-row mission and evangelism project. However, I was alarmed when a *Church in the Home* segment was to be filmed at the mission for a Sunday broadcast. I dreaded the thought of being recognized. I would be revealed as a liar and a user of godly people while I sought to remain a fugitive from justice!

I was determined to remain calm, on the outside, and acted like the intrusion of a camera crew was only a minor inconvenience. I wasn't too successful, though. My nerves showed. My head (or the "theater of my mind") played different versions of my discovery and arrest.

The word spread that a TV crew was at the Fifth Street mission for a telecast. Many of the regular faces we hosted most evenings didn't show—for good reason. It wasn't unheard of for desperate family members to search newspaper photos, TV newscasts, or documentaries to locate loved ones who dropped out of sight. Law enforcement scanned the same media to discover fugitives. It wasn't just an urban legend that the occasional "wanted" man would be found hiding among the faceless throngs of skid row. Therefore, my fears were well founded. However, I played my part, as if my life was of no interest to anyone who might see me on television.

The crew filmed the building to convey its physical updates. The men filed through the doors and were seated as Reverend Jordan's accompanist played the piano. Even with the absent regulars, we had a nearly full house.

Brother Johnson, Brother Brett, and Reverend Jordan were the speakers. No choir sang. Reverend Jordan interviewed resident assistants for their personal testimonies; these professions demonstrated that their lives had been turned around. During the filming, I spent as much time as possible with Emil in the kitchen. The camera rolled while we fed everyone stew, including Fred Jordan and Brothers Johnson and Brett. Revered Jordan counseled those who had answered the "altar call." Then, the event was over. The days and weeks that followed were torture for me. The program aired the following Sunday, and we were shown performing our tasks amongst the wretches of Los Angeles.

After that happening, every moment was akin to a death-row inmate's last hours. I feared every phone call, every stranger that approached the building, and every lingering glance at me. I fretted that I was about to be exposed. My paranoid fears consumed me. One day, I spied Brother Johnson talking to two men dressed in business suits; they were on the street. I couldn't move a muscle as I watched from the second-floor library. Each gesture fired my imagination. I wouldn't resist arrest. (I hoped they knew that.) Were they simply asking to question me? I wouldn't deny my true identity. Could I take anything with me? Maybe I could take my Bible. Nothing else was of any value.

Somehow, I found the resolve to meet my fate. I went quickly to my room, grabbed my favorite study Bible, and walked purposefully down the stairs. It was mid-afternoon and no one else seemed to be around. I was thankful of that. I wished to be apprehended without any commotion. I decided to wait quietly in the chapel with the doors propped open. I would be spotted as soon as they entered the side door. My sweating palms and pounding heart eased a bit as those anxious minutes of waiting turned into an hour. It all came to nothing. Directly, my fears drained away with the welcome routine of the evening service.

————— • ◆ • —————

The hot summer days in Los Angeles were unlike any I experienced back East. Los Angeles was often called "seventy-seven towns looking for a city." The huge LA basin cradled its urban areas; the sprawling city was larger than some states. The countless roads and freeways contributed to its smog, a detrimental environmental condition. The primary culprits—auto emissions—literally choked the city. "Living in LA was like living at the bottom of an ashtray," some raged! The polluted, warm air was trapped in the basin by an inversion layer of cool air from the ocean. Consequently, the smog had nowhere to go.

Then, the winds came! The hot, desert Santa Ana winds screamed across the city for days (that felt like weeks). The high-velocity winds cleaned out the stagnant air masses; previous breezes only moved the smog around. Those wonderful winds created a vacuum effect that left clear, pristine vistas in all directions. The purple mountains to the west of the city stood majestically!

———— • ◆ • ————

Geopolitics was a word I would add to my vocabulary by the summer of '67. I watched and read daily accounts of the six-day, Arab-Israeli war. The whole world watched as the tiny nation of Israel—threatened and surrounded on three sides by armies—outwitted, out fought, and triumphed over its enemies! It was a spectacular reworking of the David versus Goliath tale with the same God-blessed outcome!

Like most Christians in America, I felt an attachment and affinity for the Jewish people and their state. Basic Judaism, founded upon the Mosaic Code, was the taproot or "vine" from which Christianity branched. We embraced their history and their mystery of God. I felt personal empathy for Jewish people after reading books about the Holocaust.

The African continent was convulsing. Black Africa's sub-Saharan countries were challenging the control of their European colonizers. The Biafra War was a "black on black" civil war. The oil-rich region of Nigeria, dominated by the nation's largest tribe (the Ibo), was determined to set its own course and become an independent nation.

Ernesto "Che" Guvara, Fidel Castro's revolutionary comrade in Cuba, was shot dead in Bolivia where he had been fomenting a revolution

Great Britain sent troops into Northern Ireland to protect its interests there. Conflicts erupted, and the British troops sought to return law and order to the area by controlling the IRA and Catholic minority.

King Constantine of Greece was forced into exile. Greece and Turkey (its historical rival) glared menacingly at each other across their common borders. Tensions were especially high on the island nation of Cyprus.

In Southeast Asia, the Vietnam conflict became the Vietnam War, and it was raging with reverberations throughout the region.

China proved itself an international player on the Korean Peninsula, and watched jealously as the generals of North Vietnam allied themselves to China's communist rival, Russia's Soviet Union. With an empire that spanned more than a half-dozen time zones—from Siberia to Eastern Europe—the Russian "Bear" became the United State's chief rival for world power.

I had a front-row seat in this real-world, real-time class of politics. I read essays, editorials, and in-depth articles for insight into these global conflicts.

———— • ◆ • ————

Los Angeles wasn't considered a great sports town. Because residents were from all over the country, their loyalties were scattered. The local sports fans only demanded that their teams be competitive. The local college and university alumni, however, held different perspectives.

The USC (University of Southern California) Trojans and the UCLA (University of California at Los Angeles) Bruins were crosstown rivals. Both had storied histories, huge followings, and almost perennial powerhouse teams in football and basketball.

The professional sports teams were slightly less glamorous. The LA Lakers (basketball), Los Angeles Rams (football), LA Dodgers (baseball), and LA Angels (baseball) were all solid franchises at the time.

I immersed myself in the sports culture of LA. It was a welcome diversion from the chaos in my life and the rest of the world. I enjoyed the struggles of athletic competition and absorbed all I could about the teams. We were allowed to watch the 1967 World Series between the Boston Red Sox and the St. Louis Cardinals on the TV in the mission chapel.

———— • ◆ • ————

Under Emil's tutelage, I cooked for the staff. I also prepared the soup for the evening service. I was usually the first one in the kitchen in the morning. I unlocked the door, brewed the coffee, and laid out the eggs among other breakfast-prep items. The kitchen was set up with an older commercial grill, stove-top burner, and large oven. The appliances were black, solidly built units that had seen years of use.

I enjoyed working the grill in the morning. Emil taught me the care and cleaning of it before I actually began cooking. He admitted that I had an aptitude for food preparation. Planning and timing were essential elements in preparing a meal, and I thrived under those pressures.

That's when my worse moment in the kitchen occurred. The grill was warming as I prepared a tray of diced potatoes for hash browns. When I opened the oven door to insert the tray, a ball of flame raced up my arms! I cried out. I was more startled and frightened than in pain at first. The sound of the tray crashing onto the tile floor and my shriek brought Emil and Brother Johnson rushing in.

I was in shock. My apron and t-shirt were singed. My bare arms and face were left almost hairless. My eyebrows, eyelashes, and budding facial hair disappeared in an instant! Things could have gone much worse! As it was, my flesh only suffered a flash burn. I had to endure a little discomfort and sensitivity with light until my eyelashes grew back.

The accident occurred because the oven pilot light had gone out. The oven had filled with gas. When the oven door was opened, the grill's flame ignited the escaping gas. Poof!

Almost as suddenly and unexpectedly as the ball of flame burned my arms, Emil was gone. (Only six months earlier, I joined the mission.) When he did not appear for breakfast, I did not think too much of it. There were days that I didn't see him until the staff helpers cut vegetables for the evening soup.

On that particular morning, however, Bill (a sales rep for our food supplier) arrived to pick up the order from Emil. I hurried to Emil's room to retrieve the list of needed supplies. My knocks went unanswered. Emil was gone—totally gone! His room was empty, and his bed was unmade. Bed linens were piled beside the door. I walked back to the kitchen in a daze. The supply salesman and I reviewed the stock items we required.

Brother Johnson called Martin Brett, who came in earlier than planned. He pulled me aside and asked if I felt capable of handling the cooking duties until they hired someone. I said yes. My pay doubled to ten dollars a week.

I immersed myself in my new duties. Meanwhile, the unfamiliar weight of being responsible for feeding staff and service attendees settled over me. As I directed my helpers, I reflected on how I was gently prepared for this moment by Emil. Now, the kitchen was mine, for the time being. I wondered why Emil left without a clue. Of course, Old Bill thought the worst and declared that Emil had answered the "call of the bottle." He also accused the old cook of drinking regularly.

I grudgingly admitted to myself that there had been a few occasions when Emil begged off from cooking and serving. He declared that he was under the weather. I had smelled alcohol on him, but I never envisioned him not being there.

———— ◆ ————

I hated Old Bill for looking for the worst in every situation. I hated how he reveled in the agony of others! My burning anger at that miserable, old, crusty, mean-spirited son of a bitch was the main reason I doubted I was a true Christian. I wanted to strangle that little bastard! And he probably wanted to strangle me, or at least see me disappear. I know he resented me *before* Emil left, but his loathing for me increased tenfold when I took over the operation of the kitchen!

He pretended to be helpful and encouraging, but his venom coated every word he spoke. He saw through me in many ways, and this ability excited him even more. He wanted to see me fail. Old Bill knew that we were both manipulators. Yet, he hated me, while everyone else liked me.

His shadow loomed over everything I did. In my attempt to avoid his inevitable criticism, I concentrated intensely on my endeavors, so they would turn out successfully. I also felt that it was unhealthy for me to constantly be angry and fearful of him.

While I sincerely wanted to become the Christian I was pretending to be, Old Bill discerned that hypocritical part of me. He gloated and wallowed in my internal conflict. Now that I had all the keys to the kitchen, I could comfort myself with food whenever I wanted. This was truly my personal heaven—and hell!

I didn't realize how much I learned from Emil until I actually started planning a week's meals for the residents. The dinner menus were very basic. The walk-in cooler and the large freezer were usually well stocked. The pantry held staple items and some cookbooks.

Brother Bedrose's produce deliveries were my responsibility now. When he showed up a day after Emil had left, and someone told him that I was in charge, he simply looked me in the face and said, "Praise the Lord," as usual.

The soup was the thing. The soup kept the doors open, fed the hungry, helped the lost souls find salvation, housed the repentant, and encouraged the charitable. It all started with the magic soup. I made a good pot of soup. Some thought it was better than Emil's. I'd say I had a good teacher. I learned how to extract a flavorful broth from meat bones. With a good basic stock, vegetables, and chunks of meat, the soup was a hearty, delicious meal. My soup made me proud. In addition, I supervised the kitchen smoothly. My stature and authority grew.

At eighteen-years old, I was in control of the "heart" of the mission, the kitchen (and its thousands-of-dollars operating budget). I became more isolated. The kitchen duties demanded more of my time. When I arranged my schedule to have a little time alone, I cherished it. I knew I screwed up my life, but I didn't know how to unscrew it. How could Jesus save me from my sins when I was a low-life fugitive, living a lie every day? I had no one to confess to or confide in. I didn't trust anyone with my secrets. I used my solitude to search for answers to my riddles.

———— • ◆ • ————

"The World Tomorrow" boomed from the television speakers. It was a Sunday morning TV program that aired before *Church in the Home*. The host was an anchorman named Garner Ted Armstrong. He had Hollywood good looks and a newsman's voice and style of delivery. The entire half-hour program was presented as a serious news show with Bible and prophecy teaching as its foundation. I was enthralled from the first moment I saw it!

"The World Tomorrow" was the broadcast outreach of the World-wide Church of God, founded by Herbert W. Armstrong (father of Garner Ted Armstrong). With high-production values, the show utilized graphs, charts, news footage, and Bible verses. "The World Tomorrow" was unique. G.T. Armstrong spoke more like a college professor than a TV preacher. He was energetic, intellectual, and his persuasive delivery encouraged thought.

I requested the free literature the show offered, including the organization's monthly magazine called *The Plain Truth*. All of my requests were honored without one request for a donation. That was unheard of! Every ministry sought contributions. This reason, among others, was why the church was loathed by traditional Christian denominations. I kept my interest to myself after Brothers Brett and Johnson displayed disapproving looks upon spying my copy of *The Plain Truth*.

I was fascinated with some of this church's teachings, especially regarding the twelve tribes of ancient Israel. My love of history and geography compelled me to study the Worldwide Church of God's beliefs. I kept an open mind, but I identified problems with the strict dogma the church adhered to. Yet, it was refreshing to hear a broadcast ministry challenge Christian holidays like Christmas and Easter. Although the Worldwide Church's teachings were accurate and undisputed, most Western churches have continued the celebrations through the ages.

The Worldwide Church of God adopted the Old Testament and Judaic practice of Saturday Sabbath. It acknowledged that God ordained this day of worship. The church also adhered to other Jewish festivals and sacred celebrations.

"The World Tomorrow" taught that there was to be simply that— a "world tomorrow." In spite of the overwhelming problems around the globe, a divine plan was in place to guide the human race to a better day. We were to become "new" creatures on a restored planet.

The old-time religion preached about a heaven with "streets paved with gold" and saints and angels ceaselessly singing praises to God. A song, "In the Sweet By and By," offered simplistic views of the future for Christians. The lyrics were derided in a parody song that mocked its simplistic images: "You'll get pie in the sky when you die by and by. That's a lie." Through the ages, secular entertainment has loved poking fun at the images of Christians floating on clouds, playing harps, and floating around heaven.

G.T. Armstrong told his radio listeners and television viewers that during the prophesied thousand-year reign of Christ on earth, the nations of the world would peacefully undo the destructive things man had done to the planet. This concept was a practical example of mankind being taught to "turn swords into plowshares." What a wonderful idea: A loving God existed, one who wanted to teach the human race how to un-make the toxic "omelet" they had mixed themselves into.

If this teaching was true, we would learn secrets that had evaded our greatest intellects in solving our needs for clean energy. We would discover how to eliminate the danger of nuclear waste that we buried in deep caves beneath the earth or under the sea. It was almost too wonderful to believe!

I wanted to believe this idea. I wanted to believe much of what the Worldwide Church of God taught. More importantly, I wanted to believe the truth. I didn't know what the truth was, but I somehow sensed that I would know it when I found it.

The Thanksgiving holiday bore down on me with more pressure than I experienced before. All the missions were expected to serve hundreds of men a traditional Thanksgiving dinner. Our resident population at the mission grew slightly before the holiday. This swelling granted me more manpower. I organized the kitchen and directed men that were often three times my age. The pressure was great, because I wanted to succeed and justify the confidence placed in me. I had an aptitude for cooking and usually exceeded everyone's expectations.

I felt the desire to start smoking again. Some of the guys, while witnessing or on personal time, returned from the street with the odor of tobacco on them. Of course, I was a prisoner of my own fear and dared not leave the building. I caught myself more than one time, talking to someone outside the mission door as they smoked and feeling myself exhale along with them. It was comical and sad!

I could understand why so many male cooks were heavy drinkers or alcoholics. One's own internal conflicts and the drive for perfection creates a pain that one needs and fears. Alcohol was a familiar sedative to ease that pain for some. I turned to my familiar "lover"— food. I ate until the pain of the day was gone, until all pain was gone! I knew a terrible guilt awaited me in the morning.

Thanksgiving was sad, because I missed my mother, grandmother, brothers, and sisters more than ever! I knew they were worried about me, and wondered what became of me. I cried on the inside for the pain I brought them. I had no legitimate reasons for why I had done the things that brought me to such a sad state. I suffered in solitude and prayed that they sensed that I was okay. I hoped they believed that someday they would see me again.

———— ◆ ————

The Korean children's choir was featured on *Church in the Home* after Thanksgiving. The choir was comprised of young South Korean children from a Christian orphanage. They were on a multicity tour of US church-sponsored concerts throughout the Christmas season. Attractive boys and girls with angelic voices, they were the new centerpiece of the Fred Jordan ministry. The focus was changing from the broken and lost souls of skid row to these young, innocent children who sang beautiful hymns. These virtuous children were the collateral damage of the Korean conflict.

I was glad that the spotlight was off us at the mission. Each TV broadcast spoke less of the skid-row ministry and featured more of the sweet voices of the children's choir as Christmas approached. Snapshots and film footage were exhibited during program segments about the mission, but the push to donate money came when the children's choir performed.

I kept my disenchantment with the modern church's embrace of the cultural and secular aspects of Christmas to myself. It was still a melancholy season, as I reflected on my one year without family contact. Like the Thanksgiving holiday crowds, our service and meal-attendance numbers reached capacity during the Christmas holiday season. The warm weather of Southern California and the relaxed attitudes toward transients and street people helped those groups swell throughout the winter months.

The streets were alive with these transient people. Many carried their worldly possessions in shopping carts, appropriated from nearby markets. It was a common sight to see a street person searching through trash cans and dumpsters for bottles to recycle. The streets were getting younger and a few more women were living on the sidewalks of LA. Along with the "down on their luck" folks were the hobos, winos, drug addicts, and mentally deficient souls.

We welcomed 1968 with prayer. We read scripture and toasted the entry of the new year with eggnog. The rest of the world celebrated mindlessly with alcoholic beverages. Why was the new year beginning in the middle of winter? Wasn't the first of spring more like the beginning of a new year than during a time of death and dormancy? Why were we so contrary?

I was hungry for the truth. I thought that the more knowledge I had, the better able I could discern it. Since knowledge was power, perhaps knowledge was truth, as well. I questioned everything and was open to everything. I allowed myself to be teachable. Therefore, I watched and listened to all the religious- and spiritual-based programs available.

Kathryn Kuhlman, Oral Roberts, the International Church of the Foursquare Gospel of Aimee Semple McPherson, and Revered Fred Jordan were my teachers, among many others. My educators represented a wide spectrum of religious thoughts and beliefs. But what were they teaching? Each Christian sect or denomination taught a variation of the "truth." How could God's kingdom and the message his Son brought us create such confusion among people he was bringing light to? Wasn't there a way for all Christians to be?

———— • ◆ • ————

January 1968 saw America's vision of itself change again. The Tet Offensive began in South Vietnam. Millions of Americans were caught off-guard by the news. The North Vietnamese Army and its South Vietnamese communist allies (the Vietcong), staged a surprise, major offensive against the South Vietnamese Army, the Army of the

Republic of Vietnam (ARVIN), and the US forces. All over South Vietnam, major fighting broke out during the holiday period of the Tet Offensive. The Allied Forces of South Vietnam were surprised by the intensity and coordination of the attacks.

The former imperial capital of Vietnam (Hu) was captured by the communist surge, and other positions were attacked and overrun. The response by US and allied forces was swift, as positions were reestablished and the citadel of Hu retaken. But the damage was done. The huge psychological thrust that the North Vietnamese generals made far outweighed their temporary gains on the ground.

America's nose had been bloodied! This news about the turn of events was like a red-hot poker through the American consciousness, and it provoked major backlash against the war and leadership in Washington! The United States of America was engaged in yet another "shooting war" in which the use of its immense power was unthinkable.

Talk radio was alive with commentary from the entire political spectrum. The antiwar voices were raised and the pro-victory, "let the military win" voices answered just as loudly. This was one debate among many that hashed and re-hashed the argument over the airwaves. Talk radio was hosting a national town meeting.

If talk radio wasn't born in LA, it certainly was nurtured there. I lived each day to listen to average citizens calling a radio program and voicing their opinions for the benefit of their fellow citizens. Talk radio was the modern replacement for the old town squares, general stores, and post-office lobbies; the places where people met and discussed the topics of the day.

I experienced mixed feelings during this time, and guilt was among them. I languished in the bowels of an American city and observed the increasing carnage from Vietnam. I wondered if any of the recruits from boot camp were among the fighting or dead. Sadly, the nation viewed the deceased soldiers returning home in flag-draped coffins.

I was pained at not being among my former peers in the military. I also could not imagine being among those who fled across the border to Canada to evade the draft. Each group was praised and skewered by fellow Americans. On the radio show, I heard parents vehemently defend the rights of their sons to resist the draft and the war. Some kin claimed to pay for their relatives to leave the nation for the great white north of Canada in order to save their lives.

Others, including Dr. Martin Luther King Jr., raised their voices against the war and its disproportionate burden on poor minorities, and especially black Americans. The words of heavyweight boxing champion, Muhammad Ali, echoed across the nation like the crack of a whip. He declared that the North Vietnamese had never called him a nigger in a response to a question regarding why he refused to fight and kill the Vietnamese, the enemies of America.

The Tet Offensive on the ground proved to be short lived, but the reverberations of the Tet Offensive continued in the hearts, minds, and streets of America. Our nation's goals were out of focus. We questioned our resolve. How could we win a war without using our might to its fullest?

Had our military suffered their own Dien Bien Phu? The major battle that forced the French government to surrender its hold over much of what was at that time called French Indochina? Was America proving to be another paper tiger? President Lyndon Johnson, his generals, and admirals responded to those questions with a bigger and louder war. The roar of the US tiger was heard throughout the region!

African Americans were challenged over a dilemma—loyalty to their sons or loyalty to their county. The Vietnam War appeared to be a battle for an ignoble cause in a far away land. And the United States continued to be an ungrateful and unrepentant nation in regard to racism; it continued to oppress black citizens. Black Americans proudly and honorably served their country in every conflict! Almost always unheralded, the heroics and leadership demonstrated by brave Negroes in all branches of the military was widely ignored and swept into the dark corners of American history.

Thousands of Negro servicemen enjoyed freedom and respect—never experienced in their own country—when fighting abroad during the war years. Although often relegated to support units, some "colored" troops fought decisive battles against enemy forces. They were heroic and victorious! These engagements fed the suspicions of some racists who feared that blacks killing whites on foreign soil might lead to race conflicts at home; blacks may be determined to secure the rights they'd been denied in the United States—by any means necessary.

Black Americans demanded to be recognized and respected in their own country for the contributions they made to its growth and strength! America was a better, stronger, and more vital country because of the talents of African Americans—brought here in chains!

Before television, America was divided along native-born, immigrant, ethnic, racial and religious lines. This great experiment of America encouraged all her peoples to be nurtured by their heritages and cultures. It also ascribed to a higher ideal of equality and brotherhood that united all beyond any notions of class. Though a magnificent ideal, it was still a work in progress. America revealed to the Old World that the New World exceeded all of its glories by establishing a meritocracy through democracy. The United States hosted a society whereupon one's race, status, and class were not as important as one's ability, talent, drive, or determination to succeed. America worked in spite of its flaws, because most American people believed in their country, and they supported laws that encouraged and protected the rights of all.

Television was all at once a great uniter and divider of American society. While my generation peered through the window of TV into a mostly white America, we still shared its values, goals, and dreams. Television wasn't so much breaking stereotypes as it was cleaning up and repackaging them. But that's what TV did with everyone—every group—because the principal purpose was to provide nonthreatening entertainment to the largest number of people in order to sell advertising.

The television culture became our teacher—by what it did and didn't show us of our world. The first TV generation drifted from accepting traditional conditioning. Our minds were no longer being molded by our conformity or rebellion within our environment. Through mass communication, we developed allegiances to alien ideas.

Winter 1968

I was sick for days. I only performed the duties I absolutely had to complete in order to maintain the kitchen operations with the help of staff. I spent all my other time in my room. I was physically ill with flu, and the symptoms lingered. I refused to seek medical attention.

Worse than the chills, sweats, and bone-aching, sneezing fits was my heartsick depression. It enveloped me as never before! My body was gross and polluted from self-indulgence and abuse. I didn't know how to stop feeding my emotions. I prayed fervently and read my bible devotedly, searching for deliverance from this malaise that settled over my life. I learned so much about life and its' possibilities, since taking refuge at the Mission. My nineteenth birthday was approaching, and I was still confused about what to do about my trail of deceit. I was joyful for the knowledge I gained, but my personal conflicts raged on. Their weights became greater than I could bear.

The words of ancient Israel's King Solomon floored me. Here was a historic figure, revered for his wisdom and wealth, who recounted that at one time he considered ending his own life! What a shock! Here was a man, who by all accounts, had more of what every man wanted. Yet, he contemplated suicide? If Solomon found no lasting comforts in the wealth and worldly delights he possessed, what hope was there for anyone else to do so?

———— • ◆ • ————

I honored my obligation to operate the mission's kitchen. This duty was the reason I forced myself from bed for a few hours each day. I planned and prepped the meals for the staff and got the soup pot simmering for the evening service. Brothers Juan, Donavan, and

James followed my instructions, and Brothers Brett and Johnson encouraged me to rest as they prayed for my restored health.

I added a new fear to my legion of others, as I worried that another cook might take over the kitchen. I was still an amateur and over my head in some ways. I dreaded becoming just another staff member at the mission. If I was relieved of running the kitchen, I only had my organ playing. I hated the image of Old Bill relishing my fall from grace.

As I slept in fevered anxiety, I felt the fingers of a hand closing around my throat. I struggled for breath. I couldn't cry out! I was drowning in my own juices and fighting to escape dying! I wrenched myself from the stranglehold, and at the same time, I slammed my right arm onto his forearm as hard as I could! I felt his arm go limp. I threw off the covers and rolled to the other side of the bed to escape. I was drenched in sweat and gasping for air in the predawn light. I staggered to my feet and tried to focus my eyes. My heart was pounding wildly!

Then, as I braced for another encounter, I felt my left arm dangling lifelessly at my side! The blood was beginning to flow back into the limb, and I felt a tingling sensation—like pins and needles. Slowly, it dawned on me—while I stood there wobbling, feverish, and dazed—that my own left arm had tried to strangle me! What I believed to be an outside threat to my life was actually a nightmare. I used my sleeping left arm as an escape from my deepest fears!

I collapsed onto the dampened bed and wrapped myself in a blanket, as another wave of chills erupted over me. Fully awake and shivering, the intense terror eased from my body. I wasn't ready to joke about it, but I reached a new low. In some weird and twisted way, I attempted to strangle myself! I had come undone. I was unmoved by the demands of my office. I had no cares regarding the kitchen responsibilities I usually, jealously, coveted. I had come to the end of myself.

In the hours that followed, I lay in bed in a twilight zone of shifting consciousness. I drifted in and out of fitful sleep. Later, I sipped water from the melting ice I accepted; I refused all other food or aid. Somehow, I knew it was early afternoon in my dark room. I felt pitiful. Random thoughts and fragments of memories stung me in my half-wakened state. I imagined bits and pieces of my life, lying on the floor of my mind—old photos and newspaper clippings fallen from a box of mementos.

"My God, my God what will become of me?" I heard myself silently wonder. My eyes moved a little as I ached with a prayer for deliverance from my malaise. "Dear God, have mercy on me, a sinner. Please take pity on me, a wasted and broken vessel." My despair was vain! That realization brought me lower still. I found no hiding place in my mind, and no release from life. Involuntary tears streamed from the corners of my eyes. "God help me. Save me from myself!"

There it was! I instinctively recognized it as soon as I heard it. The words echoed an ache that emanated from a place I did not know, and yet, I somehow knew to trust! "Save me from myself?" Yes, yes, that was it! Where did that idea come from? What did it mean? There was no vanity in the question. I wanted a reason to live.

CHAPTER 9

AN INVITATION TO OPENNESS

Without opening my eyes, I reached over to the radio and turned the dial to find a familiar station. A classical melody was playing, so I paused to hear what program it introduced. The taste of dried tears was in my mouth. Then, I heard the distinctive voice with its crisp, clear, and very British accent. His name was Roy Masters. His program was called How Your Mind Can Keep You Well and a Moment of Truth. Directly, he launched into one of his tirades.

Masters' tirade was more of an inspired rant; he spoke like a prosecuting attorney, railing against the psychotic jungle mankind was entrapped in. He used everyday words, but in very specific and insightful ways. He was talking to me. I lay there; my eyes shut against the dim afternoon light, and listened intently. I'd never heard anyone speak so truthfully and powerfully before! My heart soared and my mind was alive with wonder. He apologized for not taking any calls (on what was usually a radio call-in show). Then, after an advertisement from his program's only sponsor (a house moving business), Masters returned to his harangue. He was a firebrand whose righteous anger was directed at shaking us out of our spiritual lethargy.

Roy Masters had to pay for his time on the radio, like many preachers on LA's religious radio stations, but he seemed unconcerned about making people feel good. Neither did he attempt to manipulate hearers into feeling guilty about their pasts, nor offer them simple-minded salvation that eventually resuscitated their high opinions of themselves.

He never spoke a word about Jesus Christ or God during that tirade, and yet, I understood that he was talking about them. "Whatever saves you, claims you!" Masters repeated several times. That notion resonated deeply in my feverish mind, as I listened to the traditional religious programs that followed Masters' show. Whatever saves you, claims you?

With my spirits slightly buoyed, I showered, dressed, and made my way to the kitchen. Weaker than I realized, I was practically useless. However, my appearance cheered everyone. Even Old Bill seemed nearly pleased to see me. From a perch in the corner of the kitchen, I did little except direct my helpers and answer questions. Immediately after the evening soup was served, I returned to bed.

The next morning, I waited hungrily for the beautifully inspiring music that introduced Masters' program. I dared not change the station. I didn't want to miss a word of what he was going to say. His early morning program was a short one, a mere fifteen minutes to deliver a message and direct listeners to his afternoon call-in show. After the music, came that voice. He introduced himself humbly and apologized for taking much of the prior afternoon's program with his tirade.

He welcomed new listeners and spoke about the purpose of the Foundation of Human Understanding, his organization that was located on Western Avenue in Los Angeles. The foundation was a nonprofit entity that depended on tax-deductible donations from loyal listeners. No dues or tithes were required, and one couldn't join or belong to the group. There were no courses (only weekly lectures) at the foundation office, which was open to the public.

Masters spoke briefly, and encouraged followers to be patient and not prejudge his program. He claimed that objectivity was required to gain insight into his teachings. He offered a meditation exercise, taught by way of a long-playing record, to help followers achieve a state of objectivity. His "be still and know" meditation was a simple technique; it addressed negative thinking, emotional damage, and stress.

With mild skepticism, I listened as he explained that he believed this wordless prayer-type meditation was practiced by the early Judeo Christians. He hurriedly explained that, although it bore some resemblance to other Eastern forms of meditation, its direction was totally different. He offered the recording for whatever one could afford. I folded some cash and a note into an envelope and set it beside the radio.

During the afternoon broadcast, he took calls. Masters spoke to a distressed caller and cut right through the caller's emotionalism. He displayed keen insight for framing the real problem. With the skill of a psychic surgeon and man of God, he exposed the caller to part of himself that he did not know he had. He asked if the caller was meditating and offered to send his recording, *How Your Mind Can Keep You Well*, for whatever he could afford (or free of charge) with no obligation. This offer was amazing!

As the conversation continued, Masters stressed that meditation would help the caller achieve the ability to be objective regarding problems. Thus, he would seek the deeper causes and discover real solutions. Masters spoke kindly, but firmly. The alert caller responded with tearful enthusiasm. I scribbled the address of the foundation on an envelope and recited a silent prayer that mediation was the answer I yearned for.

I listened to every program over the following days and became convinced that this man had something to offer that I desperately needed. I liked where he was coming from. However, Roy Masters was a very controversial figure in the area. His iconoclastic approach to traditional religion was maddening to most of the other radio preachers. Some ministers on the same station consorted to have Masters censored or removed from the air. However, the firebrand that he was, Masters trusted in the power of his message and behind his message to ensure he remained on the air.

Masters insisted that he wasn't opposed to the teachings of the other radio ministries. He simply wanted to restore an important bit of understanding to modern Christianity. Masters' contention was that modern Christianity was more "Churchianity." On the subject of the born-again experience, he criticized those believers who devoutly memorized chapters and verses of the Bible and proclaimed to assimilate the spirit of God. Masters claimed that the vast majority of Christian believers were taught the words, without the music. These insights were powerful and greatly resonated within me!

————•◆•————

I resumed my full duties in the kitchen when my health returned. Everyone was glad that I was back, and I was surprised at how much I missed the job. Even Brother Bedrose's thumping on the locked kitchen doors after closing was welcomed. I learned to tap into some of the organization's talent. I thanked God that I reached this point in my life despite my self-sabotage. A new hope was on the horizon.

I was delighted when the package addressed to William Kinkade arrived a few days later. I recognized the logo for the FHU on the mailing label. The parcel contained a book and album. I read the information on the album jacket. I gently placed the 33-1/3 LP recording on the turntable. I followed the instructions exactly. I darkened the room, sat in a straight-backed chair, and listened to Masters' voice speak to me. His tone, now familiar to me, floated into the room—and into my consciousness. As I recall, his introduction went something like this:

"You are about to take the journey...." Be sure that you do not do this exercise for the purpose of feeling better." Repeat the meditation exercise by yourself at least three times. Do not wait until you feel like doing your exercise; do it religiously. Do it each time as if it were the first time, so that it remains an observation exercise. The meditation exercise is what the name implies. The exercise will make the subconscious subject to the conscious understanding."

Masters' voice continued in a friendly and instructive manner with certain phrases standing out more than others. From my memory, I believe he spoke the following message: "The most important thing for you to experience is repentance. When you see yourself in the light, and you see your ego as part of the problem.... This meditation exercise contains all the ingredients for perfect self-control. The values accumulate only when practiced daily."

On and on, Masters' introductory words washed over me like a spring rain shower. After side one ended, I paused to savor the insights his words fired in my mind. Then, I turned over the album and began the meditation exercise.

I obediently practiced the meditation for the first time. As warned, my mind wandered, but as encouraged, I noticed it. I brought my attention back to my hand by my side. The process was harder than I thought. My attention danced away from the moment when I became aware of the needle riding the groove of the record, a door closing, and a siren sounding faintly in the distance. Then, I became lost in some daydream or other distraction before dutifully focusing on my hand again. I listened as Masters stated that he was reminding me of what I already knew in my heart.

I awoke earlier than usual to practice meditation each morning. For about thirty minutes, I attempted the observation and concentration exercises with the record. I had varying degrees of success. I disappeared for a time when my mind planned meals, conducted imaginary conversations, and relived past events.

When I became aware of those drifting thoughts, I gently returned my attention to my hand, which represented the present. The practice became wonderfully frustrating! Almost without exception, any glow I felt after meditating would vaporize once I immersed myself in the activities of the mission. Ah, but it had always been so! Now, I contrasted my newly formed self-awareness to my time as a kitchen manager. My consciousness was alive and growing.

I read *How Your Mind Can Keep You Well* from cover to cover. I didn't try to study it or learn it. As the author advised, I simply read it and let whatever message triggered an insight, do so. When I reread it, I discovered deeper meanings and whole paragraphs that I missed completely. The words hadn't changed, but I was changing! I regarded myself trying to be more patient during the day. I worked to hide my frustrations and anger by suppressing, rather than expressing, them. I internalized negative emotions to maintain my own self-image.

I proceeded to truly understand the real need for patience. That capacity was the key to the meditation exercise. Forebearance became the matrix of true character change. "Be still and know that I am God." Psalm 46:10 now had real meaning!

Acting patient wasn't good enough, but a starting place. That point was where I was. I was on an inward journey. I was determined to persevere. If what Masters was saying was true, I had nowhere to go but inward and upward.

My new attitude made a difference to my co-workers. In subtle ways, they responded to me differently. My new, internal self made itself honestly known in my behavior and speech. I had a love for words, and they became charged with meaning as my understanding grew.

My nemesis, Old Bill, tried to upset my desire to become a better person. He still got under my skin, but the effects diminished. I discerned that his compulsions were devised to create enemies. Old Bill needed someone to judge in order to temporarily escape the darkness of his own nature. We were not so dissimilar. At the mission, we harbored the same angst, because the pain of our lives forced us to judge each other. I was discovering a way out—or a way above— that pain. I thanked God for Roy Masters!

"Merry eyes twinkling...." was Masters' descriptive way of explaining a nonjudgmental discernment that came from one's patient desire to resist temptation without resentment. This was no simple "whistling in the dark" philosophy. With fear in the heart and knees knocking, one could find the courage to be still, stand his ground, and witness the opposing forces of evil.

Patience gave one the power to rise above a conditioned reflex response to life's problems. We are the sum total of our experiences and burdened by the accumulation of our wrong reactions to pressure and temptation. Trying to solve our emotional conflicts often leads to consciousness-reducing addictions. Emotional upsets destroy our objectivity, and we make terrible errors in judgment.

The predominant factor (in how rapidly or slowly one progressed) on the healing road was found in one's intent! Intent was the inclination of one's soul to seek and accept nothing less than internal self-honesty—the truth about oneself. Each searcher's journey is his personal awakening. His path is only as difficult as his pride is stubborn.

As I read the Bible, the words came alive in a more beautiful way. My meditation kindled deeper insight, and I trusted my ability to read between the lines, regardless of the Bible translation.

By my nineteenth birthday, my health was better, and my life became more purposeful each day. I took increased joy in playing the organ before services, and I nervously became the principal speaker many nights. This change was just fine with Brother Johnson, who resisted public speaking. At first, I was like a clone of all the other preachers that stood behind the podium and addressed the hungry crowds. Our guests weren't as hungry for the word as for the soup.

I selected a few verses from the Bible and illuminated them as I did at morning devotions. Then, I tied everything together before giving the "altar call." I employed some of the dramatic theatrics I gleaned from sawdust-trail preachers I viewed in the pulpit and at the movies. I held an open Bible in my left palm and strode back and forth across the stage, gesturing into the air for emphasis during key passages. I was objective regarding my performance; I tried not to be too predictable. I occasionally slammed the Bible onto the podium to startle the dozers.

Each morning, I meditated, cooked breakfast, and supervised the kitchen agenda. If Brother Johnson and Martin Brett were out of the building, I oversaw the other mission duties. I supervised the cleaning of the building and inventoried the clothing and book donations. In the afternoons, I listened to Roy Masters (and other radio programs), read, and meditated. Then, the evening routine began with supper for the staff, salvation service, and soup for the street people. The day ended with Brother Bedrose's late delivery of cast-off produce from local markets.

I got a handle on things and sensed a purpose to life on earth. The meditation exercise was the catalyst for the change in my life and mind. I could see that humans were never meant to be externally motivated beings, but our ego's weakness traps us in a world of illusion. The ego hides within the mind and knows of nothing greater than itself! We are justified in its false light, and therefore, become addicted to our own vain imaginings. That malady was my sickness, my dis-ease.

The "be still and know" meditation was my way out of that mind trap. It was not habit forming, but it proved to be like prayer, an act of dedication. Meditation was often frustrating, sometimes joyous, but mostly, a struggle to stay aware as it worked its magic throughout the day. During mundane chores, the sudden awareness of being lost in thought and dream stuff would awaken me, and I'd bring my attention back to the present moment, the now.

————•◆•————

Senator Eugene McCarthy captured the imagination of the peace movement in America when he challenged President Lyndon Johnson for the nomination of the Democrat party for President of the United States. It was a bold move by McCarthy and inspired other Democrats to demand another standard bearer for their party.

The good and liberal laws that President Johnson rammed through congress, (ground-breaking legislation that formed his "Great Society") were coming to naught, because of the open wound of the Vietnam War. In April of 1968, Reverend Martin Luther King, Jr. was assassinated in Memphis, Tennessee, where he was supporting striking garbage workers. Another giant of the times had fallen. We mourned in shock as we attempted to fathom the motivation behind such hatred and vile behavior! Dr. King won the Nobel Peace Prize in 1964 after dominating the consciousness of black and white America in a way that had never been done before. He caught the imagination and the admiration of the world as he urged nonviolent demonstrations against racial injustices. Many of these unjust acts were institutionalized in facets of American life. First JFK, and five years later, MLK killed. Two of America's bravest sons were slain in the streets of her cities.

————•◆•————

After my nineteenth birthday, I reflected on the two years since I was an angry and confused teenager in Hartford. Not a day went by without some remembrance of my family. I often spoke of them in references to my past. For a little while longer, those memories were all I clung to. I was not ready to return to Hartford, yet. My new path, incorporating meditation prayer, formed my new understanding. I unknowingly had been searching for this path all my life.

————•◆•————

As far as anyone could tell, I was a young black man who had answered a call to serve Christ, by feeding and ministering to the lost sheep of LA's skid row. I was content with this image for the time being. I was eager to change. I was learning to evolve and become better. It began with change. There was a deep mystery within the universe of my mind that I wanted to understand.

Old Bill perceived that there was a change in my attitude toward him. I forgave him by letting go of my resentment. I stopped playing the game, because I could see that we were both acting out of compulsions that fed our darker natures. Through my growing patience and insight (attributed to my meditation exercises), I grasped how helpless I was before my most powerful emotions. I couldn't hate Old Bill, because I understood that he was a prisoner of the same weakness!

I had little to do with the changes that occurred in me, except in my attempts to "be still and know." I had faith that God was at work in my life, because I was letting things go that I used to justify for my private little angers.

Old Bill was confounded by my modified behavior. I acceded my resentment of his stares, my desire to put him in his place, and the storm clouds of anger forming in my mind. Let it go! I refused to indulge myself with judging him, right there, in the heat of battle. I sought to center myself in the present moment. "Dear God, help me to be still and realize his hatred, without hating him back." If I hate the hater, I become an extension of that hate and diminished by it.

I wasn't always successful, but each confrontation throughout the day, when he tried to get my goat, there was less of a goat to get. I watched him play friend or foe in an attempt to lock me into playing the judgment game. I was learning to love Old Bill when I didn't respond to his anger with anger. This act was the forgiveness factor of the divine mathematics of God. One from two, leaves one—alone. Who he was spoke louder than what he said. Therefore, Old Bill's weak attempts to pretend to respect me were exposed by my unemotional responses.

I was sharing the patience of God. As He had waited for me to seek His purpose, I was humbled. This humility allowed God's patience to flow through me and touch the lives of others. The power of patience was incredible. Patience blessed me with insight that was far beyond my nineteen years of age. Patience impacted my life in such a positive way that I knew I would never be the same again— and that was a good thing.

I was learning to deal with each day's problems. I was still frustrated at my frustration and angry at my anger. I covered my feeling with Christian behavior. However, there was a difference now, because I discerned what was happening inside me. Then, I repented. Repentance is a willing step in the process of eliminating our self-conceit and self-will. It is voluntary suffering; we feel our selfish ego die. I was discovering how to surrender my will to God.

I discerned the conflict between my conscience and my former self. During meditation, I recited the Lord's Prayer. I grasped that I must "be still and know" the lessons, before my lies and excuses were unpeeled like layers of an onion. As we encounter the riddle of ourselves, we are brought to repentance repeatedly. Baptized with tears of repentance, I prayed for the real Jesus, not just the idea of him, to come into my life as my Savior.

I stopped judging myself. Whenever thoughts of judgment about my weight entered my mind, I had to be still and watch. Sometimes I failed miserably, as I watched the demon of self-loathing torment me. Directly, I broke down and consoled myself with food. With my youthful passions and imagination, the task of staying aware and patient during times of stress was a challenge. My faith kept me committed to the process.

When Old Bill left the mission, he may have seen this action as his final strike against me. Before I began to understand our conflicted personalities, I avoided direct contact with him. I released my part in our destructive relationship, and this freedom mirrored being released from bondage. This man was in pain, and my emotions were the "drug" he came to depend on to ease his pain. I refused to play any more by not hating him back. I tried to reach out to him, explain our compulsions, and apologize for my part. Old Bill sidestepped my forgiving attitude. One morning he was gone. He had moved on, as Emil had, under cover of darkness.

The antiwar voices forced the president to decide not to run for reelection. The earth was shaking. President Johnson was a broken man who realized that much of the good he achieved, drowned in the blood of the Vietnam War—a war that America had no will to win.

Vice President Hubert Horatio Humphrey (HHH) became the heir apparent for the Democrat nomination for president. However, HHH wasn't going to win it unchallenged. Senator Robert Kennedy, the brother of the slain president, had seen enough. America was hemorrhaging, and Kennedy decided that he had the answers; he would stop the bleeding from the Vietnam War and heal an angry nation.

Like many Americans, I was a Kennedy watcher. The family captured America's imagination like no other in modern times. In many ways the former attorney general was a better candidate for the presidency than his brother, John. Among black Americans, Robert Kennedy came across as genuinely moved by their plight and the plight of all races. An underdog, the New York senator literally rolled up his sleeves and waded into the fray.

The election primaries were furious battlegrounds. All the political pundits agreed that Robert "Bobby" Kennedy needed a strong showing in key Western states before the Democratic convention. The Northwest joined his camp, and all eyes turned to California as the make-or-break prize. Winning this state could lead to a triumphant march to the convention.

The anxious waiting was over. The California primary returns were in; the returns showed that California Democrats wanted RFK to be the party's standard bearer. Kennedy's victory speech concluded. The reporters' election summaries and campaign projections faded into background noise as I read and reflected. The forty-two-year-old Kennedy had something special. He exhibited more than just the Kennedy mystique, he also had substance. Kennedy could make a difference in the direction of the country.

The announcer's voice changed tone when he spoke excitedly about a commotion and confusion surrounding the senator's entourage as they exited the Ambassador Hotel in downtown, Los Angeles. Everyone stopped breathing for an instant. Unspoken prayers formed in their minds. "No! Please God, not again!" The radio crackled with the news flash: Shots were fired as the senator's entourage departed the hotel through the kitchen! The senator had been shot! The gunman was subdued and captured!

The tragedy unfolded over the next hours; then, it was consigned to history. A young, Middle Eastern man resented statements made by Senator Kennedy in support of the State of Israel. He allowed his angry passion to become deadly. Another light was snuffed out in America. Kennedy! King! Kennedy! All slain within five years! Even those citizens who didn't deeply mourn these losses were in shock! What was happening in our country? Couldn't lively political and social debate exist without hatred and murder? I couldn't hold back my tears.

————— • ◆ • —————

During the summer of 1968, almost everything I did was golden. The kitchen ran smoothly and the mission staff looked to me for direction. My contributions allowed Martin Brett and Brother Johnson time to work on other projects. These projects included counting mission donations and evangelizing. My ministry reflected my role in the mission as the chief cook, organist, preacher, and teacher.

I was thankful for the changes that occurred in my life. Two years earlier, I was an angry, frustrated, selfish, deceitful, seventeen-year-old Marine Corps recruit. I wanted to return to the marines, accept my punishment, and (if possible) complete my enlistment. However, my pride demanded that everything occur on my schedule.

That was my world when Brother McCue entered it. I noticed him in the audience for two consecutive nights when I preached. McCue was a large, white man with a bald head and deep-set, penetrating eyes. With his erect posture and almost placid facial expression, he appeared out of place among the usual bent and broken men in line for soup. I fought my fear of making eye contact with him, because it occurred to me that he might be a government agent searching for fugitives like me.

My preaching became more spiritual and less biblical. I was inspired (without notes) to illuminate a Bible verse in metaphysical terms in order to illustrate the point. My new understanding flowed like a wellspring from within me. The bleary-eyed, blank faces—who came to life only when we sang the old, familiar hymns—challenged me to impart a nugget of truth. My goal was to help them want to make real changes in their lives.

My fears relaxed when a bald stranger appeared with Brother Johnson the following evening. He came forward during the "altar call" and appeared to be considering a resident position at the mission. Sure enough, he spent the night and took a seat at the morning devotions. Newcomers weren't required to speak. Consequently, he remained silent, as a few of us spoke or read a Bible passage. I was slightly relieved to see him. I didn't believe that a fugitive-hunting government agent would go so far as to join a skid-row mission to catch a suspected fugitive!

The stranger listened intently as I spoke that morning. Our eyes met a few times when I glanced around the room. After my comments and a prayer, this new fellow, Brother McCue, helped rearrange the chapel chairs. "You're a bit high minded for your audience," he said, as I passed him on my way to the kitchen.

I was taken aback by his sudden comment and only managed a weak response: "Yeah, you're probably right."

I felt strangely drawn to him as he moved gracefully about the building, performing chores. When he spoke, the timber of his voice was powerful. It was obvious that he was no street bum, druggie, or wino. He was quiet and introspective. When he did speak, he selected me to fix his gaze upon. He spoke fluently and eloquently, and he was economical with his words.

Brother McCue was a man's man. He had "command presence" or that special aura that natural leaders possess. So why was he on skid row? His personal demons weren't obvious, so I was extra cautious around him. He was never overbearing or dictatorial. Instead, he applied himself to any task he was assigned. By his third day, I assigned him to work with me in the kitchen. This move was purely selfish on my part. I hungered for knowledge, and I noted that he was a storehouse of information.

McCue was in his fifties, I guessed. He was from Missouri, but had traveled much of the world. To my ear, he had no recognizable accent. Staying true to our unspoken code at the mission, I knew not to probe into his past. I gathered bits of information about him when they came out during our conversations about current events and history.

McCue spoke about the national political scene. He talked about the powerful Prendergast political machine that took Harry Truman from being a Kansas City haberdasher to being the vice president of the Unites States. He spoke, at times, as if he had some first-hand knowledge of events during those times. President Truman was in office when I was born, so that piqued my interest. I couldn't determine whether he admired or hated Truman's powerful political machine.

Most of our talks took place in the library, which had practically become my personal study. McCue spoke in depth on virtually any subject with a little prompting, or sometimes, he remained quiet. "Even a fool is counted wise if he holds his peace; unless he opens his mouth and removes all doubt," he said with a hearty laugh.

I felt like I was learning at the feet of a master. Had Alexander the Great looked on his teachers, especially Aristotle, with any more admiration? Had the older and wiser man brought the known world into clearer focus for the Macedonian Prince?

McCue expounded on the domino theory and its influence in shaping American foreign policy in Southeast Asia. With intense clarity, he talked of how the East versus West power struggle was being played out in pro-Communist verus anti-Communist regimes. I responded to his white-hot intellect. I warmed myself by his glowing insights and passions when we talked about the maneuvers of despots and civilizations throughout history.

Brother Mac liked my mind. He enjoyed my hunger to grasp the concepts and insights he shared about global politics. I was no super intellect, but something amazing was happening. "When the pupil is ready, the teacher will appear," he said in response to my enthusiasm regarding our talks. I was a willing pupil for whatever he was sharing. McCue was the Renaissance man I so wanted to be.

He never questioned me about my being in authority at a skid-row mission, when it was clear that I was the proper age for combat in Vietnam. He honored the code of silence about past lives.

I surprised him with my knowledge of history. The Punic Wars between Rome and Carthage; and the Peloponnesian War between Greek rivals Athens and Sparta were very familiar to me. I still spoke with boyish enthusiasm about Hannibal's invasion of Italy after crossing the Alps. McCue smiled when I talked about the great military genius of commanders from Alexander to Napoleon to Patton. Directly, McCue's smile faded. I sensed that he knew the truth of war. The reality was frequently too painful to talk about. I felt chastened, because I indulged an old passion that conflicted with my evolving Christian world view. "Wars can be justified, but there are no just wars," he said softly.

McCue furrowed his brow and rubbed his hand over his bald head whenever he made a point. I paid attention to whatever he was saying. I loved listening to his self-assured and focused views. Was he the dad I never had? Someone who could stimulate my mind and be an example? Our connection made me want to confess my sins to him. My strong impulse was to bare my dilemma to him and see if he agreed with my plan to turn myself in. Instead, I kept my secrets to myself.

Mc Cue watched from the dining room doors when I spoke to a small group. I said that our carnal nature was enslaved to our pain-based, conditioned reflexes. That was why we were, trapped in the cycle of self-defeating behavior. I wove verses from Proverbs, noting the metaphysical principles they revealed. I spoke straight from the heart, without notes or preparation. I felt truly inspired, but raised barely an eyebrow.

"You're too high minded for this lot," McCue said again, as we hurriedly set up the soup pot. Once again, I had no response other than to shrug with a slight nod of agreement.

"I decided to stay here because of something you said at the service last week'" he told me later that evening. He'd asked me if it bothered me that he said I was high minded.

"No," I said. "I try to preach and teach what I see. Believe me, I'm not that smart." I said.

"You're a pretty smart lad, but you've got something else—spiritual insight." He rubbed his head, as he searched for the words to say.

"I came in that night for something to eat. Then, I heard you tell these men that, let me see, how did you put it? 'Don't try to change the world you see, change the way you see the world.' That nearly floored me," he laughed and slapped his thigh. "I mean all those guys were just looking for some soup and you're telling them that! You weren't the run-of-the-mill, holy-roller, soup-and-salvation, Bible-thumping preacher! It sounded kind of new age, but I knew you were coming from a different place."

"I saw you here the next night, too," I added to let him know I noticed him.

"That's when you said that the most important goals were to find interior silence and discover our true selves. Aspiring to any other purpose was living an illusion.

"Yeah, that's exactly what I said." I marveled at his recollections.

"Well, that's what convinced me to find out where you were coming from," he confessed.

It was a key confession. As much as we talked over the past week, we didn't have any discussions about religion.

"So you're the one person who liked my metaphysical approach to the scriptures," I said lightheartedly. "I do give the glory to God, as they say, and I also thank God for a fellow named Roy Masters. He teaches the Judeo-Christian meditation that changed my life," I added emphatically.

"That's interesting," he said after a pause. "Do you use a mantra?"

"No, there's no mantra. It's not like those Eastern meditations. This meditation is really a concentration, an observational exercise that centers you as you learn to detach your mind from random thoughts," I explained.

"Yes," he said, as he looked off and back at me. "The desert fathers didn't use a mantra, either, but a phrase like in the Jesus prayer. Whenever they sat quietly, but had various thoughts take their attention, they'd say something like 'Lord Jesus' to bring their thoughts back to the present moment."

"Well, we don't use any words, phrases, or imagery. After awhile, your thoughts wander down stream, and you suddenly are aware that you're literally lost in thought. As soon as you realize that, you're back in the present moment! Our ego constantly seeks to escape the present moment, but our honest intention will bring us back." I continued, "This meditation teaches an awareness of the right hand to help bring your mind back to the present. It's a very gentle awareness of the right hand and the forehead."

"Yes," he nodded. "That's the hand-and-eye connection. The "transcendental eye" it's called, in the center of the forehead," he explained.

"Wow," I exclaimed with delight. "You're familiar with it?"

"I read about such practices during my studies of ancient mysticism. It was perceived as a tool to achieve the mind-body connection. Some of the early orders of desert monasteries preserved the practice, and some adherents evangelized it in their journeys." I listened intently, amazed at the complexity of this man.

"Before the great schism, many priests and others practiced a type of quiet, contemplative prayer," he said. "Unless you can put your attention where you want it, you will never master yourself. Beware of thought control and escapist practices."

"Well, this meditation process is not escapist. It's frustrating to see yourself struggle to be still and aware of-the-present moment. And seeing your own frustration is part of the process! I'm not really a good example of it, but the meditation helps you find the power that can change your life," I said, trying to end with an encouraging tone.

McCue rose and held his coffee cup in the air as a way of invitation. I nodded. He returned with two cups of coffee, and I was resigned to the prospect of a long night.

"If God is that immovable object you believe you found during your meditation exercises, then you know now that this world is the irresistible force!" He looked at me intently. "Life demands strength," McCue said forcefully. "It will destroy those unfit to survive. That is its purpose," he said slowly, emphasizing each word.

"The phrase, 'the spirit is willing, but the flesh is weak' is a loser's mantra. It's what someone cries when they're justifying their weaknesses! You're young, Brother William, and you have wisdom beyond your years, but you have many wars yet to be fought in this life," he said prophetically. "You must fight to keep this honesty you have. It will serve you well in the long run." I felt awkward during our sudden silence. Had he seen through me? Did he suspect I was a draft dodger hiding from authorities or a loser using religion to conceal my fear of dealing with real life?

"When I leave here, I want to go back to school and eventually become a missionary overseas or something like that," I said boldly, but it sounded pathetic to my ears. I couldn't tell him of recent thoughts of returning to the marines without confessing my deserter status. The idea of missionary service was one I had entertained from time to time.

His eyes opened wide and he smiled broadly. "I once served in the mission fields abroad," he announced quietly. "It can be rewarding and challenging. I was a teacher for a time in Eritrea Province in Ethiopia," he continued, as he answered my unspoken question. "You have a good spirit, you like history, and you get along well with people," he continued, turning the conversation back to me. "You could do well in the mission field. You're a young man with a good mind and an old soul," he smiled warmly and touched my shoulder to emphasize the compliment.

"Thanks, but I have no illusions. I'm learning to deal with my dark side every day. I've done some bad things to other people and myself, but I didn't know any better. Now I do. I can't make amends for all the bad things I did, or to the people I hurt, but I can continue to submit myself, my ego, my pride, to this light that is showing me my errors," I explained.

"You continue to live your life with that attitude and you'll be fine, William," McCue said with his eyes ablaze. "You'll have many ups and downs, periods of faith and doubt. But that self-honesty you have will save you from destruction. My God, you are a pleasure to know! Stay true to that insight you have, and you will learn to live without fear."

"Give yourself time," he continued. "We all come to hate ourselves at some time in our lives, but only the seekers of truth let it change their lives for the better. I don't see that you have any guile in your heart. That's a beautiful thing for a "colored" boy growing up in America these days! There's a lot of rage out there over racism.

McCue took a breath and resumed his discourse. "I could see it coming years ago! I served with black men of high intellect, courage, and honor. Most of the blacks had to suffer in silence as they were passed over or promoted slowly. But the black race has endured! Your people have outlasted the powers that made racist attitudes legal, even though they were always immoral! Your race has suffered terrible abuse and injustices."

"I know, I know," I interrupted his tirade. "I'm still learning and understanding about that part of human history. The Afro-American experience is unique to us, but humans have dominated and enslaved each other throughout the ages. It's the unrepentant, un-awakened human mind that can justify these crimes! I grew up with all sorts of people: black, white, and indifferent. I'm thankful for that, but even without that, I don't think I could ever see a person's skin color or racial classification as the single identity of the person. Something in me always rejected that attitude."

"I see that spirit in you," McCue said. "People like you, because you don't have that judgmental attitude they're so used to dealing with. You've got a spirit like Billy Budd, the character in Herman Melville's novel," he added hurriedly. "Billy Budd had no animosity toward others—a guileless lad."

"I'm no goody-two-shoes, Brother Mac." "I'm too much of a people pleaser," I added. "I see that about myself. I'm dealing with my anger. But you're right about me not judging people based on their race."

"The old saying, 'don't judge a book by its cover' applies. That proves my point about you. There's another quote I like," he closed his eyes and tilted his head back slightly. Then, after he secured the memory, he looked me in the eye and said, "It goes something like 'as far as possible without surrender, be on good terms with all people.'"

"Sounds like 'Desiderata,'" I interrupted enthusiastically, because I recognized the verse.

"You know 'Desiderata?'" he asked with obvious delight. "Why should I be surprised? You really are something," he said, laughing and shaking his head. "That's amazing," he said, still chuckling.

Suddenly, McCue turned serious. "I confess to you that I have my doubts about a loving and all-powerful God, given the state of the world. With all the pain and suffering we experience or see everywhere, it's hard to believe in a just God."

I was shocked. McCue recited Bible verses and prayed in morning devotions. He had Christian knowledge that impressed us all. Now, he was telling me that his faith was weak.

"Your preaching, if you will, was different," he said. "It wasn't the standard fare. I was impressed and thought maybe this place was teaching something different. Now, I know it was just you."

"I was searching without knowing it," I confessed. "All I can tell you is that I do believe that Jesus taught the way to salvation and atonement with God. I have a stronger faith now, because I see reality in a new light, and because of the meditation exercise. It really helps you see the way."

"Some who wander are not lost," he stated. "I grew up in a Christian home, went to Christian schools, and was a committed born-again Christian and church attendee. Now, I've lost my faith. If there is a God, I don't believe he is a personal deity who intervenes in our personal lives. There's just too much agony in the world with drought, famine, war, and disease! I can't have faith in a loving God that could permit these things to dominate life in most countries!"

He stood up slowly. "I know all the Bible answers for human suffering," he sighed. "Some show God punishing sin directly, others reflect that suffering comes as a consequence of sin. Where is the love?" he made a gesture with palms open and walked away.

Brother Mac left me with the memory of that night. He shared more of himself with me than anyone else had in a long time. Yet, he was still a mystery man to me. Was he a warrior-priest who had lost his way? He was a spiritual master, of sorts, with an expansive knowledge of religions. His discipline and commanding presence spoke silently of his ability to be a leader of men. We were each contradictions who had met in the unlikeliest of places for a brief period of time.

I didn't have a response to McCue's spiritual doubts. I had been through that nightmare, but was now awakened. My faith wasn't coming from knowledge alone, but from an experiential relationship with God that was developing within me. I shared with McCue what I could.

The New Breed

"Jesus, Jesus, Jesus! The sweetest name I know," they sang with untrained voices. They were the new breed of Christian youth from the hippie subculture. They called themselves "Freaks for Jesus" or "Jesus Freaks." They were searching for values and meaningful lives, and ironically, these young people were now embracing the "faith of their fathers," but in their own form and fashion. Many of these youth now rejected the sex, drugs, and rock and roll that they had so heartily embraced! Finding redemption in the Jesus movement, religion now became their passion!

Reverend Fred Jordan and other evangelistic ministries bemoaned the youth of America, because they rejected traditional values and lost their way. Overwhelmingly—white, city, suburban, middle-class, wealthy—all rejected the values of their parents' generation. These new, young "rebels without a cause" had found a cause—truth and justice. (Spelled "Jesus!") Passionate youths wanted honesty in regard to real life, and they became more and more cynical about the world their parents created. They wanted to believe in the idealism inspired by the slain leaders (JFK, MLK, and RFK) who strived to make the world a better place for all people.

Some were inspired to join the Peace Corps or VISTA (Volunteers in Service to America). Each young adult imbued the belief that he or she could make a significant contribution to the future of the country. Rather than "turning on" and "dropping out" of society, they were going to engage in societal change.

The "Jesus Freaks" tended to come from the group that promoted positive change. These young souls rejected the secured lives their parents structured for them. Instead, they explored the ever-beckoning counter-culture on college campuses, city streets, wayside communes, or other alternative-lifestyle habitations. Now, they were turning to Christ for direction. He was their new "drug of choice." He was the Good Shepherd, leading them from despair and showing them how to prepare for his coming kingdom!

On *Church in the Home*, stories were featured about the youth ministry of Reverend Jordan. There was an outreach by his organization to direct the passion and energy of the reclaimed youth for

Christ. Many young people left distraught families wondering what had become of them. Now, they told their stories of redemption—between singing songs and handing out religious tracts. They traveled in small groups, as they sought out at-risk, young people to witness to and convert to Jesus. The Christian ministers wanted to reach these young people before the Hare Krishna or other competing religions got to them.

Almost equally divided between boys and girls, they were reprogrammed—from long haired, dope-smoking, free-love, rock and rollers into long-haired, freshly scrubbed, gospel-singing, Christian soldiers. Their families did not completely understand what they were becoming, but at least their kids were back in touch and on a seemingly saner path. The bands of youth drove through communities—in retro-fitted school buses with Bible verses and religious symbols painted on the sides. These illustrations and verse reflected the freaky, eye-catching art of the hippie movement.

The bus parked at a local church or community center, Then, the "Jesus Freaks" would enter neighborhoods in pairs. They'd hand out Bible tracts and invite young people to a Christian youth rally to be held in the area.

The movement enjoyed great success, and donations poured in from across the nation. Caring Christians were deeply moved by the stories and testimonies of the young prodigals. They marveled at the youth who had come to Jesus. As never before, people were apt to dig deep or "give until it hurts" to help the youth succeed.

———— • ◆ • ————

It was late summer, 1968, when we got the word of changes to come. Brother McCue and I were only a couple of days beyond our deep discussion. I looked forward to further talks. I loved his mind, but was even more curious about the man and his life. His self-confessed struggles with his faith prompted me to seek a way to reach him.

I studied and learned that faith comes in two ways. One course is when the mind accepts as true the testimony of another. The second approach is a spiritual gift from God. We cannot give ourselves faith, but in wanting to acquire Godly faith, one must believe that there is a God and that He rewards anyone who diligently seeks Him. I wanted to encourage McCue to learn and practice the foundation's meditation exercise. I believed that if he suspended any preconceived ideas about it, he could find the clarity and stillness he needed to renew his faith in God.

The mission Director called a meeting. Martin Brett told us that some of these youth for Christ were coming to stay at the mission for a time. The Rescue mission would be the home base of operations as they set-up and ran Youth for Christ rallies.

He couldn't hide his awkward position during this transitional period. His job would be the same, but its mission was different. The streets were younger now. The prior generations of "losers" were being replaced, or rather displaced, by young people. These youth could be their children or grandchildren in some cases. The younger faces were better as poster children for the mission's outreach. Their plight might not be as pitiable as a wino's, but their chances for long-term redemption seemed greater.

I left the meeting feeling like it was déjà vu, all over again. The fears I had, when the Korean Children's Choir heightened the visibility of the mission, were back. But this would be worse! These Christian hippies would live in the same building much of the time. I felt a little guilty that I resented them for intruding on my turf. It was selfish of me to be jealous of young people, because of the different demands they would make on my time and solitude.

I had a separate meeting with Brother Johnson and Martin Brett about reorganizing the kitchen to accommodate approximately a dozen young men and women. They assured me that I could handle it. There would be an adjustment period, and some of the kids would be assigned to me to help with the extra workload. We adopted a "can do" attitude to the new challenges before us, because there was nothing else we could do.

I poured out my concerns to Brother Mac when we worked in the kitchen, taking inventory, and preparing an expanded list of items to order from our food salesman, Bill. I was surprised at the sudden frustration I felt. A feeling of helplessness, I had almost forgotten, charged back into my mind. My world was turned upside down in a way I couldn't have anticipated!

McCue spoke quietly. "I don't believe in coincidence. Some say coincidence is another name for God. Our meeting was no accident." He continued after a pause. "You reminded me of some very important beliefs I once held. To learn to accept all that life brings, as if it were from the hand of God—the good and bad alike," he said sincerely.

Bill, the salesman, was at the door. He was delighted with the larger order, but he also saw my concern over the drastic change in the direction of the mission. He reminded me that he serviced other accounts that could use a good cook.

The next morning Brother McCue was gone.

The psychedelic school bus parked next to the main entrance. The voices of the riders flowed through the open windows, as they sang songs of praise. Director Brett and Brother Johnson, greeted the bus. Someone from Reverend Jordan's staff snapped photos of the group being welcomed to the skid-row section of Los Angeles. There were a dozen "Jesus freaks" that would reside at the mission; these new guests would sing at the evening's service.

There were six girls and six boys separated into two dormitories. The girls were on the second floor at the opposite end of the hall from the staff, and the boys were assigned to the third floor. Each dormitory had a bathroom. The kids were smiling, hand-clapping, singing, bright-eyed, and born-again Christians who loved Jesus. They were all white. I had never seen anything like it.

I was nineteen; the age range of the youths was from eighteen to twenty-four. This chapter was a new one for the Christian Evangelistic movement, as groups like these were spreading over the country. They were "on fire for Jesus!"

"Praise the Lord!" and "Thank you, Jesus!" were spoken liberally in their conversations. "Yes Lord!" and "Amen!" were mixed in. This was the same language used by new, reborn Christians to validate their images and prove their minds were right.

This "God talk" was seductive, and one could lapse into it easily. It offered a natural way of reinforcing one's new identity and belief system. These new "babes in Christ" were heavily influenced by the special language of other "saved" individuals. They spoke the names of "Jesus" and "God" with closed eyes and outstretched arms!

For me, with roots in the black-church experience, it reflected the emotional expression that I rejected when I switched to the Methodist church. This Pentecostal enthusiasm and emotional release was hypnotic and dangerous, I thought.

Thanks to my meditation exercise, I was being "sorted out," and growing in a different direction than that espoused by the born-again practitioners. I managed to form a space between the traditional "salvation gospel" of Reverend Jordan's rescue mission and my evolving, internal enlightenment. That space was about to be challenged!

———— • ◆ • ————

They were an attractive-looking group. The male cluster dressed plainly in trousers with shirts neatly tucked. The girls wore long dresses or skirts below the knee. The boys had short haircuts while the girls' hair was shoulder length, and some had much longer. These female, apple-cheeked ladies wore no makeup and no jewelry, except for some crucifixes.

Basically, these youth looked the way their parents wanted them to look. Their appearance contrasted that of the rebellious kids and hippies they saw panhandling for pocket change on the streets. While their new "uniforms" symbolized a break with their past, their name changes were a break from their origins. They believed a new name signified a new direction in life.

The leader of the entire group was called Joshua. He, like the others, adopted a Biblical name for himself. The Biblical names they chose made them feel more in touch with historic Christianity. They deemed that names like Daniel, David, Michael, and Jonathan along with Sarah, Leah, Ruth, Naomi, and Rebecca had spiritual qualities to them. It was all part of the program of illusions that they bought into. Who was I to criticize their name changes? Hadn't I done the same thing for less noble reasons?

———— • ◆ • ————

I was teaching myself to play a donated Kay guitar using a beginner's book. I played only simple chords, but garnered great joy from the feel and the sound of the instrument. The guitar was just for my personal enjoyment.

——————•◆•——————

I hadn't been around young females for two years. It felt strange to have the young girls in the building. However, these women took great pains to be helpful when needed, or subdued and quiet when not.

The brightly painted school bus attracted attention wherever it went. The infectious enthusiasm of the kids—singing songs of praise, passing out tracts, and inviting young people to youth rallies—was very successful. Our building became their base between tours.

Daniel was the second in command to Joshua. He had a gentler approach in dealing with the kids, so I tended to use him as a go-between whenever possible. Joshua tended to be overbearing. Although we were cordial, it was evident that we would not be friends.

Michael was the quiet one, and his fraternal twin brother, Jonathan, was the joker. Jonathan had the cherished knack for making people laugh. The unspoken rule of our mission applied to the new, young visitors. Unless they volunteered their own stories, during testimony or in conversation, their past lives were personal and private.

Three of the kids were assigned to work with me: Miriam, Michael (the quiet twin), and Luke, the youngest boy. Miriam was overweight and had a pretty face. Her raven-black hair was thick and framed her face and hazel eyes. She had a gentle nature and a pleasant personality.

Peeling vegetables was still like therapy to me, so in a relaxed and conversational tone, I shared my struggles with being overweight with Miriam and the others. "Isn't it strange that whenever you decide to make any change in your life, all types of new temptations suddenly appear?" I said, and we all laughed. "Since I had a weight problem all my life, you know I wouldn't want to be around food all the time. So where do I end up?" More laughter.

When the boys were doing other chores Miriam responded to my confession. "You said you were larger than you are now. How much weight have you lost?" she asked.

"I stopped weighing myself every day. The last time I did, I'd lost twenty-five pounds," I said.

She reacted with a smile, "That's great!"

"I never thought I'd be cooking and around food all the time. I hated myself for being so weak, but that just made it worse. I struggled with weight. Sometimes I'd win, but mostly, I'd lose. Now I'm learning to be patient with myself. I can recognize the emotions that make me want to overeat, and sometimes I can let them go."

"I pray I'll be delivered of this burden when the Lord is ready," she said softly. I don't fight it, either. I just give it to Jesus!" she said.

I paused for a while. "Miriam, remember this, you must also be a partner in your own rescue," I said. "What I mean is that those of us who struggle with self-abuse problems—with food, alcohol, or drugs—must learn to 'let go and let God' *in the right way!*" I said, emphasizing the last four words.

"But that's what I said," she protested slightly.

"I know that's what you said," I responded gently. We were no longer working—just standing and talking. "Let me tell you what I mean," I continued. "What you said sounded like resignation, like you were just relieving yourself of any responsibility for your actions or choices. Correct me if I'm wrong."

She pondered my words thoughtfully. I could almost see her emotions swirling around inside her, as she fidgeted with her hands. "I don't know," she finally said softly. "Maybe I'm doing that."

I reached over and touched her on the arm for a moment. I crossed a line I never intended to, but still had a strong impulse to continue. At my gesture, she raised her head and looked me in the eye.

"Miriam, I don't want you to feel good or bad about your life right now," I said sincerely. "I just want you to be aware of it. Look, I'm right there with you, but I've found the stillness within myself that gives me the patience to see negative feelings before they're able to trick me into following them. I'm not saying it well. But there's a way you can reach an objective place within yourself, where God offers you the strength you pray for! There's an opportunity to make a real conscious choice, not simply follow old compulsions or emotional conditioning. It's what the Bible calls 'taking thoughts captive for Christ,'" I said passionately.

Miriam listened intently as I continued. "I don't understand all this that well, myself. I'm still discovering stuff about how messed up I am. But I know this for certain, this meditation process—which is like a silent prayer to God—saved my life, and it's helping me gain victory over my self-destructive impulses to medicate myself with food," I said finally.

I could see I had somewhat overwhelmed her, but much of what I said registered as she nodded attentively. "Wow, that's heavy," she said. "Deep stuff. I've been on diets most of my life. I go down; and then, I put all the weight back on, and more."

Her shoulders slumped, as she reexperienced her frustrations. The pressure from her past visibly bore down on her. Her spirit gripped her there, so I spoke before the moment was lost. "The most important thing you can learn to do is find the patience to be still. Then, you'll notice that your emotions start upsetting and frustrating you. It's a cruel game we play in our minds without knowing it. We sabotage ourselves. We judge ourselves. Something in our minds whispers that we're not worthy of God's love, so we secretly agree to punish ourselves. It's scary what's going on inside you, but Miriam, it's wonderful, too. If you can recognize these mind games, it means you're alive. You're waking up to a reality that will save you! Be honest with yourself about the forces and thoughts that are keeping you emotional, and sometimes," I paused for effect, "you'll be able to watch them dissolve, because you didn't get involved with them."

I was amazed that I was learning how these things fit together even as I listened to myself. This was the truth! And this truth was what I was living in my daily life since I began meditating. I never articulated it before. I spoke with passion, driven by sincerity.

"You sound like a psychiatrist or something," she said, laughing nervously.

"No, no, no," I said quickly, as I noticed Michael eavesdropping. All truth, real truth, must be self-evident. You must discover it for yourself, otherwise, how do you know it's really the truth? I'm only sharing what I've gleaned from experience and observation. Another thing to remember is that when we ask God for wisdom, we get problems to aid us in reasoning our way through. If we pray for courage, he sends danger and challenges to overcome! Do you see how beautiful that is? What our Creator does to promote the character we need to change ourselves?" I asked joyfully.

She was getting it! Miriam could see where I was coming from, so I went on a bit longer. "My weight problem is simply the evidence of the problem I have with food. I eat when I'm happy; I eat when I'm sad. I eat, and overeat, because food is my first savior. I learned to have faith in food to relieve my pain—from when I was angry for not having enough to eat as a kid to my fears and frustrations today. Now, with prayer and meditation, I'm unlearning those behaviors. What that means is that I may get my weight down to where it's supposed to be, but I would still have a problem with food. Unless I deal with the root anger and resentment that binds me to food, I will struggle with my weight. And that's the way it should be. I need to go back the way I came to identify the source of my problem."

I walked over to my shelf of cookbooks and took a brochure from the Foundation of Human Understanding I kept tucked among them. I offered it to Miriam. "This is a helpful pamphlet: *What You Should Know about Being Upset.* You're welcome to read it. See if it makes sense to you. You may garner some insights." Miriam took the brochure and flipped its few pages.

"Thank you," she said politely, and tucked it away as she nervously smiled at me. Miriam had a lovely smile that highlighted her pretty face, but as she tucked away the brochure, I noticed her hands. Her nails were short and irregular like she chewed them.

I felt drained and exhilarated. I touched this girl's mind and hopefully, her heart. Something in her spirit called to me to help her find hope.

———— ◆ ————

The door to my room was slightly ajar as I played my guitar one afternoon. I stopped when I heard the knock. It was Michael. Known as the quiet twin, he opened up when talking about sports.

Once he knew that I kept up with sports teams, I was his new best friend. After we chatted about professional athletics, Michael lingered longer than usual. I asked if anything was on his mind.

"Do you play chess, Brother William?" he asked, looking in the direction of my chessboard.

"I haven't played the game in a long time," I said. "I keep that board set up in order to solve the chess problems in the Sunday paper. Do you play?"

"Yes."

"Well, I was never that good at it, so maybe you can teach me some moves." I said.

We decided to play a game without any time limits. It would last over a few days with each of us present during moves. The match would take place in the library, and occasionally, Jonathan would join us. They enjoyed teaching me some classic attacks and defenses. The two brothers' personalities were very different, but they appeared to be each other's best friend. I liked seeing that bond.

One of the extra rooms on the boys' floor was transformed into a game room with a Ping-Pong table and some donated board games. Some afternoons, with the others out of the building, the brothers, Miriam, and I would play Ping-Pong in the game room for an hour. It was a sweet time. This hour was our time for helping each other to mend.

All three liked my evening sermons and the messages I taught during morning devotions. It appeared that with no desire of becoming a shepherd, I gathered a small flock.

Brother Reggie returned to the rescue mission in October of 1968. (He also bunked at the mission a year before I arrived.) Reggie was a slender, good-looking, black man with big, brown eyes. He had a crooked smile and years of hard, street life etched into his handsome and craggy features.

"Hey there, young brother," he said to me in a friendly tone, as he stuck his wooly head into the kitchen. "Brother Brett said to see you about workin' in the kitchen. Brother Emil's workin' at the Midnight Mission. I seen him about a month ago. I worked with him here," he rattled on without taking a breath.

"It's good to see a brother in charge," Brother Reggie said as we shook hands. "Brother Martin said you're doin' a good job. I been sober now for awhile. I'm tryin' to get back on my feet. I worked here for Emil, and I cooked in the navy before that. I'll do whatever you say. You're the boss! You the man!" he said with a raspy laugh. He said he was sixty-years-old, but not until he relaxed with a cup of coffee and gave me the *Reader's Digest* version of his story did he begin to look like every one of those sixty years.

"I was raised in the church," he stated with a mild Southern accent. "Shit," he winced. "Excuse me," he quickly apologized. "I know the Bible. I was saved when I was fifteen-years-old," he said.

As we talked in the dining hall, my little crew gathered. I introduced them to Reggie. He had a wonderful and an entertaining way of storytelling. We listened raptly to his tales from his journey through life. "I know the Lord only gives you so many chances to get your life turned around. This might be my last chance. I don't know," he said softly.

"Do you mind if we pray with you?" I heard myself ask. We joined hands and bowed our heads. I recited a short, heartfelt prayer to give hope to this broken man, and I sincerely asked God to heal all of our lives. There were times when flesh and blood needed flesh and blood. I knew this was a time when words meant less than human interaction. We sincerely ached for this man and prayed he found the strength to endure his journey to salvation for a little longer.

Brother Reggie's story wasn't so significant in and of itself. In fact, his tale was so typical of the lost men on skid row that made it rather unspectacular. However, his pain and passion became the key in a series of events to follow. The sharing of Reggie's saga motivated my helpers to unburden themselves to me. The door to my room was always open for our conversations. I would hear a knock at my door when the kitchen or dining hall were not private enough. I grew comfortable with my new role.

Miriam was a different person. She told me she was meditating. She learned from reading the instructions in Roy Masters' book and recording. Miriam wanted to be secretive, so I went along, but her attitude was changing. The only real tragedy in life was to suffer repeatedly without learning. Miriam was teachable.

Miriam, the twins, and I were hanging around the third-floor game room. "I have a son," she proclaimed. "I have a little boy," she went on. "He's probably in Indiana or Illinois. Today's his birthday. He's five–years-old today," her voice trailed off, as her mood shifted slightly. We were silent. The pain of missing her son's birthday prompted her sudden confession.

Miriam explained how she was forced to give up her out-of-wed-lock baby at sixteen-years-old. She recounted how strict and loveless her "Christian" parents' discipline had been. Her angry rebellion prompted her to run away with a teenage boy that she thought she loved. Their weird odyssey of stealing cars, shoplifting, dope smok-ing, and sharing the cramped confines of a VW Bus with another vagabond couple, ended with her pregnant and the one-time boyfriend in reform school. With tears falling, she rushed on to clar-ify that an adoption was arranged by her parents before the baby was born. "I agreed to it, but I hated them for it! After I went into labor, everything happened so fast. I just cried and cried. I never got to name my little boy." After a long pause, she added, "I never told any-body this before. Well, that's not accurate. I told Sarah after the youth rally where I accepted Christ. She told me to forgive my par-ents, and I thought I did. Now I can see," she said, looking at me as she smiled and wiped away her tears, "that I still harbor a lot of resentment toward them."

Change was in the wind. The winds of change can be deceptively calm in the beginning, because they arise as a refreshing breeze one may not notice. Hence, I resented this group of young Christians when they first arrived, but tempered my resentment as we bonded. I greatly appreciated them now.

————— • ◆ • —————

The meditation-observation exercise was a nonhabit-forming practice. That was the bad news. One must commit to practice it each time like new. Unfortunately, there was never any compulsion or external motivation to meditate. The desire must emerge from within; the yearning for the right way to be must gently prompt one to be still. We must surrender to his light. This was true prayer—an embodied prayer, as one becomes quietly aware and perceives one's swirling, hypnotic thought patterns.

Then, you disappear, but you don't know you're gone. You're no longer observing your distracting thoughts, but dancing along with them in a toxic mix of past pain and future joys. You're lost! Lost in the space between your ears—the fantasy zone where the mind is a slave to puppet masters within one's haunted imagination. Next, the silent mystical prompt to awaken and detach from the wandering imagination appears; we return to the "neutral zone," the quiet center of self-observation. That gentle prompt to become aware and awake was from God.

We need salvation from our sleeping, hypnotized mind that is dreaming it is awake! The still, small voice—like the sting of conscience—guides us back to the present. The present is the only place we can ever be saved. The present is where real self-awareness causes real change. The God of patience waits for us to surrender our wills, as we submit to his Spirit within us during each aware moment.

While I was the confessor to many at the mission, I couldn't share my story with anyone. The closest I got to revealing my truth was upon telling my kitchen helpers that I was born out of wedlock. I added that I wondered what it would be like to meet my real father. That was the most private information I dared reveal of my past. I was still living a lie!

———— •◆• ————

Sarah poked her head into my room. "I heard you playing," she said with a pleasant smile, "I didn't know you played the guitar, too."

"I'm not very good. I just fool around with it," I explained. It's relaxing. Do you play?" I asked, hoping she lingered a while.

"No," she said, as she stepped all the way into my room. "I don't play anything really, unless you count the tambourine," she laughed. "That doesn't take much skill."

Sarah looked lovelier than ever standing in my room. She was tall and slender with strawberry-blonde hair that cascaded over her shoulders and almost halfway down her back. She had a lovely face with gentle freckling. After viewing Sarah interacting with the other kids, I appreciated her pleasant personality. The self-assured way she carried herself reflected a strong character. Whenever the youth group sang at the mission or on the Sunday telecast of *Church in the Home*, Sarah was the one who stood out. She was the stuff of fantasies, even with her striking beauty subdued by her humble manner of dress.

"It's so neat in here," she said, as she walked in slowly and glanced around the room. I was glad that my things were in order. The only other female who visited my room was Miriam.

"Thank you," I managed to say. I felt foolish for not inviting her previously. Yet, I could hardly believe she was there. I was sitting in a rocking chair, where I liked to read or strum the guitar. Sarah walked to my "meditation" chair, opposite me, and sat down gracefully.

"Miriam tells me about your talks with her, Brother William," she started, looking directly at me. I tensed up involuntarily. "She said you've helped her so much! More than anyone else! I could see the recent changes in her—in her spirit," she added. "I thank the Lord for your kindness."

"Thank you," I responded with a twinge of adolescent awkwardness. "I don't think I did anything special," I went on, not wanting to project false humility. "I thank the Lord for any insight I can share about being overweight and learning how and why food can dominate our life." I stopped myself at this point.

"She thinks so much of you. We all do," she stated, as she touched my knee with her hand and held it there for a moment.

A pause settled between us. Her legs were crossed, lady like, and her long dress hung loosely around her ankles. She was in her stocking feet; her socks reached midcalf, but were turned down above the ankle. She sat hunched over her lap with her raised legs bouncing slightly. She appeared as if she wanted to say more.

"I just shared my personal struggles and understanding with her, about how we get caught up into using things, like food, to save us from the pain of living. Like with drugs, booze, or whatever, the escape doesn't last. You have to keep returning to your fix for comfort." I set my guitar aside. I felt comfortable again.

"What I told Miriam is that with food problems, there are no quick fixes! For some of us, it will be a life-long struggle, but not in a willful or egotistical way. It's so complicated. When we push our pride out of the way, it becomes easier. Food feeds our proud egos, but we are acting under a compulsion that puts us into conflict with our true identity—where God wants us to be," I finished, hoping I didn't sound too ponderous.

"Mike, Miriam, and Jon said you were deep," she said smiling, as she leaned back in the chair. "We've been praying for Miriam to overcome her problem, but like you say, I knew it went deeper than just overeating."

"Yes, we're eating our emotions," I interrupted "We're trying to conquer our resentments and frustrations. Normal eating is guilt free. Abnormal appetites expose a problem. We're full of resentments over our past sins, because we haven't really forgiven! And we're frustrated with our present lives because they get in the way of our idea of happiness! That same frustration makes us want to eat again to ease our conflicts." Once again, I was realized the truth as I was speaking it!

"Interesting," she said thoughtfully. "That's interesting. Miriam said you showed her a meditation prayer. How does that help her any differently than regular prayer?"

I took a deep breath and slowly exhaled as I sat back in the rocker. I couldn't quite believe the moment was happening. I viewed Sarah and admired her from afar. Like a love-struck school boy, I took extra pains with my grooming and dress since the girls invaded our domain. I never allowed any serious fantasies about Sarah to play out in my imagination, but the temptation was there. I had a warm and loving feeling for Miriam, but Sarah was the unattainable beauty that only the fearless dared approach. I savored the way she said, "We all do," after telling me how much Miriam and the others thought of me. Here Sarah was, in my midst, and our minds were connecting. I wanted each word I said to her to be inspired. I wanted to touch her soul in a way that it had never been touched before.

"Sarah," I said gently, "regular prayer, as you call it, is usually humans talking to God. We're either complaining or begging for something," I paused for effect before completing my thought. "The meditation prayer is more about *listening* for God. It's is the, 'be still and know that I am God,' from Psalm 46:10. This meditation teaches us to 'be still and wait,' patiently, for the Lord's light to reveal us to ourselves; so, we can see ourselves as God sees us. There're no words, no chants, no music, no incense. This place is where your ego self—your true self—and God meet in the present moment, when you are still and he is ready."

"It doesn't matter what you call him, but when you sincerely practice this silent prayer, you're answering his invitation to openness by surrendering your egotistical will—if only for a fraction of a second. For only a few seconds each time we meditate, are we able to be still."

"Only a few seconds?" Sarah questioned with surprise. "Is that in the beginning?"

"Yes, it's like that in the beginning for sure, but years later, it may not be different. Look, the main thing is that we see how crazy we are. How un-sane our minds work most of the time.

"Un-sane?" Sarah asked.

"Yes, it's a word that perfectly describes our mental condition. Most people are not completely sane, or they wouldn't do the irrational things that they do and later, regret. Neither are folks usually clinically insane—a term used by professional headshrinkers. Most humans are in a place dominated by "un-sane" thoughts and actions, because we are in hypnotic trances. Our thoughts are toxic. Our behavior becomes addictive and destructive, because we don't exercise impulse controls."

Sarah was giving me her full attention so I continued. "Each of us lives in his own little, psychotic cocoon whereupon he compulsively dreams that he is a wonderfully brilliant and beautiful human being. We like other sleepwalking dreamers that mirror us. We judge everything as if we were God! Our minds are in perpetual judgment mode. We're in angry denial most of our lives—resisting this truth! If we are still enough to see our passions—and our poisons—our honest hearts will cry for salvation!" I stopped, fearing I had gone too far.

"What about Jesus?" Sarah asked so sweetly that I smiled.

"Jesus is our Savior from our mind tricks!" I said forcefully. Only his sinless life, death, and resurrection can save us from ourselves! It's all so wonderful when we can see for ourselves that our true nature is trying to answer His Call! Jesus shows us the way to reverse the curse of Adam! When we choose Jesus as the tree of life, instead of the tree of knowledge that Adam and Eve chose, we embrace God's eternal life! It's all part of God's divine plan. Our conscience is endeavoring to bring us to the light of God's life! We need to learn how to let go of who we think we are and learn to grow from Christ's light."

Sarah caught me glancing quickly at the clock on my nightstand. Sarah stood. She was the tallest of the girls. I could see her shapeliness when she adjusted her dress. I rose slowly, thinking she'd start toward the door. She didn't move, so that now we stood uncomfortably close. I awkwardly stood there. Sarah had something else to say. "I'm sorry for taking up so much of your time," she said as she searched for words. "Can we talk more about this meditation another time?"

"Yes, anytime," I said quickly. "Stop by anytime," I added. I winced at the open invitation, but doubted that she would follow up on it. If she did, it would be just for what she said. I was coldly realistic, and I knew there was no romance budding.

I watched her walk down the hallway to the girl's dormitory. I pushed my door closed and meditated before returning to work. I settled into my chair; I could still feel the warmth of her presence. A light fragrance of soap and shampoo lingered; I breathed it in as I tried to center myself.

———— • ◆ • ————

The black-and-white–checked trousers I wore as head cook were beginning to hang loosely on me. I would be able to order a size smaller for the second time in as many months. Brother Donavan trimmed my hair neatly with scissors and a comb. I searched through our donated clothing for smaller items to wear. It was a good time for me. It was a humbling victory to be shedding pounds during a stressful time—when I would otherwise be growing out, rather than growing up.

———— • ◆ • ————

The Youth for Christ group was away for a few days; they were scheduled to return before Thanksgiving. I looked forward to seeing my crew again. Miriam, Michael, and Jonathan became my surrogate siblings. Perhaps, in some mystical way, I was discovering how to be a good older brother—the type I should have been to my real-life brothers and sisters.

I was eager to see Sarah again. I felt strange. I didn't want to embrace the teasing fantasies that slipped into my consciousness. How silly to feel like a kid with a crush on his classmate. I did not choose to have these feelings but they were there.

"Brother William?" Finally, I heard the voice I longed to hear.

"Hi, Sarah," I said. "Come in." I was calm and casual, but I was also thrilled with her presence.

The youth group had been back for two days, but Sarah and I were too busy to say more than hello. I put my guitar aside, as she walked to the meditation chair. I still hadn't deciphered her. She didn't seem to have any demons. I wondered how she came to be a Christian "gypsy," considering she was so together.

"Things have been so crazy lately," she started. "I swear sometimes, Joshua acts like such a jerk," she proclaimed, obviously agitated.

I was puzzled. I had no idea what Sarah was talking about. She crossed her legs and leaned toward me; then, she took a deep breath and exhaled slowly. "He's away for a while, so I wanted to tell you what's goin' on." She paused while she fingered the small crucifix around her neck. "Joshua's discouraging us from talking with you about anything other than work stuff," she said.

I was stunned and perplexed. What was going on? Someone wanted to outlaw the friendships I formed with this lovely person and others? What was that about? "What happened?" I asked.

"Joshua said that you're confusing us with ideas that are not biblical," she said somewhat apologetically. "I just wanted you to know," she went on. "That's why he sent Leah and David to work in the kitchen yesterday."

I gathered my thoughts. I wondered about the abrupt change, but figured they were put in place because of other circumstances."Why does he think I'm against biblical principles?" I asked, not really expecting a detailed answer.

"Because, you gave that pamphlet to Miriam about practicing meditation," she answered. I nodded slowly.

"Joshua said it's not biblical. He said that new-age religions are godless and dangerous, and so are you. I don't agree with him about you," she added hurriedly. "None of us do, but...."

"He thinks he knows a lot about that stuff," I said mockingly.

"Well, he does have some background in religion. I think he went to a Bible college, and his father is a minister," she added. "Miriam and Joshua had a big fight. He was real mad when he saw her reading that brochure. She came to me afterwards and told me about it. She was crying, but she stood up to him. She never could before. Miriam thanks you for that," she said. Then, she smiled. "I confronted Joshua and told him he was wrong about you. I explained how much you had helped Miriam, but there's no talking to him when he gets like that. He can be very domineering," she said as she stood up.

I remained a bit dazed. Sarah stepped toward the door, turned, and faced me. She took my hands into hers. "I know you're a good person. You have a good spirit, and I think you're coming from a good place," she said, squeezing my hands tenderly. Then, she slipped within my arms and embraced me with her head on my shoulder. I squeezed her body firmly and patted her back for a moment. The hug had caught me by surprise, and I tingled as we parted.

"We'll still have our talks when he's not around," Sarah whispered. "God bless you, Brother William."

———— • ◆ • ————

I loved the story of the birth of Jesus. However, the blurring of the lines between the nativity and Santa Claus disgusted me. I did not approve of the pagan icons that American cultural Christianity embraced. The "Jesus freaks" rejoiced during the Christmas festivities. The pagan influences didn't dissuade them. They celebrated the birth of Jesus, the Savior of mankind.

My little flock and I spoke about this commemoration. I explained why I refused to be caught up in the hysteria, although I didn't wish to dampen their enthusiasm. After all, they were in the mind-set that the more they celebrated Jesus, the more real he became. They embraced the spiritual parts of the holiday and down-played the secular factors, because they were born-again Christians.

Miriam, Sarah, Michael, and Jonathan met with me in the rec room, library, or dining room while Joshua was away. Never again did we meet in my room. My books made them uncomfortable. Mere Christianity and *The Screwtape Letters* by C.S. Lewis were not as suspect as some of my other volumes (*The Forgotten Books of Eden*, *The Lost Books of the Bible*, *A Brief History of the Inquisition*, *How the Great Religions Began*, and some biographies).

———— • ◆ • ————

It was early December and the skid-row missions teemed with winter transients. I wasn't scheduled to speak at services, but became a last minute fill-in. The youth-group members and my kitchen staff listened from the rear of the chapel. I felt inspired, as I winged it without notes or preparation. I wished to say something meaningful."The pains of our haunted lives are unrecognized bless-ings to us. We curse them, because we don't understand that they are awakening us to our errors. The Bible calls them, sins. We are slaves to these sins," I said in a tense whisper. "We are prisoners of our own toxic natures, under compulsions to live contrary to the laws of God—the law of love!"

I clasped my hands in the air and paused until I was sure I had everyone's attention. "What are the laws of God?" I laid the Bible on the podium and walked to the edge of the stage. "Jesus of Nazareth answered that question when he said, 'You should love the Lord your God with all your heart, all your soul, all your mind, and all your strength.' And Jesus went on to say, 'Love your neighbor as your-self.'"

I dropped my hands by my side, walked to the podium, and leaned forward. "Who was this man named Jesus? Why do his words—from almost two-thousand years ago—still echo throughout all of human history? Jesus and his Word are the truth," I said softly for dramatic effect. "They were spoken by a man who was not a slave of human nature. His nature came directly from God, his Father, mirroring the nature of the creation of the first human being. That first man—we call Adam—didn't know how to love his creator, as he was loved. Because he allowed himself to be corrupted by an outside influence, Adam disobeyed God and broke the direct connection of life they once shared. In time, Adam eventually died, as a consequence of their broken relationship."

I opened the Bible. As I glanced around the room, I noted that Sarah and Miriam were on one side of the room; Michael and Jonathan stood in the rear beside Joshua and Daniel. "So Jesus was the second Adam, but he lived his life in total love and obedience to God, his Father. His life was lived without sin and was sacrificed for our lives. 'For God so loved the world that he gave his only begotten Son, that whosoever believes in him should not perish, but have eternal life!'" While I spoke the passage, I watched many members of the audience mouthing the words.

"That Bible verse, John 3:16, reveals to any searching soul how to reconnect with our Creator," I said forcefully. Jesus is the link to reconnection with the Creator. The pains in your heart and life are signs that you should question yourself. Ask who you are, and why you resist your conscience. Why do you refuse to admit your life is out of control?" I asked, raising my voice. "We'll change everything about ourselves, except the realization we're trapped by our pride and unable to stop feeding our self-defeating nature! There is a light that shines in the darkness inside each of us," I went on. "That same light of conscience is the 'still, small voice' that guides us to the meaning of life."

I was going off the reservation. I silently prayed that I was making enough sense to reach the few I could help. "Our real selves—our true human nature lays dormant, like a seed, at the center of our beings. If we can be still long enough to become humble, we can be brought to repentance. Then, the process of turning our lives around begins.

"Jesus, who was the second Adam and God's only begotten Son, will join his sinless life to yours. Jesus lived a sinless life, because he was born with the original human nature. He possessed direct knowledge of God and his purpose. Jesus enjoyed the perfect relationship with his heavenly Father, that of love and devotion. His perfect life tormented the power structure and the lives of many others, and he was killed for obeying the higher laws of God's love. His perfect nature was killed, instead of mankind's imperfect, sinful nature. He died for you and me, but his godly spirit could not be killed and was resurrected to eternal life by God. His Holy Spirit will enliven the seed of God within your soul, and you will start to be born again! That means a new order of life and a godly understanding of your purpose." I spread my arms out before them.

"I'm sorry for being so long-winded tonight. Brother Reggie already gave me the sign to wrap it up." Laughter erupted. "This is about life and death," I resumed. "My God, I wish I heard some of these messages when I was hungry for truth. Too many churches have forgotten the meaning behind the message. They preach like robots."

With sincerity in my heart, I continued. "I'm not the best messenger, but you need to hear these ideas spoken this way! Accept your pain! Emotional, physical, and spiritual pains are mostly sensed in order to wake us up from our dream states. Look at your constant discontent with everything in your life! We are lost and angry. We irritate the life from each other, as we die from our self-inflicted wounds! Our culture or family connections cannot save us! Our lifestyle cannot save us! Our politics and education cannot save us! Good deeds and a good life cannot save us! Even religion cannot save us; it cannot restore the connection we need with our Creator." I paused to let that sink in.

Directly, I shouted, "It can't just be a religion! The whole planet stinks with religions! Everybody's got a religion! Even when we say we don't, we are lying to ourselves, because we repeat the same behavior over and over! Why? Because our stubborn pride is our religion! We think it will save us! How far must we fall before the pain of life awakens us? There's a higher knowledge than most churches teach. Knowledge that all true religions point us toward. It's a guiding light that makes all truth self-evident! We must yearn for that light within our hearts, and it will show us the "door" at which Jesus is knocking. He wants to enter your life and change your nature.

My passion and yearning to reach each member of the audience provided me energy to continue. "You will become a new creature, living the blessed, fearless life that you were meant to! The seed of your true identity will bud, flower, and grow from God's light of love, and from your willingness to surrender. Somewhere in your heart, you know this is true. You tried the rest, now I invite you to try the best. I ask each of you to search your heart tonight,"

I gave the cue for the "altar call." The music was softly turned on. "Come to me, all you who are burdened and heavy ladened. I will give you rest, the Savior promises. God is calling you to try his way—his right way! The only thing you can really change about your life is your attitude! Change your attitude tonight. Let go of your pride and willfulness or seek to learn how. Repentance can begin here. Repentance can begin now! This can be your moment of truth, stop outrunning your conscience and be still! When you begin to question your attitude, with real self-honesty, you'll discover that your conscience was never your enemy! It is your guide to a healthy relationship with yourself. If you're ready to ask God to help you change your attitude toward him, I invite you to come forward for a public testimony tonight."

I heard a few of the youth-group members say "Amen" out loud. The song, "Just as I Am" played in the background while I held my outstretched arms over the congregation. A few people walked to the front. "I ask each of you who would like to make a public acknowledgment of your change of heart and attitude to come forward. To others who prefer to remain seated, yet want to make real changes in their lives tonight, your new attitudes are blessing you right now!"

I was sincere, but uncomfortable, as I gave the traditional "altar call." My talks were typically so different from the norm that few attendees came forward for prayer. This evening, some members were already standing and humming along with the beautiful hymn. A few more folks came forward. I greeted each one with a handshake and thanked him or her with a heartfelt "God bless you."

Then, I motioned for everyone to stand. "Our Father, I pray your spirit moved me to speak to the hearts of those who endeavor to make changes in their lives tonight. I ask that you bless these souls who came forward tonight, and the others who asked you into their hearts. And I pray for this entire congregation and this ministry, and its work! Bless each of us and teach us your way of embracing each moment that life brings to us. I ask these things in the name of Jesus, Amen." There was an echo of "Amen" from the auditorium. Off to one side, I gathered the dozen or so penitents that came forward. I didn't feel tired at all.

There were times when I felt tremendous personal power—times when I could think clearly and everything seemed to go well. During these moments, my confidence was infectious. I could be intense and inspiring or calm and comforting. The pendulum swung both ways. I struggled to stay focused and noticed a kind of disconnected sensation enveloped me. I called it being "partly cloudy." During these junctures, more effort was needed to make decisions, and sometimes, I made dumb mistakes.

When I spoke that night at the mission service, I was at my peak. I was pleased by my ability to articulate so many key points to so many needy people. I was humbled by the thought that God's power was at work through my life. The next morning, my four friends gathered in the dining hall after devotions and chores. We prepared for the Christmas holiday. I assigned them various tasks. On Saturday morning, it was like old times. We sat around the table and talked in a casual way.

"Brother William, I really liked your message last night," Michael said, dispensing with the small talk. "There was a lot of good stuff in there," he added.

"Yeah, I liked it, too," his brother chimed in.

Minds were unbuttoned, and openness of thoughts was being shared. "Weren't you a little too strong when you talked against the churches?" Sarah asked.

"Not really! I could have been a lot stronger!" I said forcefully. "Religious organizations serve a purpose that's within the divine plan," I said confidently. "But I attacked the churches, because I wanted to encourage people to question what they're taught, what they believe, and why they believe it."

"The churches do way more good for people than bad," Sarah countered. "I just feel it's good for people to seek the Lord, and the church is the first place they go. I think it turns them off—gives some an excuse not to go at all, if you leave the impression that they're mostly bad," she added sweetly.

It was now our familiar point and counterpoint, and we both enjoyed the discussion. I embraced her with my eyes. I loved her spirit and her mind. I agreed with her view.

We talked about the First Council of Nicaea (presided over by Roman Emperor Constantine I), "Apostles' Creed," and the doctrine of the Trinity. I questioned the doctrine of the Trinity. "The Father, Son and Holy Ghost are in the Bible."

A booming voice interrupted me, and into the room strode Joshua and Daniel. "The Holy Trinity is part of historical Christianity, and…." Joshua bellowed until I cut him off.

"The word "Trinity" is never mentioned in the scriptures," I interrupted.

My group's chemistry altered when Joshua joined them. With piercing eyes, he glared at each member; he saved his most intense scowl for Sarah. She simply peered back at him. Joshua walked within a couple of feet of me and folded his arms across his chest. His body language expressed that I was in for a rough time. "My point was," I continued before Joshua interjected his next thought, "that the Nicene Creed was forged by religionist intellectuals who were determined to explain, to our feeble, little brains, the unique qualities of God!" I sounded more superior than I wanted to. "They might have meant well, but they ended up putting God and Jesus into neat, little boxes—the same boxes that they utilized for worshipping Gods before Christianity took over as the state religion! The Godhead may be a Trinity, but that assumption has become a dogmatic article of faith," I added emphatically.

Joshua rolled his eyes. This was the first pitched battle in our undeclared war, and I could feel the adrenaline rush through my body. Then, Joshua spouted, "The triune Godhead is a historic article of Christian faith. The Holy Bible is the authority from which it derives. Because you're confused about the Trinity, doesn't mean you should spread your confusion, brother. The Reformation restored the church to its original condition. The Gospel is the only thing we care about. We're sharing God's plan of salvation and soul winning!

You're talkin' ancient history," Joshua continued. "The true Gospel will not be hidden under a bushel, praise Jesus?" he challenged and clapped his hands.

"Praise Jesus; praise the Lord," echoed the others.

Joshua shot a steely stare at me, as he folded his arms again. He nodded with self-satisfaction and exuded supreme confidence.

"Joshua," I spoke his name in an attempt to soften the rhetoric. "The Reformation didn't change that much at first. Actually, all of the organized churches and religions that evolved from that period still bear fruits from the poisoned tree within their doctrines." My tone was instructional and friendly, and I could see I caught him off guard.

After a pause, Joshua asked, "Brother William, do you believe that the Bible is the inspired Word of God?"

"Yes," I said firmly.

"No, you don't," he shot back quickly. "You don't believe that every word of the Holy Bible is the inspired Word of God, do you?"

"Joshua, I said I do," I responded. I wasn't going to walk into his trap. I would make him work at tripping me up.

"Okay, you say you believe in the infallibility of the Bible, but you don't believe in the 'Sonship' of Jesus, the Holy Trinity, Bible prophecy, or soul winning!" he stated. He wanted a fight.

"I do believe each of those things. I do believe the Bible is the Word of God, the Word from God, and the Word about God as he revealed himself to man," I said slowly.

"All scripture is inspired by God and profitable for doctrine and instruction in righteousness. Second Timothy 3:16!" He said haughtily.

"Look, are we gonna have a dialogue or a debate?" I asked. "The Bible, as it is compiled, has a vast store of wonderful books and texts, loaded with wise, spiritual, and historical insights," I proclaimed. "But whole books and other writings were not included in the Bible for a variety of reasons. Many of them are obvious, but others aren't so clear. It goes to the paternalistic attitude of historic church elders; they didn't trust that these other writings could be judged by unlettered common people! That's all I'm talking about."

"Study the Word to show thyself approved." Joshua pointed at me, ignoring my point. "I see the unbiblical books you have in your library," he went on. "The *Book of Mormon* and Catholic Bible shouldn't be there! And the so-called Church of God stuff is full of lies! You need to contemplate the Word of God and the Old and the New Testaments; these hold inerrant truths and reflect the absolute authority of Jesus Christ! Study to show thyself approved," he instructed.

"'Of making many books there is no end; and much study is a weariness of the flesh,'" I countered. "Don't use the Bible to prove the Bible," I said angrily. Can't you see that all truth must be self-evident?" I pleaded, a little frustrated. "The Bible shouldn't be the object of worship—but its author should be!" I emphasized. "You can quote verse and chapter all day and use your knowledge to pull rank on others, intimidating them into agreeing with you. Forcing people to memorize chapters and verses of scripture does not turn the Word into flesh! The truths and principles of the Bible are eternal—like their author! We need the book to testify of him— to introduce us to him! Then, the Holy Spirit will lead us."

Joshua gestured toward me dismissively; then, he waved me off with both hands. "You're just another free thinker," he said to me as an insult. He was just short of calling me a heretic. "I'll pray for you, Brother William," he went on sarcastically. "I'll pray that the Lord opens your eyes to the infallibility of his Word. The reliability of scripture is the basis of our faith. Free thinkers are lost and condemned." Joshua turned to walk away. I blocked his exit without thinking. I was invading his comfort zone, and he involuntary stepped backward.

"I'll take that as a compliment," I said, as my voice rose. "I am a freethinker and that's not a sin! I think all Christians should be! You think you're saved, because you can quote chapters and verses all day? The Lord wants us to worship Him, in spirit and in truth! What you believe may be right," I went on, "but there is a right way to come to believe in the truth, and it's not to simply repeat it proudly like a parrot! That just makes you a hypnotized Christian—a hypno-Christian!"

"That sounds like your new-age, religious teacher talking," he said.

"Brother Joshua, stop being so close-minded for a minute," I said with frustration creeping into my voice. "Open your mind! Jesus didn't come to start a new religion, but to free man from religion. Listen to the words of Jesus; he taught us to learn to worship God in spirit and in truth, because the time was coming when people wouldn't worship on one mountain of one belief and another mountain of another belief," I said with finality.

"I don't understand you, Brother William," Joshua said, as he shook his head and threw up his arms. "You employ quotes from the Bible, but you don't believe the Bible is the Word of God!"

"I never said that, Joshua!" I took a half step toward him. "Stop twisting my words!" I demanded forcefully. "I can see that you're into your born-again, self-righteous, judgmental, Bible-thumping attitude!" I spat angrily. Suddenly, I felt weak, but I was determined to stay strong. I continued my attack. "I honestly believe that if Jesus came back right now, most Christians wouldn't even recognize him! They would question his un-emotionalism! They would say he doesn't use enough 'God talk' or quote the Bible often enough! They would claim that he sounded funny, because he didn't speak in a King James Version of English," I chuckled at that, but no one else did. I noticed everyone watching we two combatants.

Advancing my point, I asserted, "I truly believe that most Christians today would persecute Jesus, because he would not represent the image that they hold of a Christian or Christ! He would tell them—in modern terms—that the scriptures testified of him. And that these Christians didn't recognize him, because they never knew him; they never had a real relationship with him except in their imaginations. They accepted the facts about him and his teachings, but never grew in spirit, because their minds were filled with chatter and vain repetitions of chapter and verse. Christians never learned the message that speaks to their hearts: 'Be still and know God,'" I concluded.

"You shouldn't even be here, brother," he said. "If you don't believe the Bible and the message of Jesus—to go into the world and preach the Gospel—why are you here? If you died tonight, brother, where would you spend eternity?" he challenged me.

That was frequently a question during a "soul-winning" foray. I knew it well, yet he caught me off guard with it. "I believe in the Lord, and I trust the Lord. And I believe he's preparing me to be with him in paradise," I said. I glanced at Sarah; she was contemplating me. I acted confident in my answer. Daniel and Leah whispered. I wondered, if during this oft-anticipated shootout, I was outgunned in a battle of wits. I sensed that I held my own, and now, I was mentally, physically, and emotionally exhausted. My anger drained me. I wasn't going to argue with Joshua about born-again, soul-winning Gospel, although I had one time embraced it. "I do believe in the great commission to preach and teach to the unsaved," I said.

"You don't know where you're gonna spend eternity," Joshua said smugly. "You need to get right with Jesus! You need to be washed in the blood of the lamb. Amen?"

"Amen," some responded.

"If you were ever saved, Brother William, you're now a back-slider! You're a freethinker, a false Christian spreading unbiblical beliefs! You should ask God's forgiveness for rejecting the true Bible-based church and its authority! " Joshua removed a small New Testament from his back pocket and held it between us. "The Bible must always have the first and last Word in our lives! The Bible is the ultimate authority for every born-again Christian! We don't just study it; we fill our minds with it so the Holy Spirit can transform us. And yes, we memorize the Word! Idle minds wait for trouble, so we remember the God of our salvation and his Holy Word!" he exclaimed.

I thought for a moment. "People like you transformed historical Christianity into hysterical Christianity," I shot back. "People like you turned many people away from the real message by intimidating them with chapter and verse! Rather than teaching them, you confuse them by cramming the Bible down...."

"I could say the same thing about you," Joshua interrupted. "You're the one who's confusing people! I'll tell Martin Brett that I don't want my people around you! The Bible says 'do not be yoked together with unbelievers Second Corinthians 6:14,'" he said; then, he started toward the door. Everyone stood, as if to follow him.

"Speaking to people about Jesus is a good thing. I do believe in the great commission to preach around the world, but it shouldn't be some kind of game! The more souls you "win," the more you please God? Doesn't that sound like trying to save yourself with works? Isn't it a prideful ego trip? 'Let your light so shine among men, that they may see your good works, and glorify your Father, which is in heaven," I added.

"We'll pray for you, Brother William," Joshua declared from the doorway. "You like to express yourself with Bible terms, but you're a false prophet. God is using us to tell others how they can have eternal life. I think you need to get saved! You need Jesus in your life!"

"'They honor me with their lips, but their hearts are far from me,'" I proclaimed loudly.

The doors swung closed and he was gone. I had spoken from the heart and wanted Joshua to understand where I was coming from. We were not that different. We both strived to be important and true to our beliefs.

"I think it was a draw," Jonathan said, breaking the tension. I smiled.

"I can tell he knows the Bible backward and forward," I said. "I didn't want to get into a Bible-quoting contest. I love the Bible and believe in it, but I don't worship it." There was silence. "You guys know that I'm not trying to confuse you," I sighed.

I felt Miriam's gentle touch on my arm. Her eyes were moist with tears. "He was so arrogant just now," she said. "He was frightening! He always gives me a hard time, but he's never been that angry before!"

"He's a control freak," Michael said. "We all know that, but he's a strong Christian soldier and a natural leader, too." They all agreed.

"He's a "'P.K.'" Sarah said, "a 'preacher's kid.' He's trying to find his own pathway now. I know he rebelled and got into some bad stuff—like we all did—but when he came back to the church, he tried to be the best Christian alive," she said knowingly. "He can be too intense."

The thought occurred to me again that perhaps Sarah and Joshua had a history. I searched her face for a clue.

"It's not about us," I said exhaustedly. "It should be about what's right—not who's right! We really believe the same things, basically. It's just that he's into "Churchianity" more than Christianity. I'm sorry if you're in more trouble, because of me."

The doors opened; Daniel poked in his head and glared at our group. "Joshua's calling a meeting in the chapel—now!" he announced. Michael touched my shoulder, and Sarah touched my hand before they obediently filed into the chapel. I stood alone. What had we debated? My point was that the historical churches wanted command and control over the beliefs of their converts and hysterical Christians were judgmental, narrow-minded, and dogmatic parrots, spouting chapter and verse without getting the message. Joshua's attitude proved my point, I thought.

CHAPTER 10

ENEMY MIND

The library continued to serve as my refuge, and I relaxed there before the service preparations. One evening, my heart leapt for joy when I spied Sarah, standing alone among the books, looking out the window. She turned slightly, and I feigned that I did not want to disturb her. She smiled and motioned me toward the window. We viewed the converted bus with the John 3:16 verse surrounded by biblical artwork. We stood there in silence for a moment. Then, I studied some street people leaning against the building. "They're lining up early today," I noted.

"We're starting our Christmas tour next Thursday," Sarah said while looking outside. "We'll be away for a week. Some of us are going home for Christmas," she added with a sideways glance. She regarded me, as questions formed in my mind. Was she going home? Was there a history between her and Joshua? I had no right to ask, and I had no reason to know. There was no future for us. I wanted to say something but I just stood there.

Joshua stuck in his head. "'He that hath the Son hath life,' Brother William," he proclaimed; then, he departed. The next few days passed in similar fashion with Joshua ambushing me with Bible verses or questions. If he saw any of his group speaking with me—about anything other than a specific task—he made a point of interfering. "I have the promise of eternal life, Brother William," he'd say or "Heaven is my home, brother. Do you know where you'd go if you died today? Where will you spend eternity?"

When I fired back, sometimes Joshua's surprise attacks turned into skirmishes. He converted our battle about Christianity into a war over the allegiances in the youth group. However, I simply yearned to share the little bit of light I discovered. The true Gospel message was liberating and beautiful when properly understood. I thought Joshua was misguided, because he was unaware of the forces that controlled his emotions. I wasn't working to undermine his authority.

During a conversation with Miriam and Jonathan, I ascertained more about Joshua. He was a preacher's kid who attended a Bible college with strict rules governing behavior and dress. He rebelled and was dismissed from school. Then, Joshua drifted into a hedonistic lifestyle. Like many others, drug use turned into drug sales to support his habits. Minor scrapes with the law and a short stint in jail convinced him to seek redemption. He returned to his family and Bible college. Joshua quit school before graduation to begin his own ministry; he wished to serve wayward youth, because the lifestyle of unruly young adults was familiar to him, having lived it during his rebellious period. Joshua called his ministry, "Freaks for Jesus," and it grew quickly—with youth rallies and prayer-group encounters. Eventually, his fledgling movement attracted the attention of traditional ministries. At this point, Joshua and Fred Jordan formed an alliance.

Jonathan suggested that perhaps some of the animosity Joshua directed toward me stemmed from his racial views. I disagreed with Jonathan about that. I wanted Jonathan and the others to realize that Joshua, like all of us, used his mind and knowledge as a shield and a sword. Joshua was determined to protect the only world-view belief system he knew; he attacked those who challenged him.

"Joshua is a control freak," Miriam said. "We needed that domination in the beginning, but now, he tries to control everything about our lives. That's why we like working for you."

"Yeah, you're smart, funny, and helping us be better Christians," Jonathan added.

"I don't know about all that," I said quickly.

"You promote our knowledge and commitment to the Lord," Miriam added. "I love the Lord, and I think he's using you in a powerful way. I don't know why Joshua is so upset with you. You're not leading us astray. The meditation exercise helps me."

I spoke to them about my early frustration with Sunday-school classes and forced church attendance. They shared similar stories.

We enjoyed these moments of openness. I remained guarded, though, because I feared that someone would eventually ask questions about my past life. I wasn't ready to reveal my history.

I heard a familiar knock on my door, and Sarah stepped into my room. The door remained open as usual. I closed the book on my lap as she approached. "How are you feeling?" I asked her.

"Much better," she said, as she touched her throat and chest. I sent her bowls of soup for two days while she suffered with a cold. "Thank you for the soup," she said politely; she sat in her favorite chair. She missed the Christmas tour because of her sickness. Everyone was due back later that day. "I wanted to tell you that I started meditating," she said with a smile. "Miriam gave me the book you loaned her. I got the basic idea, I think," she said.

"Wow," I said with obvious delight. "That's great. Is the meditation helping? Do you have any questions?"

"I don't know if it's helping yet, but I know I'm doing the right thing. I don't have any questions so far. I even listened to Masters' show yesterday afternoon."

"Sarah, you've been a bad girl," I said jokingly. "I hope I haven't led you astray," I added with mock fear in my voice. We both laughed.

She looked lovely sitting there, leaning forward with her legs crossed and long strands of hair glistening in the afternoon sun. My heart was full of love for her.

"You know that we think a lot of you," she divulged, as she touched her throat and swallowed gently. "You've been a real blessing to us," she added.

"Maybe some more than others?" I queried.

"Well," she sighed. "You know how that goes. Listen, even Joshua's impressed with you. Sometimes, I think he's afraid of you. He's terribly domineering and strong-willed, but you don't give in to his bullying. You stay so cool and calm. It blows our minds. You're so together, Brother William. I love that about you!"

I shook my head in disagreement. I knew better than anyone that my insides had twisted into knots since my running warfare with Joshua began. If I seemed calm, it was in contrast to Joshua's rage.

Sarah took a deep breath and continued. "I know Joshua loves the Lord, but I see how controlling he is. In the beginning, we depended on him for so much. Now, he won't let us question anything or allow us to grow at our own paces. He's changed a lot, too. He's critical of everything. He's always looking for faults. He's too judgmental— just like you said—but he's the one who brought me to the Lord. I'm thankful for that," she said faintly. "I know that Miriam told you about her baby and everything. She gave her heart to the Lord right after I did. Miriam confided in me, and I didn't tell anyone else. We joined Joshua's "Freaks for Jesus," (and took it as a compliment when people called us that name), but now I'm starting not to like it."

Placidly, I listened to the music of Sarah's slightly hoarse voice. My romantic fantasies started teasing me. She further intimated. "I heard what you said the other day about soul winning and I kind of agree. I don't like it when it's a competition. I like the way you kind of say your truth quietly without beating people over the head."

"It's not my truth," I said defensively.

"You know what I mean," she laughed.

"I do," I admitted. "A proud person can never really know God, because the proud look down on everything and everyone."

"I like that," she said, as she stood. We walked to the doorway. "It's funny," Sarah continued. "I feel a little sad that I don't have exactly what I thought I had. But I'm thankful that I see that now. I just hope I can stay on this path until I learn God's plan for my life," she added with a sigh.

"You'll be fine," I said. "Keep meditating, praying, and being totally honest with yourself—that's the key. Now, I realize that true and lasting beliefs had to be *shown* to me. Words are not enough. Meditation isn't the only way to see the truth, but it is so pure and uncomplicated once you get the hang of it. Just yearn to be patient, forgiving, and non-judgmental," I said, as I touched her shoulder. "That's what Jesus showed the human race. He revealed God's love to the world by not giving in and hating the injustice being done to him! It's so beautiful," I said emotionally. "It's so beautiful." Sarah took my hand into hers and kissed me on the cheek before she left.

After chapel services, Miriam and Jonathan helped unload the produce from Brother Bedrose's car. While Brother Bedrose ate heartily and repeated "Praise the Lord," the kids and I got into one of our discussions. In short order, Sarah, Leah, and Michael drifted into the dining hall. "Class" was in session.

I talked about Greek civilization, the Peloponnesian War, and Alexander the Great. I mentioned how Pax Romana (or peace through Roman dominance) made the Mediterranean a safe region for the Gospel to be planted among the Greco-Roman world. It was the perfect time and place for God to plant the seed of regeneration.

"Some cultures are better than others," I stated. "Although the Romans were pagans, they governed through law and order. Palestine was in turmoil, but the Jewish people were ready for fulfillment of the promise of God to Abraham and his descendants. Only a precious few men understood that the peace the Son of God revealed and taught was the only cure for man's alienation from God and hatred of each other. If you could magically take away all cultures, all governments, and all religions, you know what you'd end up with?" I asked.

No one hazarded a guess. "Just people," I explained. "Of course, eventually, all those elements would return unless the people were 'in-dependent,'" I said, scratching my head. "Being governed from the inside by the internal guidance system we all have access to— that's what living by faith really means," I said. "That was the good news Jesus awakened man to. The symbolism in the Bible is like a code or universal language that anyone from any time can understand. But the timeless messages in the scriptures are only perceived by the searching soul."

I imparted more of the truth: "We need a special stillness to help our souls reach awareness—which some might call 'enlightenment.' This enlightenment is only a glimpse of the timeless Godhead that we were created to serve through faith. Faith, not feeling, is what saves us. 'For by grace are you saved through faith; and that not of yourselves: it is a gift of God: Not of works, lest any man should boast.'" I quoted Ephesians 2:8-9.

"Amen," they said automatically. Suddenly, the double doors exploded open. Into the dining hall stormed Joshua with Daniel.

"You should all be studying before evening prayers!" he screamed. "Jonathan, aren't you the prayer leader tonight? What are you doing hanging out down here?" he shouted and glared.

"Hold it, Joshua," I interjected calmly, as I stood. "I needed help unloading Brother Bedrose's produce. It's my fault they're still here," I explained.

"You're a wolf in sheep's clothing!" he spat at me. "You're working against the Lord! You're sowing confusion and wickedness among God's people!" he shrieked in full-out attack mode. "The Bible is the authoritative standard for my life," Josha barked. "Like I said before, you like to quote Bible verses, but they're not the first and last words in your life, because you'd rather be a freethinker and a self-styled philosopher. You need to find out what the Bible really says about salvation and fill your mind with that! Trust God's Word. Study it. Fill your mind with it. And let the Holy Spirit change you, if it's not too late, brother!" Joshua was right in my face, and everyone watched, suddenly transfixed by our exploding drama.

"You don't know me," I hollered, trying to match his intensity. "You don't know anything about me! I love the same God and Jesus you do! We shouldn't get into a pissing contest over who's the better Christian; there's no victory in that! We should dialogue. Why are you so upset? Free your mind and your ass will follow, Brother Joshua."

"Watch your mouth," he sneered. Then, he stretched his arms into the air and rocked back on his heels. "You're something else, brother," he said with venom. "You never go out! You never go outside of this building to spread the Word of the Savior you claim to serve! You're just a fat loser, hiding out here from life. That's what I think! You sneak around behind these walls, confusing new Christians with your pseudointellectual, age-of-Aquarius nonsense! You might have Brothers Brett and Johnson fooled, but I'm going to make sure that Reverend Jordan knows the truth about you! You're sowing confusion and a false Gospel among these babes in Christ, and you need to be exposed!"

Joshua pointed his finger at me. "Roy Masters is a cult leader! I know about Roy Masters now, and the local churches are working to expose him! He says he's not, but he's just another new-age preacher! Reverend Jordan doesn't know that you're working against his ministry! What are you hiding from?" he asked again. If you were ever a born-again Christian, you're a backslider now—a fat reprobate who is going straight to Hell! You need Jesus to come into your miserable life, before it's too late, brother!" he said sarcastically.

I was dumbfounded and in a temporary fog. Joshua was nearly unhinged. I regarded his rage. My face was flush, as I felt conflicting emotions. Yet, my hands were ice cold! I saw Miriam crying, and Sarah shaking her head as she comforted her.

"And you two are on probation until you learn to submit!" Joshua said angrily to the girls.

"You can't bully everybody all the time!" I blared suddenly, finding my voice again. I longed to rescue the girls, or was it Sarah I wanted to impress? "You are wrong!" I proclaimed emphatically. "You're being wrongheaded! You're twisting my meanings to make them seem unbiblical! We can disagree about that, but you have no reason to get personal! Personal attacks reveal how small-minded and petty you are!" I growled angrily.

Joshua ferociously turned. "Get thee behind me, Satan," he blustered before leaving with Daniel and the others.

Alone I stood, quaking inside, as the scene replayed in my head. I should have said this! I should have said that! My thoughts raged! I was beaten! I was destroyed! I was exposed as a weak and deceptive recluse, a lukewarm Christian or a fraud! I was devastated.

I sat in my room, crestfallen. I was unable to meditate as a compulsive replay of the contest humiliated and angered me. Why did Sarah have to be there? Was the root of my conflict with Joshua about Sarah, I wondered? There was no romantic future for us. Yet, we connected on a spiritual and emotional level that we both enjoyed! We had different paths to travel. We both realized that. Didn't Joshua understand this as well? Or was it all about power? Was he jealous of me as a rival? "You must submit to your leaders as you would to Christ," I heard him say often. What a dramatic turn of events. I was a fat loser. Joshua won the power struggle.

I had difficulty falling asleep, and when I did, it was fitful. I was unexpectedly awakened from a dream; it seemed so real that my heart beat rapidly. In the dream, I was sitting in my room. Suddenly, a window opened, and a beautiful girl climbed through the open window. She danced and seductively smiled at me. The girl was entrancing in her sexy outfit, as she danced about the room to music I could not hear. She gyrated and writhed rhythmically; I was unable to take my eyes off her. She beckoned me to follow her, as she climbed out the window. Then, both she and the window disappeared! I quizzically glanced at my large clock, but I couldn't tell what time it was. The hands were gone! The hour and the minute hands were gone! I had lost time! A wordless voice said that the girl had stolen my time! That's when I woke up.

What was the dream about? Was there any real significance to it? I didn't know what to think. Was the dancing girl, Sarah? Miriam? I wept bitterly in the wee hours of the dark for several moments. Next, I washed and dressed somberly. I stripped the linens from my bed. Then, I sat at my desk, and with my hand shaking slightly, I wrote three notes and placed them in envelopes. I took two of the envelopes and an armful of books and quietly walked down the hall. I placed the books in the library and slid an envelope under Brother Reggie's door and another under Brother Johnson's. When I got back to my room, I tore the third envelope and its note into tiny pieces and flushed them down the toilet.

Beneath my mattress, I had hidden an envelope with money. I counted it—two hundred dollars. One last time, I looked around my room. With my three precious books and a bag of clothes, I walked quietly downstairs to the director's office. I unfolded a small piece of paper with a phone number scrawled on it and dialed the number. I hadn't used a telephone in over a year. The phone rang, and I prayed for an answer on the other end.

"Hello?" the voice said sleepily.

"Bill?" I asked in a tense whisper. I never considered that I would be waking his wife. I felt stupid and thoughtless.

"Who's this?" the voice asked with some agitation.

"Bill, it's Brother William from the Fifth Street mission."

"Oh, Brother William," he said, as he recognized who I was. He had given me his number the week before when he introduced his replacement.

"I'm sorry to call you so early Bill, but I need to find out if they filled that job you told me about a couple of weeks ago?"

"You mean the position at the Volunteers of America? I don't think so. Why, are you changing your mind? You're gonna leave the mission?"

"Yes," I whispered into the receiver. I didn't want to be discovered.

"When are you leaving?" he asked. "When can you start?"

"I'm leaving now," I said tensely. "I can start today," I added confidently, although I didn't have a clue of what I was getting into.

"Wow!" he said surprised. "Okay, that's great. Do you know where the organization is? It's not too far from your place."

Bill gave me directions and the name to ask for regarding the cook position. He said he told them about me when he first heard of the opening. I thanked Bill and apologized for the intrusion. I left my keys on Martin Brett's desk and scratched out a thank-you note in the dim light from the street lamps.

As I walked down the streets of skid row, I resolved that I would get a job of some sort with the Volunteers of America. Bill was my reference. I was sure that God was opening another door for me, because a big door had closed. Here I was again in the dim light of morning, leaving unfinished business. I was running away again! Sneaking away like a thief in the night! I pulled up the collar of my jacket to protect my neck from the cool morning chill. I needed a little more time to do things my way, and I prayed to God this change was part of his plan for me.

I never heard of the Volunteers of America until I was living at the mission. Sometimes I watched their trucks go down the streets; the vehicles were decorated with the distinctive patriotic colors and name emblazoned on the sides. Occasionally, I wondered who they were and what they were about. Now I was standing inside their building, only a few city blocks from the place that was my home for almost two years. I talked to a handsome, Italian-looking fellow in gray slacks and a starched-white shirt with captain's bars on the shoulders.

"I'm Captain Briscoe," he said, as he extended his hand. He had a strong grip and powerful forearms. I matched his firmness. He was about six-feet tall; we stood eye-to-eye in his office. Briscoe had a full head of wavy, black hair and a smooth, freshly shaved face. His eyes were kind, and he had a friendly smile. He talked with a definite New York accent. I introduced myself.

"Bill called me a little while ago and said you'd be coming by this morning. Here, have a seat." he motioned to a chair beside his desk.

We talked a while as the building and the streets came alive with activity. He asked about my cooking experience and told me that the job only required cooking for the Volunteers of America workers who lived in the building. We walked upstairs to the kitchen facilities; the equipment was slightly newer than at the mission. I checked out the walk-in cooler, freezer, oven, and grill. I demonstrated my familiarity with a commercial kitchen. The steam table was positioned as a divider between the kitchen and dining room; several large round tables were arranged around the institution-looking room.

Briscoe and I walked through the rest of the building. There was a large day room with a pool table, Ping-Pong table, and card table for card or board games. Easy chairs and folding chairs were scattered about the room; some faced a television. A large shelf was stocked with books, magazines, and newspapers.

Captain Briscoe explained how the Volunteers of America had splintered from the Salvation Army. That's why the Volunteers still used military-rank designations for their executives. However, the Salvation Army was considered a religious organization, and the Volunteers of America was a business that created jobs for the destitute. The Volunteers were more about redeeming men's lives than saving their souls. I was fine with that. When I said I wanted the position, he showed me to my bedroom, just down the hall from the kitchen. Briscoe offered me a small sum of money in addition to room and board.

There hadn't been a regular cook at the Volunteers for a few weeks. I quickly managed to familiarize myself with the available supplies, and in short order, I set out a lunch of tomato soup and grilled-cheese sandwiches for about a dozen men. I was an immediate success!

During the meal, I met the head honcho of this Volunteers of America division. His name was Major Schwartz. He was average height with a stocky build; full, round face; and a nearly bald head. Major Schwartz was friendly, but all business. He didn't have the easy charm of his brother-in-law, Captain Brisco. Nevertheless, he gave me a hearty handshake when he welcomed me to the facility. I found a new home, and I thanked God.

The events of the day didn't catch up to me until I was alone in my new bedroom that night. The room was much smaller than my large room at the mission. By comparison, this room was Spartan. The room featured a single twin bed, a small night table (with a lamp and clock radio), a tiny clothes closet, an upholstered easy chair, and a four-drawer bureau with a mirror suspended on the wall above it. No TV, no record player, no guitar. And no books except the three precious volumes I'd brought with me. (*Amplified Bible*, *Strong's Concordance*, and my dog-eared copy of Roy Master's *How Your Mind Can Keep You Well*) I placed those volumes in the compartment beneath the night table. I left many other treasured books at the mission. These three I refused to part with. One large window overlooked the street.

Although my door was shut, I heard the muffled sounds of activity. I dropped my head onto my chest. I was broken. Had I lost all hope for my personal redemption? I was vanquished, and now, I was drained. What had I done? I had quit and run again. I returned to the form and comfort of my half-buried past. I stole away like a thief—with no warning or explanation. The short notes I left for Brother Johnson and Martin Brett simply said that something important developed suddenly, I had to leave immediately, and I added a brief thank-you and good-bye. My message was one of those half truths I was comfortable telling people. I sighed deeply, as I knew the "something important" was to get out of there before Brother Joshua complained to Reverend Jordan about me!

In a twisted type of revenge, I turned rabbit and ran! It was my perverted victory—a hollow triumph. What had I learned? Had I really changed from a confused and angry loser into a truth-seeking child of God? It was doubtful. I was a fat loser living a life of half truths and hiding in the shadows. Yet, I believed I was being transformed into a servant of God and Christ!

Joshua's unrelenting and ferocious attacks had broken me. Like with Old Bill, my anger ignited. It pained me deeply to taste my rage again—so much so, that I physically ached. Sarah's lovely face came to mind several times. I remembered her and Miriam hugging each other when Joshua went ballistic. I loved them both. I wrote a note to them that I destroyed at the thought of Joshua discovering it. I surely dashed their love and trust in me by leaving the way I did. I prayed that the time we shared would prove valuable to them.

Had the will of God been in anything I had done today? Had I deluded myself into believing that the Lord opened this window for me? Had I been too despicable a creature for him to continue to shepherd through my own folly? My heart ached, as I turned the Words of Jesus into my own pitiful cry:

"My God, my God, why have I forsaken thee? You straightened my path and directed my wandering to your secret place within me. You opened my mind and breathed new life into my bitterness. Your sweet forgiveness blessed my days when I yearned for comfort and sought peace apart from the knowledge of you. Your patience mended my broken vessel. Now, I have turned from you, and the darkness of my false heart has overcome me! I have been brought low, oh Lord, and deserve the disdain that has descended on me! Search my soul, dear God, and find the spark that had glowed so brightly—the spark that is from you! Preserve my soul, Lord, through this wasteland that I have embraced. Lead me in your loving way to correction. Teach me to hear your breath, and to breathe in your sweetness. Forgive me, Lord, as I forgive! Lead me to the path of righteousness through my darkness. Amen."

I woke early the next morning. I lay there for a moment before I realized where I was. I turned off the alarm, before it sounded. As my eyes became accustomed to the darkness, I viewed my little room. I thanked God that I was warm, dry, and safe. I spoke the Lord's Prayer and began my meditation. I felt in deep despair, but somehow, I knew it was a condition I must not resist. I gave into hating my tormentor again, rejecting the clear opportunity to forgive. So, I fell from my lofty self-image of my growing holiness into despair! Joshua's actions tempted me to resent him, and now, I admit that I was enraged by how he attacked me. I felt humiliated by my reaction to him. My enemy mind was exposed as a liar and a betrayer of my spiritual principles.

I thanked God for routine! Routine often bears a secret joy for those who need healing. I found this idea to be true for me, as I worked in the kitchen of the Volunteers of America. In the VOA, everything was new and yet, familiar. Once the coffee was brewing and the grill was warming, the sweetness of routine kicked in.

I was a welcome sight in a kitchen that had not hosted a regular cook for a while. For some time, lunch was cold cuts and rolls for the workers; the same fare was presented for evening meals.   My only assistant—the man who brewed the coffee before I got into the kitchen—was Gale. He was the official coffee maker and served as the cook's helper. He placed cereals out for breakfast along with white bread for toast. Gale cleaned the kitchen between the self-service visits of the staff and ordered the supplies. I relied on him to learn where everything was stored. This morning's meeting was my first one with Gale. (He was away during my arrival the previous day.)

"I'm Gale Norman, sir, and you are?" he asked, as he extended his hand. He peered at me through thick glasses with his head slightly cocked to one side.

"I'm William," I said, catching myself before saying Brother William. "William Kinkade," I added and shook his hand.

Gale was about six-feet tall and slender with a well-muscled build. He had straight, platinum-blonde hair that he combed back from his face. That face was chiseled into a severely handsome Teutonic-type countenance. The glasses he wore were thick, but didn't detract from his intense hazel eyes. Gale's hair was moderately graying around the temples and receding along the hairline. He struck me as being in his mid to late thirties.

"It'll be a pleasure to work for you, sir," he said politely.

"You don't have to call me sir," I said with a nervous laugh, highly conscious of our age difference. "I'm not one of the officers here. Just William or Bill is fine." I added.

"Very well, sir," he said with a thin smile. "Forgive me for my formality. When I remember, or find occasion to, I will refer to you by your Christian name."

That was my introduction to Gale. Reserved and formal to the point of being severe, and yet, he displayed friendliness that seemed stiff and studied, but sincere. Sincere, because it represented who he was. Gale stood ramrod straight—like an Aryan angel—dressed completely in white. He wore a white T-shirt beneath a white dress shirt along with white, beltless slacks; white socks; and plain, white tennis shoes. With his gray-blond hair, ghostly pale complexion, and white garments, he suggested an impressive bleached entity.

Every movement by Gale appeared deliberate and efficient with no wasted motions. He was always in step with his own personal drumbeat. Though he could move swiftly when necessary, he never seemed to be in a hurry. Gale lived on black coffee, and a steaming cup was never far away. That was his only apparent vice. He ate only one meal a day and didn't carry an extra ounce of fat on his body. His intense manner; piercing eyes; and precise, deliberate movements made the other men reluctant to work with him. Consequently, Gale was assigned the position of kitchen helper or solitary laborer.

In the fraternity of manhood and maleness, Gale stood out. He didn't use profanity; he didn't speak loudly or abusively. Gale wasn't aggressive or defensive, and he never complained. He could sit or stand perfectly still for hours with just his cup of coffee. All the while, he would never do or say a thing to another human being. This quietness made the men feel uncomfortable around him.

Gale had a quick wit and a keen, disciplined mind. (Yet, he was no more in touch with reality than the rest of us.) Like Gale, I stood out from the other fellows, because I didn't curse, display anger, or throw tantrums. My contrast to the other men may be why I was a curiosity to Gale.

And we were the two odd balls. The men treated us differently. Gale was teased and ridiculed; I was welcomed and accepted. Although the men respected Gale's intelligence, they were put off by his attitude and lack of personal warmth. I, on the other hand, respected each man as an individual. My obvious youth and equally noticeable weight problem hinted at my hidden personal problems to the perceptive eye. Yet, the men felt comfortable around me, and I with them. When you factor in that I was a decent cook as well, I had a new home for as long as I wanted.

I stepped into the rhythm and routine of the place. There were usually approximately a dozen men living at the building. They straggled in during the breakfast hours (6:30 to 8:30 a.m.) and order a hot breakfast from the grill or simply eat cold cereal, pastry, toast, or canned fruit. The real early risers purchased the morning papers and read them in the well-lit dining room. After breakfast, the kitchen was closed, so Gale and I could clean and prep for lunch and dinner. The men reported to the street-level warehouse work area and busied themselves under the watchful eyes of Captain Brisco and Major Schwartz.

This was the Los Angeles Volunteers of America. The organization put willing and able men to work. Whether he was on his way up or down, a man could find a helping hand to aid him in his own rescue. Most of these men were rough cut and crude, displaying no pretense of Christian virtues. The men were mostly white, with an occasional black or brown face, and the age range was between thirty to sixty years. After my cloistered-living circumstances, the bold vulgarities of life among the "unwashed" and "unpretentious" were sudden assaults to my senses. This was still skid row—the "school of hard knocks"—not charm school.

The building had rules: Doors were locked each night, no drinking of alcohol on the premises, no smoking in bedrooms, no fighting, and no visitors! The work week was five-and-a-half days.

I noted the irony of all my free time without having access to religious and philosophical books to study in a library, as at the mission. Though, the day room had a collection of books and magazines. Copies of *National Geographic*, *Reader's Digest*, daily newspapers, and weekly magazines informed us of current events. The day room housed an old upright piano that needed tuning; it offered a pleasant diversion at times.

The work took place in the street-level warehouse and work area. That's where VOA trucks came and left with pallets full of computer punch cards. The processes began when long, narrow cardboard boxes of these computer cards were brought into the warehouse. They were trucked in from businesses all over the region. In the warehouse, they were transferred to shipping pallets, wrapped for shipping, and placed on trucks for transport to a shipping port, like the one in San Pedro. From there, they went to a processing plant in Japan!

The ever-industrious Japanese were flexing their resurgent industrial power with aggressive innovation and cheap labor. The pallets of punch cards were put through a reprocessing procedure in Japan and shipped back to the US as recycled cards, ready to be reused. I remember my amazement when Captain Brisco explained to me that it was less expensive to ship used punch cards across the Pacific Ocean—and back again—than it was to reprocess them in the United States.

The Volunteers of America made money from this business, and the organization was providing meaningful work for struggling men. My new responsibility was to provide meals for these men—three times a day, six days a week.

Idle time was suddenly more than I had in two years. After reworking the menu and placing a large order with Bill, the food salesman, things fell into place nicely. I thanked Bill for being responsible my new position. Bill told me that both Captain Brisco and Major Schwartz were impressed with how I organized the kitchen and menu. Everyone was pleased, even the enigmatic Gale.

Not having to prepare a large cauldron of soup every day or wonder when Brother Bedrose would arrive revealed to me how much those two events had dominated my life. Now, without those obligations or evening services, I was alone at a time when I felt fractured. In my solitude, I tried to maintain a personal routine. I completed my meditation, recited my prayers, and read my Bible. I repeated these exercises a couple of times each day. I never left the building and rarely watched TV, but I listened to the radio and read in my room.

I understood the uneven ground that leads to salvation. I had been tried and found wanting, as I experienced a meltdown of confidence over my conflicting hypocrisies. Joshua had merely been the torch who set me aflame. Now, I had to be still and suffer my disintegration. I yearned for the faith to know that my healing had begun.

When I meditated, I perceived the tugs of war between thought and awareness, emotion and discussion, and agitation and stillness. In that stillness, I tasted the bitterness of my anger at Joshua for embarrassing and attacking me. I suffered the guilt of my slow and reluctant forgiveness of him. It would be some time before I understood that forgiveness was not an action, but an attitude. Forgiving is what we are before it's what we do. It's an expression of the internal experience of God's grace that we share.

As the new year of 1969 passed through January, I made mental plans to return to Camp Lejeune in the spring. It seemed a possible venture, because my job at Volunteers of America paid more than the mission's. I imagined the scenario of returning to Camp Lejuene after having been a.w.o.l. for three years. I had no idea what fate awaited me. I anticipated that I would have a year to serve, and I would accept my punishment. I was ready to face whatever came, as long as I was able to return at my own choosing, tell my story, endure my sentence, and become a productive member of society again— in or out of the service.

———•◆•———

I heard the train only a second before I felt its power vibrate the building. My bed shook me awake. I sat up, startled. I realized I overslept by about fifteen minutes. The lighted dial on the clock said 6:02 a.m., as it danced on the nightstand, jittered to the edge, and fell. I caught it. The whole room was quaking wildly, and in the dim light of morning, I viewed the items on my bureau falling to the floor. I couldn't hear anything, but a rumbling roar. The mirror on the wall above the bureau dropped with a crash and shattered. Only the wall calendar remained in place; it swung like a pendulum.

It was an earthquake! I sensed it before I knew it—not a train, but an earthquake! On the edge of the bed I sat, perfectly calm, but unable to move. My chef's checkered pants were folded on the chair across from my bed. I only had to rise, lean over, and grab them— yet, I couldn't move! My legs wouldn't work! I couldn't make any part of my body move! I was totally present, totally aware, as I watched myself and waited. I wasn't afraid or nervous, just immobile. The thick plaster on the inside wall of my room suddenly cracked in an uneven, ragged gash from ceiling to floor! Then, it stopped, as suddenly as it started. It was over. The earthquake—earth flexing its fury—only lasted a minute or two. It was February 9, 1969, and the San Andreas Fault made its presence felt.

It was my first earthquake. Like anyone who lived in Los Angeles, I experienced tremors at times. Sometimes, your mind could not understand what your body was feeling until you spied lamps swaying or other people reacting to the phenomenon. An explosive release of pressure thunders in cascading waves through the earth's surface and rattles everything from the mountains to the sea.

An earthquake is a terrifying calamity. Everything is suddenly a threat to you! Walls, ceilings, and bookcases, as well as telephone poles, buildings, and bridges are subject to collapse, turning anyone into a victim! And it doesn't end when the big quake ceases. That's when the aftershocks start! These powerful tremors can collapse a structure that was badly damaged in the primary earthquake. These events remind us that we are only visitors on a living planet!

I finally got dressed and joined the chorus of voices in the halls and day room. The power was out, and the gas had been shut off at the mains to avoid leaks and possible explosions. The VOA building didn't sustain any major damage, but a two-story building down the street, totally collapsed. It was unoccupied.

Other places weren't as fortunate. A nursing home that housed approximately fifty people collapsed. With other deaths, the total hovered at one hundred. However, the drama didn't end right away. All the local television and radio news programs dusted off their old stories about what and what not do during an earthquake. Most of the stories offered spins on commonsense tips: Don't touch downed power lines; don't ride in elevators; perch under reinforced archways and doorways; and seek shelter from collapsing walls. Special counseling was available for children, who were often more terrified by the overreaction of their parents than the earthquake. And pets needed special attention and care.

A grand drama played out over the next few days in true Hollywood blockbuster fashion. The Van Norman Dam developed a dangerous crack. The rush was on to lower its water level before the dam burst and flooded the San Fernando Valley (affectionately referred to as the "Sin" Fernando Valley). We witnessed an hour-by-hour tension convention, as engineers and workers labored feverishly to get the water level below the crack before the valley was turned into a lake. Evacuations began, just to be cautious. It all ended with a Hollywood finish. The valley was spared devastation, and the city returned to normal. Fade to black, roll the credits. This is California. Get used to it.

————•◆•————

Once again I was privileged to meet a singularly interesting character. Gale proclaimed that he was a Stoic. He practiced Stoicism, a belief that utilizes self-control in overcoming destructive emotions and placing one's spirit in harmony with nature. I gleaned this information about Gale after he probed me about what made me tick. (I knew I was intriguing to him.) "Are you a believer in Christianity, sir?" he asked in his usual direct interrogative style.

"Yes, Gale," I responded. When he said nothing more, I added, "Why do you ask?"

"No particular reason. I just noticed how you carry yourself. I knew you cooked at a rescue mission. However, you don't talk like a born-again Christian. Yet, you display a depth of character and self-control that I rarely observe," he said, getting to the point.

"The born-again Christians and I have our differences," I chuckled. "We believe essentially the same things, but I avoid that 'God talk.' I think that's what you mean."

He sipped his ever-present coffee, as I talked about "primitive Christianity" versus "born-again Christianity." I explained, "I'm into religious enlightenment while many others are into religious excitement."

When I asked him if he was an ascetic (assuming that word would favorably describe someone who was as disciplined as he was), he raised his eyebrows and gave me a quizzical look. "Do you know who Marcus Aurelius was?"

"You mean the Roman emperor and philosopher?" I returned. He wasn't surprised, because he knew I had an amateur knowledge of history.

"That's very good, sir. Marcus Aurelius was a Stoic. He believed in Stoicism, a Greek philosophy based on logic, personal discipline, and the brotherhood of all men," he paused to let me digest that information.

When I responded that I recognized Aurelius as one often quoted, because of his philosophical writings, Gale was quite pleased. Gale went on to describe Stoicism, in general terms, during the Greco-Roman world dominance. Because this was a pagan philosophy with many parallels to Christianity, we had a lively discussion about the two. Gale's most startling lesson for me was that the world famous Serenity Prayer—which virtually every alcoholic knows—was inspired by the Stoic's view of life. Like countless others, I loved the insightful simplicity of that plea for personal clarity during times of struggle.

This discussion was the closest Gale came to offering a glimpse at the personal demons that drove him to this oasis in the skid-row desert. We were respectful of each other's beliefs, and each of us, at one time or another, was teacher and pupil.

———— • ◆ • ————

Jack was working at the VOA shortly before I arrived. He appeared like a nobleman—elegant and respectful—yet, out of place, as he made his way through the food line during lunch and dinner. He was pleasant and went out of his way to compliment me on my cooking. Jack was tall, about six feet two, and always appeared neat and clean, even in his second-hand clothing. He wasn't rough and gruff like most of the other men; yet, he was comfortable among them, and they liked him.

Jack had a subtle leadership quality that inspired confidence. We talked on several occasions. Jack had been an executive in the industrial world. At the VOA, his talents were utilized in the warehouse office. The captain and the major were impressed with his abilities.

And I was impressed. This intelligent and polished man talked to me as an equal. Between him and Gale, I enjoyed hours of stimulating conversations. Neither man suffered fools gladly, so I felt privileged that they thought I had something to contribute.

There was also sadness about Jack that wasn't obvious at first. Eventually, he spoke of the pain of falling from grace in the business world and losing his family during his descent into alcoholism. I understood his story, his pain, and his ongoing redemption.

Jack was thankful for his three months of work in shipping and receiving. His health was back, and he was attending his AA meetings regularly. His next step was to redeem himself in the business world; and then, reclaim his family. Jack confided his ambitious plan to me. He made it our secret. Jack would return to the corporate world, in short order, and he wouldn't forget those of us still down on the bottom. He was a changed man.

I loaned him my book, *How Your Mind Can Keep You Well*, prompted him to order the record, and encouraged him to meditate. He expressed anger at organized religion, so I felt he might be open

to meditation as an observational exercise; it could guide him in iden-
tifying real causes to his problems. In addition, meditation could
improve his understanding of Christianity's true message. "This meditation practice will make your Serenity Prayer come alive," I said.

"I'll take a look at the book," he responded, flipping through the
pages. "You know. I'm not so keen on religion. I do believe in a
higher power, though. Church is too controlling for me," he said.

Jack was raised a Catholic, so I believed that introducing him to
Masters' meditation would make him objective regarding his anger at
his religious upbringing. We discussed meditation for a bit, and I cor-
rected his impression it.

A few days passed with no sight of Jack. Then, I purposely
sought him in order to determine why he was avoiding contact with
me. Jack told me that there was no problem. I grasped that he was
depressed. He eventually confessed to me that he had met with several headhunters in order to land a job; Jack needed money to put
these men to work, finding him a position. He said that the big corporations tapped specialty firms to hire key executives for their divi-
sions. He went on to explain these firms were called headhunters,
because they often secured employment for department or division
"heads." Two types of these firms existed in the marketplace—those
that worked for an individual job seeker and those who worked for
the corporations. Both types of agencies used national searches.
Jack needed these services so that they would shop around his
resume. Starting salaries—at the level he was used to—would be in
the high five-figure range.

I wanted to help this man who had become the closest thing I had
to a friend at the VOA. What could I do? He needed money, at least
five-hundred dollars, as a deposit to the firm to prove he was serious
and marketable. Then, he required another five hundred after they
got him a job—plus a small percentage of his salary for the first six
months of employment. That's how the headhunters made their
money, Jack explained. He would be marketed like real estate, so
they would spend quite a lot of money to get his credentials in front
of interested parties.

It all seemed so simple. I had money he could borrow. I had
saved over four-hundred dollars. I could loan Jack that money, he

would land a fancy, high-paying job, and he would pay me back with interest. In return, perhaps I could request a reference from him, or possibly, secure a good job. I was delighted with this scenario. I could help another person—one I genuinely liked—and at the same time, I could reap short-term benefits (interest from my loan) and long-term rewards (if things really went well).

Jack, of course, declined my offer. However, I convinced him that it was his best chance and the time seemed right. He said that he had a little over a hundred dollars of his own and with my four hundred he would have the five-hundred dollars for the deposit. We agreed not to say a word to anyone until he had good news to share.

I was happy to be part of this bold endeavor. Jack modeled his business attire for me on the morning of his appointment. He looked so natural and professional, dressed in a gray suit, white shirt, and navy-blue tie. His black, wing-tipped shoes were polished, his face was clean shaven, and his hair was neatly trimmed. He looked every inch the high-level executive someone would be searching for. I gave him a brown envelope with four-hundred dollars in small bills. He slid it into his breast pocket and thanked me graciously. He was feeling a bit nervous. I wished him luck as we shook hands.

Jack didn't come back that night or the next. All of us wondered what had become of him. I was the only one who had a clue. He left his clothes in the closet with a few other items, including Roy Master's book. After a week, Jack's few belongings were put into a cardboard box for storage, and someone else was assigned his bedroom.

I was too ashamed and embarrassed to say anything to anyone. I was devastated! It was so much worse than if someone had stolen my hidden stash of money. This was someone I trusted with my friendship—and my future!

Now, I was destitute again! Why had I made such a poor decision, when I was so close to turning myself in and going in the right direction? A few weeks before this fiasco, I celebrated my twentieth birthday; my future looked bright and I was upbeat. Now, I had to admit that I was used like the naïve boy I was. I was angry at myself, as I realized that I was a foolish, unworldly kid with a Messiah complex. Was I so hungry for manly respect that I became gullible to this smooth operator? The sad truth was self-evident! I wanted to do a good deed, but it was tainted with a selfish motive. Consequently, I turned a blind eye and a deaf ear to any warnings my intuition gave me. I hit another bottom. I came undone, again.

———— •◆•————

The radio remained my most important window on the world. I listened to Roy Master's broadcasts. Masters' tough love and corrective advice echoed my own understanding of callers' problems. Jack's betrayal of my trust revealed another fault in me. I forgave Jack. I still felt the sting of his betrayal, but I held no bitterness toward him.

In addition to Masters' radio program, I listened to radio evangelists of many beliefs. Each had a significant following, and each offered a unique view of scripture and Christianity. I had no fear of listening to those with whom I disagreed on aspects of practices or beliefs. I also felt sadness over the state of public Christian worship that was presented. The hypnotic practices of ritual-and-rote learning prompted masses of church goers to "Amen" and parrot phrases in trance-like unison. Who was I to question their beliefs or challenge them as ungodly? I discerned mass hypnosis and a herd mentality; these attitudes stunted the spiritual growth of most of those attending! I thought that many of these followers were sincere in their beliefs, but also, sincerely wrong in their practices! I tried to be that type of Christian and failed, thank God.

———— •◆•————

Lonny was a black guy who came to work as a building custodian at the VOA in the fall of 1969. He was twenty-five, but had lived a lifetime already. Lonny was a dark-skinned kid with an Afro hairdo and a heavy-set frame. At five feet six, he was somewhat shorter than me. With practically no neck and a very large head, I understood why he got his nickname, "Fathead."

"I'm Lonny, bro, but you can call me Fathead," he said, as we shook hands.

"Fathead?" I asked. "Like the musician?" I laughed with delight.

"Yeah, man," he said with surprise. "How you know that?"

"I listen to jazz," I offered in explanation. "I never heard any-body else called Fathead, except David "Fathead" Newman."

"Well, man, I used to hate the name growing up! I caught hell all the time! I'd be getting my ass kicked regular for fightin' peoples callin' me that! Then, I hear from my cousin about this cool jazz guy named "Fathead" Newman. So, I'm down with bein' Fathead!"

We both laughed and became instant friends. I opted to call my new pal by his given name, Lonny. We were the only blacks working at VOA, but that was not the only reason for our bond. We shared similar temperaments and interests; we would have become friends anyway. And we both liked jazz. Lonny also liked other forms of music—except classical. Sometimes, I played the classical music station when working in the kitchen, and Lonny would make a face and roll his eyes.

When Lonny learned that I played the piano, he wouldn't let me rest until I agreed to work with him on an idea he had for a song. We marveled at our similarities in musical styles. Working with Lonny inspired me to write melodies for some poems that I composed. Lonny had no interest in religious songs; he wanted me to help him compose a popular tune based on his experiences growing up in South Central LA. Lonny proudly shared his hand-written poem entitled "Gotta Leave This Place." It was a sad poem based on a young man trying to escape his drug-infested world. ("Gotta leave this place, snow flakes comin' down like rain.") Lonny explained to me that "snowflakes" was a drug term. Then, he gave me a quick les-son on other street terms.

At the piano, I played a melody that we both liked; then, I added some chords. Lonny reacted instantly with enthusiasm. Lonny liked my way with words and the basic melody. We rewrote his lyrics and eventually came up with a song we thought could actually be mar-ketable. Lonny was anxious to copyright our song and get it pro-duced. This world was one that I had no knowledge of. He explained that the best way for amateurs to get a song heard by producers was to hire a professional collaborator. This collaborator would add style and professional polish to our basic song; then, shop it around the music business.

Lonny wanted the two of us to visit a collaborator he was referred to. Because I never left the building, I had no intention of going to Hollywood to visit this guy in his office! So, I told Lonny I would only go, if absolutely necessary.

When Lonny mentioned money, I thought to myself, "Oh no, here I go again?" I had saved a small sum, since watching my four hundred dollars walk out the door with Jack. I was leery of handing over any amount to anyone else.

Lonny had issues like the rest of us at VOA. It was difficult for some of the guys to like him. Lonny's off hours were frequently spent away from VOA, so that he minimized his interaction with the other men. He wondered why I never went out; I convinced him that I was devoted to my religious studies.

Lonny was a fellow, black youth with whom I shared more of my personal story than with anyone else. I perceived his short attention span for anything that didn't entertain him. I mentioned this short-coming to him as a way of introducing him to meditation. Meditation could help him focus his nervous energy. If I hadn't discovered Roy Masters' radio program, I could be living Lonny's life. I loaned him Masters' book and prayed he would read it.

The music industry was like any other business. It was always a bit easier to navigate, if you had a guide who knew the terrain. A pro-fessional collaborator knew the language—the ins and outs—and even, the secret handshake. As unknown and unpublished amateurs, our venture was going to cost us money. Were we untalented? Before adding that trait to the list, we decided to take a chance and find out for sure.

The two "colored" boys—from the way station on the outskirts of oblivion and whose lives were broken—thought they could print a ticket to paradise via a hit song. The ticket would grant them a ride past obscurity to recognition and success. I was still my mother's child, and I wanted to believe in this new dream.

I gave Lonny my portion of the small down payment, and he signed a contract for us with Mr. Cousins in Hollywood. We received copies of the contract that named David Cousins, Lonny Ellis, and William Kinkade as collaborators. We were nearly professional songwriters. The contract stated that there was no time limit on paying the full fee to Mr. Cousins. However, we wouldn't receive his full services until he was paid in full. Mr. Cousins assured us that he would begin working on our song right away.

So, I was broke again, but this time, the payment went toward a possible, triumphant future. I knew it was a long shot, but it was a shot. Directly, I had to focus on cleaning up my past. My lack of funds made me feel as if I'd taken a big step backward again. Yet, in a strange way, I embraced a different future than I thought possible.

Lonny left the VOA a few weeks later. The pressure from his past and the lure of the streets was too much for him to ignore or outlast. Around the time of my one-year anniversary at the VOA, he departed with barely a warning. Lonny said all the right things, promising to stay in touch and work with me on the song, but he needed to get back to the real world. Unfortunately, Lonny returned Masters' book unread.

As the new decade began in 1970, the world looked uglier than ever. The Vietnam War still raged, and the American cultural revolution polarized citizens even more. The racial divide widened, as power politics took center stage in big cities across the country.

I let Mr. Cousins know that I would continue paying for his collaboration while I was away. I promised to follow up when I returned to LA; he agreed to put things on hold. My next step was to purchase a one-way ticket from Los Angeles, California to Jacksonville, North Carolina.

I was finally coming to terms with my past.

CHAPTER 11

THE HUNGRY I

After the shock treatment of INDOC the brig was a welcome change. Most of the incarcerated were waiting for some type of discharge from the Marine Corps. I received a sentence of eight months at hard labor, reduction of rank, forfeiture of pay, and a bad conduct discharge. At my trial, my appointed attorney read a brief statement to the court-martial judges; he prepared this statement during our consultation. Then, my attorney called me to the witness stand to make my case for leniency. My lawyer, a white Marine Corps captain, appeared to be moved by my insightful recounting of events that led to my eventual desertion. As he hoped, I eloquently defended my case that day. I was emotional, passionate, and reasonable about causes and effects. I didn't blame my life's circumstances, but explained how my poor reaction to them doomed me to repeat errors in my life that alienated me from reality. I didn't expect the court to grant me a citizenship award for finally growing up and turning myself in after three years. However, I hoped that I was able to assure these men that I now appreciated the opportunities I had, and I deserved whatever punishment they saw fit!

My lawyer said the eight-month sentence was fair and reflected that my testimony had a positive effect on the judgment. He assured me that with good behavior, I could be released in a couple of months. My excellent behavior before my trial bore some weight, as well as my determined return to surrender myself.

As I settled into regular brig life, I found I was a minor celebrity and topic of curiosity. Everyone liked the way I talked, or at least they found my speech amusing. The nickname of "Brother Heavy" stuck with me. My large size guaranteed a nickname and this one had a double meaning. It also conveyed respect for my philosophical persona as a deep thinker and former member of a religious mission.

"Listen to the brother man! He sounds like he's been wiping his ass with the dictionary!"

As always, not everyone was enamored with me. Some detainees were downright hostile at first. The racial attitudes in the brig were as dangerous as those I noticed upon returning to the corps.

The brig was laid out like a prison dormitory. Our facility featured a large picnic table near the center of the room. A row of bunk-bed racks ran along one long wall and another wall was made up of heavy metal bars with a sliding-bar door. A bank of windows overlooked the basketball court below.

Our dorm held more blacks than whites, and I was assigned a lower bunk in the zone between the white guys and the black guys. At first, I didn't realize that the racial climate was fluid, but it didn't take long for me to grasp this reality. Sometimes, we were all "green"—just a bunch of hard-luck, loser marines doing hard time. Other times, the tension was palpable; some of the black guys would choose a target to harass. Then, they would swoop down him like ravenous vultures! I was disgusted by their petty, small-minded and wrong-headed attitudes, and I said so! That's when the hostile guys started giving me the evil eye.

Ted, a white inmate on the adjacent lower bunk, and another white guy called "Lil' Mississippi" (or "Lil' Miss" for short) was on the bunk above him. Ted and I immediately became friendly, and most of the other brothers were cool with Ted, too. He was married, mature, and likeable. Lil' Miss was a short, white kid with ears so big, some of the guys called him "Dumbo." He was from Yazoo City, Mississippi, and he sounded like it. Lil' Miss and I played chess, and I learned the lesson again: Don't judge a book by its cover. Lil' Miss was good! He was the dorm champ and possibly, the facilities champ. His slow southern drawl and big ears obscured his keen mind and chess savvy.

I had no bunkmate in the rack above me, but beside me on the "black" side, was Flowers and Hector. The two were friendly, and along with Sam and Leon, I formed a small group of buddies within a few days. We had work assignments, but we also had a lot of free time. We hung out outside, weather permitting, or inside around the picnic table.

Although tension around the incarcerated, young men persisted, there were few discipline problems. Most of the guys learned their lessons. Our dorm didn't have the real bad actors. We were focused on doing our time and going back into the world.

The topics of conversation were about just that—the world. What would it be like to be a civilian again? Discharge was the goal. The discharges we were designated weren't going to help us in the world. We understood that.

There was the prized honorable discharge; all of us had forfeited this coveted release due to our crimes. Then, there was a general discharge with honorable conditions. Next, was the Bad Conduct Discharge (BCD), which most of us were anticipating. Lastly, there was the Undesirable Discharge (UD). This form of release was the worst one that you could be designated; it was said to be reserved for homosexuals, murderers, and IV (intravenous) drug users.

Our dorm had its "jailhouse lawyers," and they enjoyed discussing cases and the possibility of a discharge upgrade after one had been out of the corps for a while. No matter which discharge we were assigned, our youthful errors were going to plague us forever.

The terrible burden of being a fugitive and living as a recluse didn't fade away until I was back at Camp Lejeune on my own terms. It was a slow, but steady release of fears. Now that my trial and the rocky beginning of incarceration were over, I grew more lighthearted each day. I was ashamed of my past, but I was letting it go. I was now buoyed by my potential to become a good person and a good citizen.

I couldn't meditate openly in the dorm during daylight. So, each morning and evening, I lay quietly on my rack and practiced the exercise; I allowed the random noises to pass through my consciousness. It was good practice.

I had a spirit unlike others in the facility. I stood out because of it, even though my inclination was to be on good terms with everyone. I didn't use profanity when I spoke, and that difference was the most obvious.

"I don't trust anybody that don't swear," someone said in a group that gathered to figure me out.

"The brother's got religion. He was in a seminary, man, but he's cool," said a defender. That response was sufficient for some, but others remained suspicious.

One of the most enjoyable episodes in our cell occurred because of the best-selling book by Mario Puzo, *The Godfather*. I delighted in listening to some of the black and white guys, sitting around the picnic table, recounting scene after scene of the book they committed to memory. The black guys indulged in hero worship of the Corleone family. Their envy of the gangster culture was troubling and understandable. If I had not a change of spirit, I could imagine myself being fascinated with the lifestyle of the thugs and murderers in the book; their world of merciless power and ruthless aggression were gilded with codes of honor.

Because the book had a compelling storyline, the guys performed sections of the novel for our entertainment; they were talented theater players. I didn't weigh in with an alternative opinion about the Corleone family for quite a while. When I did say something, a lot of the fellas listened. "That gangster-hood thing is just another fantasy world," I said when we were commenting on yet another revenge killing in the book. "They're all living these phony identities, centered around an honor code which parallels the same old eye-for-an-eye evil!"

"You're wrong, bro! They don't take shit from nobody! They got a real code of honor—you break it, you die!" James chided me.

"Yeah, but that doesn't end the cycle man," I protested. "They're all livin' in some kind of upsidedown reality. That's why it's called the underworld!" I said, and people laughed. That's how it went. Sometimes it got ugly, and sometimes it got personal.

A lot of tensions that built up inside, were released outside on the basketball court. We established a few four-man teams. Although I didn't play, I became the coach of one of these teams. At first, I simply watched the guys practicing, and I sometimes played around a little. When Flowers, Ted, Hector, and James formed a team, I made suggestions for plays. As coach, I organized workouts and taught strategy. When we played games, I offered key pointers from the sidelines. It was school-yard stuff with players calling their own fouls and arguments that threatened to explode until cooler heads prevailed.

We were winning games, and I got some of the credit. I took it in stride, because I knew it wasn't really deserved. Yet, I experienced a layer of respectability I seldom felt among athletic males before. In a weird way, it was my second chance at playing the childhood games I was formerly intimidated by. There were still parts of me that were nine-years-old and buried deep in my psyche. Those roots of self-conscience awkwardness had withered, but not yet died. I opened up honestly, as I explained my thoughts to my guys. "The boy is father to the man," I said, as we rested in the shade near the court. "That means that what you are as a boy, lays the foundation for what you will be as a man. "The boy is father to the man," I repeated slowly with emphasis.

"I can dig that, coach. That's why we all ended up in here, right? 'Cause we were all fu—, messed-up as kids?" James asked.

"Yes and no," I responded. "See, what's so wonderful about human beings is that we can change in our own lifetimes. I mean, you can start off like the worst person alive and end up a saint. As a matter of fact, there's a saying that 'every saint was a sinner.'"

" Oh, oh, Brother Heavy's gonna start preachin' now."

"Remember when you were nine?" I asked rhetorically. "Think back to when you were just nine—a single digit. Wasn't the world kind of cool? Then, things got complicated sometime after that, right?" I paused for a while, and guys joked about childhood memories until Flowers spoke up.

"Ya'll shut up now. I wanna hear the man. His shit is together, not like you knuckleheads! Go on Brother Heavy—teach these fools something."

"I'm just talkin' about myself," I said humbly. I'm still dealin' with stuff I didn't handle right as a kid. I'm so glad I can see it now! I wish someone could have told me why I was so screwed up when I was a kid, but nobody I knew had any answers. Some time, when I was around thirteen, I started hating my life. I never knew my real father and was never close to my stepfather. I seemed like the good kid, but I was livin' in a fantasy world, because the real world was so ugly! Basically, what I'm saying is that when you're a young kid and painful stuff happens to you, the only thing you can do, sometimes, is find a hiding place deep inside yourself. I loved my imagination, because it was my best friend!"

"That's some weird shit man," James interjected.

"The brother's making sense, man. He's sayin' when you're a kid you got to swallow your anger, so you don't get your ass kicked by grown-ups, right?" Flowers asked.

"Somethin' like that! What's important to understand is that getting angry and being helpless is the problem. So, like you say, the only victory a kid can have over adults is to hide his anger. You might show a little frustration, but you hide the rest, and it festers and ferments until it's like a secret rage against all the hypocritical grown-ups."

"Whoa, whoa, you're saying we're supposed to take all that shit without getting mad?" James queried. "That's bullshit man!"

"You're' right, it is bullshit when you're a kid. People talk about forgiveness, but we don't really see it much or understand it. Anyway, that rage we have growing up acts like a spiritual tumor in our soul. It poisons our thoughts and makes us do self-destructive stuff—hurt people you don't mean to! So, I built a prison for myself out of fear and anger! The poison from my toxic emotions twisted my thinking, and my pride led me to make selfish and bad decisions!

I had their attention, so I continued. "The beauty part is that I really wanted to do what was right. I had to come completely undone and realize that my mind had a mind of its own that was confusing me, distorting my thoughts and will. I had to stop running from myself—stop and learn to be still—so I could see the wrong mind that was my enemy mind!" I said enthusiastically.

I explained further. "Our self- centered enemy mind dominates our thinking. That ego mind loves darkness! It is never satisfied and is always feeding us problems to solve to keep us distracted. Our shadow minds distract us with problems and entertain us with empty amusements, so we can't see how it dominates our life!" I exclaimed.

I knew I said too much, but I couldn't unring the bell. It didn't really matter anyway, because the consensus of thought was that I was talking about science fiction. So, I went on. "Look we're born with a physical, a mental, and a spiritual self, but the spiritual self is dormant. Our mental self is a shadow self driven by emotions and ego, and it reflects how we learn from, and react to, the world. Basically, that self is who we think we are, but the quiet spiritual self is who we *really* are. That's why we're so confused and angry—we're at war within ourselves!"

"He's talkin' about body snatchers and shit, man," Leon piped in from the group that gathered around our spot. We all laughed.

"Hey it is kind of like that," I added.

"Leon, Brother Heavy is talking about good and evil. What I don't get is how come the good self is so weak? I mean there're too many assholes around! You gotta be strong and not take shit from other people," Flowers stated forcefully.

"Let me say it like this," I interjected. "The good self isn't weak, it's young and immature. That's why I said it was a dormant kind of asleep. I call it the "hungry I"—or the good, true self— that's hungry for truth and understanding about life's purpose. The good self doesn't grow totally from this world; it needs spiritual food from a heavenly source. The good self is powerful when it's in a relationship with God, but it requires that our minds and ego be still in order to make that heavenly connection.

I continued. "The bottom line is that the human mind is a terrible thing to watch. The biggest secret we keep from each other is how crazy we are! If you watch your mind, you'll see that your mind has a mind of its own. You can see your mind wrestling with itself. Well, the light that shows you this wrestling match is the light that is your guiding light to the truth," I ended quickly.

I knew I was talking about subjects that the inmates had no interest in pursuing. These topics were hard for the fellas to hear and understand, because they were unaware that they existed. We all wanted to believe that life was one huge buffet table loaded with delectable choices. Our generation didn't want moral absolutes. My lesson was to accept their resistance to my awakening and my message. I could not awaken those who were determined to remain asleep! Their lives would need to unfold, according to the inclinations of their true spirits, as mine unfolded. I learned to speak the truth—quietly and tactfully—when so moved, or to hold my peace (which was sometimes a more powerful statement). The only people who felt threatened by the little light I shed were the manipulators.

Things turned ugly one day in the prison dorm, when Leon—a smart, good-looking black guy—decided to go after Ted, the white guy in the neighboring rack. Ted was no wimp; he wouldn't back down when challenged. Admirably, he managed to avoid a major battle each time. But a confrontation had been brewing for some time.

When the group wasn't talking about sex, cars, or sports, the subject returned to race. Naturally, I endeavored to elevate the conversation. I believed that I had a lot to contribute, because I was an expert on the subject. After all, I grew up among all types of people and was an insider and outsider in both white and black groups. More importantly, though, I had an objective insight I loved to share.

The dispute erupted after three days of rain kept us inside. The chemistry among incarcerated youths is always fluid and can easily turn incendiary with the right provocation.

"Hey ya'll," Leon shouted during a quiet moment in the dorm. "No white boys on any teams, starting tomorrow!" he finished with an arrogant gesture. Most of us looked up from what we were doing and laughed nervously. Leon's taunting statement was made to get a reaction, but we did not take it seriously.

"Nah, nah, nah, ya'll, I'm not jokin'. If I see a white boy playin' basketball when we're on the court, I'm gonna kick his ass!" Leon threatened slowly, so there would be no misunderstanding.

With Ted on my team, this was a direct shot at me. I decided to make it a teaching episode and be philosophical regarding the racial topic that we were repeatedly drawn to. "Race is an illusion," I said to get everyone's attention. "Racial classifications, ethnic groups, even nationalities are all artificial barriers that men created to divide people."

"That's bullshit, man," Leon shot back. "You're talkin' outta your ass!"

"It sounds far out, I know. We identify races, nationalities, and ethnic groups; yet, they develop from natural selection. Negro blood, Oriental blood, and Caucasian blood are all the same! Unless you note skin color or facial characteristics, there are no distinctions among us. We share the same fluids and organs! That means we're all the same human beings in reality, in God's sight," I concluded my message, and arguments broke out around the room.

"Niggers been catchin' hell from the white man for three-hundred years, and that shit ends now! Leon shouted. "No white dudes on the court!" he added and gestured. "It's simple! You come on the court while the black brothers are playin', and your white ass gets kicked," he ended his rant; it was followed by a chorus of laughs from his stooges.

"That's wrong," I said, as all eyes looked my way.

"Well, you don't have nothin' to say about it. You're just a part-time brother anyway! You can't hang with the whites *and* the blacks! You need to dig yourself, bro, 'cause the revolution is comin!'" Leon said, as he walked toward me.

I watched his taut and muscular body as he sauntered. I scanned for body-language signals that might indicate he was ready to throw a sucker punch when he got close. He veered from me toward Ted, who was sitting on his bottom rack. Leon placed one hand on the upper bunk and leaned toward Ted. "When the brother's play, you go away," he rhymed. "No white boys on the court," he said forcefully. "You got a problem wit dat?" He sounded like a thug.

Ted had grown up around "colored" guys and had some basic survival instincts; he knew when to confront and when to back off. However, Ted wouldn't back down to Leon, and we all knew it. "I think your mouth is writin' a check, your ass can't cash," Ted said calmly. The room rocked with laughter—even Leon smiled. This was the verbal combat before the real thing.

"Well, you step on that court and see what happens to you. Shit, I should beat your ass now just on general principles!" Leon barked, but didn't move.

"Hey, Leon, homeboy," Ted said, as he stood. "If you feel froggy—then jump!"

They glared at each other for a few seconds. Leon didn't let a muscle twitch. Ted was equally calm. Both men were fit. This fight was one that many wanted to watch.

"Be cool, guys," I spoke, as I turned to face them. I wanted to be a distraction, but not a target. There was excitement in the air.

"I'm cool," Leon said calmly. "I stay cool. But you better get your boy out my face or...," he said without finishing the threat. Then, he turned and walked away.

It wasn't over. After evening chow, the stares became more intense. Before lights out, one of Leon's "cling-ons" whispered to me to stay out of it. He divulged that they were giving me the heads up, so I could stay out of the "blanket party" Ted was getting that night.

I was never a hero or brave. I questioned my physical courage, and I retained precious little moral courage. But, I wasn't going to let it happen again! I still felt sick when I thought back to how I lay in my top rack during the beating my bunkmate got in boot camp. I wasn't going to let that happen to another guy who didn't deserve it. And maybe it was a chance to redeem myself. Perhaps I could change the course of events. Consequently, I approached Leon and his "cling-ons" at the picnic table. I sat next to him and didn't say anything. I didn't know what I should say. Then, a thought came to me.

"If you start somethin' tonight," I said in a conversational tone, rubbing my palms together, "you will be a loser!"

"Why? You think that punk-ass dude can kick my ass?" he asked while he chuckled, stretched, and crossed his legs.

"He's not gonna have a chance if you're giving him a blanket party," I responded. "What I'm sayin', is I gotta get into it."

"Oh, so *you're* gonna kick my ass?" he asked with surprise and delight.

"No, but you will know you were in a fight!" I promised boldly. "And you'll still lose," I added, "because even if you beat up both of us, you won't feel good about it. This is all on you." I accused. "Look man, everybody wants power, possessions, and position out of life. You want to dominate every situation and intimidate anybody that doesn't agree with you. That's being strong before the weak, but there's no victory in that," I said with a clinched fist.

I persisted. "You're looking for some action, and you don't like it that Ted's not afraid of you! You don't have to be a bully," I said, and I stood to leave. "You're too smart to think you have to go around intimidating people to get respect," I finished. Then, I walked away.

Later in the cell, I felt grimly determined to put up the best fight I could. With one of Leon's "cling-ons" observing me, I openly pushed a bar of soap into one of my socks to create a sort-of weapon. I wasn't going to war unarmed.

After lights out, I lay there, thinking about being beaten up or ending up in the dispensary or hospital with time added to my sentence. My right hand clasped the top of the sock, which lay by my side. Under my green, wool blanket, I tried to meditate and stay alert.

I dozed fitfully and woke with a start several times. Silence. I didn't move, as I strained to hear the faintest sound. No movement. For the next two nights, I slept armed with my sock weapon. When the rains ended, I coached basketball. I didn't make any changes to the team. Everyone had come to their senses.

———— • ◆ •————

In the brig, we rejoiced in each other's release dates. Just like in the rest of the corps, and indeed, in the rest of the military, we celebrated short timers. A short timer could count his release date or discharge in weeks or days, and loved to talk about how "short" they were.

Sex was another constantly discussed topic. This was not unusual among young men, and especially, among those restricted to male company exclusively. Some of the guys teased me (and others) about being virgins. The taunting reflected a need for release due to their hormones being trapped in their imaginations.

"I never heard anybody talk like you Brother Heavy," Flowers said. "You got somethin'. I don't know what it is, but you definitely are different."

"He's got bullshit, that's what he's got!" Sparks interjected. "He's talkin' about consciousness raising—like the age of Aquarius and shit. I mean, I'm down with that, if it helps you keep your shit together," he explained. He went on. "I had a buddy in the 'Nam' who meditated and prayed. Even when we were in the bush, he did his thing. He still came home in a body bag! That's the real world!"

"How come as soon as you come over here, Sparks, I knew you was gonna bring up some negative shit?" Flowers asked after we all paused for a while.

"Yeah, consciousness raising is good, but I need my dick raised!" Sparks said, and everybody laughed.

"Oh. man, don't even talk about that!" Ted jumped in. "I'm so horny that a good breeze gives me a hard-on!"

"At least you got some waitin' for you!" someone else mentioned regarding the married Ted.

All I could do was laugh along with everyone else. It was on everyone's mind at some time or other. Guys wondered if we were given saltpeter, or "soft Peter" as someone called it, in our food to suppress sexual urges. That was as good as it got in the brotherhood of young marines.

———— • ◆ • ————

I was in and out of the brig after two months. I awaited my paperwork, processing Private Rose out of the USMC with a Bad Conduct Discharge. It was a final humiliation; my day of shame. I had failed at many things in my young life, but this failure was permanent! An indelible stain! There wasn't going to be any officer candidate school, no chaplaincy, or an upgrade to a General Discharge. That chapter was closed.

All I could do from this point on was to be a better person and a good citizen. I thought of these ambitions, as I sat in the Trenton, New Jersey bus station. I was waiting for my Aunt Bertha to pick me up. It was the same bus terminal where she'd left me three years earlier.

I wanted it to be different this time. If I could have afforded it, I would have taken a taxicab to her house. As it was, I barely had enough cash to make the trip to her place and eventually, New Rochelle, New York. I was returning the way I had come.

I realized how different my thoughts were from three years earlier. I ran away as a boy, and I returned as a young man. No one could tell the difference more than me. The scene of meeting Aunt Bertha played over and over in my mind long before it finally took place. Directly, I spotted Aunt Bertha in the bustling terminal. She hugged me and cried with joy! She covered my face with kisses. She smelled of coffee and cigarette smoke.

"William Lloyd, William Lloyd, you look so good! Thank God, you're fine! I knew you were alright when you called, but I had to see you for myself!" Aunt Bertha said, and she gave me another hug. I guessed that I did look good to her. The poor woman had suffered a lot because of me.

————— • ◆ • —————

We made small talk, as we rode to her row house in Trenton. In a short time, I was in the guest room where I stayed before I decided to desert my family and the Marine Corps. I unpacked the few things I had in my bag—a few clothes and letters from my family. My grandmother and mother wrote me. My sister, Dorcas, sent a nice picture of herself along with her letter; she relayed that she was attending the University of Connecticut (UCONN). I was proud of her. She was smart and pretty! I missed out on so much!

Aunt Bertha knew what to cook for a young man who was away from his family for so long. A platter of fried chicken was on the table when I came downstairs along with mashed potatoes and sweet peas. I was definitely feeling closer to home.

Aunt Bertha enjoyed a shot or two of booze before dinner, but she was fine. We ate and talked. Then, I kept eating while she had another drink. After we chatted about life and politics, she said, "You're so smart, William Lloyd." Aunt Bertha inadvertently slurred her words a little.

Aunt Bertha exhaled a cloud of cigarette smoke and asked achingly, "William Lloyd, why'd you leave that way? Run away like you did?" Her eyes were moist, and her whole body collapsed in relief after finally asking that question.

Hearing that question out loud—spoken in a dear human voice—hurt me deeper than I had imagined it would! I heard the question so many times in my head, but now, hearing it asked so sincerely, gouged my heart! I couldn't respond for a full minute. I closed my eyes to hold back the tears, yet they slowly flowed down my cheeks. I sighed deeply and heard my voice quiver as I weakly answered. "I'm sorry. I'm so sorry." I would be apologizing to her, my mother, and my grandmother, too! My amends would never be enough, and I knew that.

I reached to touch her hands on her lap. She contemplated me. "They all blamed me, you know," she said painfully. "They said I was the last one to see you—that I should have looked out for you! Nobody knew what happened to you," her voice trailed off into a whisper.

"I don't have any good reasons that could justify what I did," I said calmly, as I rubbed her hands. "I was a mess. I was angry and confused. I'm just sorry I made all of you suffer, too! I didn't know how to deal with things at that time—not like a man. The lessons I learned while I was in California saved my life! I grew up, and I became a Christian.

Aunt Bertha listened intently. "I discovered so much about myself and life. If I had to go through everything again, I would. Although, I recognize that I did everything the wrong way! I'm sorry others had to suffer! I hope everybody can forgive me for that."

"Everybody forgives you, child," she said quickly. "We didn't know you were in such pain! We just want to know that you're alright now—that you'll be alright," Aunt Bertha assured me. She kissed my hand and held it to her tear-dampened cheek.

"I'll be alright," I assured her confidently. "I'm a different person now. I thank God I finally woke up to the real purpose of life," I went on enthusiastically. Aunt Bertha wasn't a devoutly religious woman, but she whispered, "Thank God."

I told her why I stayed away so long. I admitted that I was stupid and stubborn—yet, determined to turn myself in to the Marine Corps. Everything I explained to her was a live rehearsal for the rest of my family. This step was part of the healing. I marveled at the irony of confessing my deepest thoughts when, not long before, I concealed the fermenting poisons that churned within me.

I told Aunt Bertha that I learned how important forgiveness was. Not just the feel-good concept of forgiveness, but the real letting go of resentment! Aunt Bertha accorded no interest in my new, philosophical outlook on life. She only wanted to be convinced that I was alright and had resolved my mental or emotional problems.

I waded back into the waters of family life in Aunt Bertha's New Jersey home. My visit was good for both of us. She answered phone calls from family members eager to talk to me, and the experience heightened her sense of belonging.

New Rochelle was next on my itinerary. After my days in California, I expressed a higher love for these women who dominated my young life. They did the best *they* could, to help me be the best *I* could. I loved them for that. Forgiveness unshackled my heart from resentment.

The projects where nana lived—81 Winthrop Avenue—hadn't changed at all. The tall, six–story, brick buildings and play areas were the same. The elevator ride to her fourth-floor apartment was eerie. The creaking noises and ugly graffiti were more frightening than the actual elevator ride. The taxi driver, who took me from the bus depot to nana's courtyard, knew I was Mrs. Ingram's grandson; he was an old timer who knew my mother and uncle when they were kids.

The greeting at nana's was the same as Aunt Bertha's! Hugs and kisses, and tears of joy shared between us. This small, brown woman—the cornerstone of the family with more backbone and perseverance than anyone else—melted in my arms. I tasted the saltiness of my tears with surprise. I thought I was out of tears, but they flowed. The tears of a woman can melt the heart of any man. So, I cried with her for the happiness she felt and the pain and anguish I inflicted on her.

Her apartment was like a time capsule. Everything was as I remembered. Her home was comfortably cluttered with pictures and mementos of children, grandchildren, nieces, and nephews. I was close to home.

I formed a master plan while in California. I couldn't wait any more than a day before approaching nana with it. First, I announced what she already knew: "I'm going home in a couple of days, nana." Then, I revealed my master plan. "I can get a job for a while. Then, after New Year's, I want to go back to Los Angeles, California," I avoided her reaction.

"I started writing music when I was out there," I went on. "My writing partner and I got a kind-of agent to help us get our song produced," I added.

"You're writing music?" she asked.

"Yes, nana. I write lyrics—the words for music. I have a partner. We wrote a song that was pretty good. The agent can help us publish it!" It sounded like childish enthusiasm.

"You have to go to California to write songs?" nana asked.

"Well, that's where I got things started," I explained. Fear was gripping me. Did she wonder if this story was just another lie or fantasy? I searched through my papers and found the receipt for the money I paid Mr. Cousins Production Company in Hollywood, California. The song title was printed on the official-looking paper: "Gotta Leave This Place." Nana studied the paper.

"That name, William Kinkade, is me," I said. "That's the name I used out there. I told the agent that I was gonna change it to my real name before we publish the song. And I'm going to write some spiritual songs, too," I added, hoping to draw her interest.

"You mean Gospels?"

"Yeah, like Gospels. Like I told you, I played the organ at this mission for a while. I wrote some inspirational poems, and I might put them to music later," I added, sounding like a kid trying to convince his mother why he needed a new bicycle.

"You know your grandfather wrote poems and plays," Nana said wistfully, as she handed me the paper.

"Oh, I know, nana. Ma was always talkin' about that. And she was always saying that she was gonna publish her poems." I didn't want to travel too far afield, so I steered the conversation back to where I wanted it.

"So, I'm not going to college, nana, at least not now. I was hoping to use some of the money you had for me to go to college to help me get started when I go back to California".

I said "some" but I really meant all. I imagined an amount around five-thousand dollars or more. Perhaps, I could put a couple thousand in the bank. The rest could pay my expenses until I got a job or hit it big, I thought.

The silence hung above us like a rain cloud. "There's not much money left," I heard her say.

"No!" I screamed inside my mind. All I could manage to say was "What do you mean?" I attempted to soften the edge in my voice, although admittedly, I felt entitled to it.

Nana sighed softly, fidgeted with her apron a bit, and looked me in the face. "Whenever you all needed help, I'd send what I could. You needed school clothes and money to pay bills. When I didn't have enough cash to help, I used some of the money I put aside for your college." she said gently.

My shoulders slumped, as I let out an audible sigh and the air went out of my body. I felt her soft, brown hand touch mine. "When you were first born I started that fund. It was two-thousand dollars when I told you about it. I wanted to inspire you to do well in school. You were my first grandchild, and you were smart. When I took money out of that account, I used to put it right back as soon as I could. Then, when things got worse in Hartford, I had to help your mother even more," she stopped and let that sink in.

There wasn't any need to say more. My emotions were churning, as the past came back to haunt me. Nana was incapacitated in Hartford after she broke her leg—because of me! Though her employer, Mrs. Coleman, and my Uncle Buddy took care of her obligations. Her temporary disability put her in financial jeopardy. Combined with my family's difficult months in Hartford, nana was left without extra money. My mother tapped her for cash when our phone was shut off or bill collectors threatened action! Nana had to dip into my college fund so that we could survive those tough days between welfare checks after daddy left. I should be thankful. I remembered how selfish and reluctant I was to help ma during the few times I had money. I couldn't be angry at anyone. Now, I could see how foolish my hopes were.

"There's not much left now. Only a few hundred dollars," Nana said gingerly. "We'll go to the bank tomorrow and close the account. It's your money, so you can do whatever you want with it."

I told nana that I also needed a copy of my birth certificate. I was going to use my legal birth name. She agreed to get that document when we went to the bank. She asked me to attend church with her. I replied that I probably would. I didn't want to commit myself too soon.

"Is my real father dead?" I asked.

"Yes, a long time now," she said delicately. "I told your mother when he passed. It was in the paper, the *Standard Star*."

"Ma said it was a drug overdose," I said.

"That's what people said, but the paper didn't say anything about that," she responded.

"What about his parents?" I asked, wondering about my paternal grandparents, "Are they still alive?"

"Yes, as far as I know. They stopped going to our church years ago. They didn't want anything to do with you, when they found out their son had passed," she went on, sensing that I wanted as much as she could tell me.

"John Withers." I said the name that really had no meaning for me.

"Uh-huh," she replied. "Johnny Withers. He was always quiet and moody—stayed alone a lot. Your mother, Liz, was just the opposite. She was outgoing and popular. After her father died, I kept her busy with school and church. She was smart, but headstrong. I don't think anybody thought those two would get together. She sneaked around to be with him. She went behind my back," she said with the sting of betrayal in her voice.

"Was she always gonna keep me?" I asked honestly. I never thought about it before. I was familiar with adoption. Abortion was a different issue; the debate regarding abortion divided the American people's consciousness.

"We don't kill our babies," nana said without hesitation. "Every child is precious. We never even considered somethin' like that. I was so disappointed in your mother, but once we were sure she was pregnant, I tried to make things right." Nana tilted her head back and looked beyond me into the distant past. "I had your mother confess before the church about what she'd done. She was unhappy about that."

Nana delicately continued. "I took her to see Johnny's mother and father, but they paid me no mind. They even acted like Johnny might not be your father! They were shameful the way they protected that boy! They didn't think that they should get married or that he had any responsibility to you," she spoke with her voice full of bitter emotions. "They knew I was naming their son as your father. Your dad never showed his face or said a thing. We never saw any of them again."

Nana summarized. "After you were born, I thought they'd want to see you—get a look at you. I guess your father was too far gone on drugs." Then, she beamed at me. "William Lloyd, you were always precious to us! You had no control on how you came into this world, and we always loved you! I prayed and prayed, all the time you were gone, that we didn't lose you for good. I thank the Lord that he brought you back to us safe!"

"Me too, nana," I said with my heart full of thanksgiving, "Me, too!"

I decided to let it go. My father was dead, and I would never know him. In some ways, there was a lot of him in me, and that's where I started to forgive him. I extended that forgiveness to his parents. I would never know my paternal grandparents, but from this point forward, I hoped to live a life that would make it their loss to not have known me.

When I said good-bye to my grandmother at the bus station, I had a little over three-hundred dollars and a new copy of my birth certificate. I had clothes and a decent suit that came from the thrift shop where nana and Aunt Burt worked as volunteers.

I wore the suit to church. The service was much like I thought it would be. Everyone was friendly and respectful of Mrs. Ingram's oldest grandchild. The service, conducted by Reverend Crutchfield, was emotional, but dignified. Aunt Burt sang with the choir. I felt welcomed, but also, like I didn't belong there. I went, because I knew it meant a lot to nana. She was pleased when I told her that I played the organ and preached sermons in LA. When nana asked if I would attend evening services with her as well, I declined.

I explained that I cared about church people, but not church organizations. I believed that the church served a useful purpose in God's overall plan, but for the most part, the dogma and denominationalism of (modern "Churchianity") was a turnoff for me. Nana had no concept of what I was criticizing or talking about. To her mind, God was good, and God was in church. Fellowship was in church, and the Bible said fellowship was good. Nana wanted to be a good woman who loved God and served her people. She could do both of those things through the church. I blessed her for that. I thanked God for her and all those like her.

On the bus ride to Hartford, I was reflective. My Hartford upbringing appeared in random flashbacks. Many of the childhood aspects of me—that determined my reaction to circumstances—

were still part of me, but greatly diminished. I was genuinely sorry for the resentment I demonstrated toward my mother during those years. We became emotionally distant from each other during crucial times.

Thinking back, I realized that ma needed me to be less judgmental of her romance with a much younger man. Julio was kind, thoughtful, and loving to my divorced mother; she had never enjoyed that type of devotion before. I was respectful, but cool toward Julio when he visited our home. I couldn't understand my mother's emotional need for male validation. Their relationship was dignified and discreet, yet, I hated her for it.

During those tumultuous years, I didn't comprehend that I needed my mother to share power with me. The ugly turning point in our relationship followed her rejection of my offer to help manage the family finances! In hindsight, I know I wasn't ready for that much responsibility. Now, I grasped that allowing me to lend a hand would have been the right thing for her to do. During my youth, weak male and strong female role models dominated my life. My potential manhood could have developed positively if I was co-head of the household. My mother's pride and resentment of male domination did not allow her to think of me as a helpmate. Those dark days doomed us both to disaffection, anger, and alienation.

My mother expected my knock on the door. She flung the door open! Before I knew it, ma was hugging and kissing me like I never remembered her doing! "My son, my son, my son," she said, as we swayed side to side. "My oldest son has finally come home," she declared with tears in her voice. "I was trying to keep it all together," she confessed through her sniffles. "You sound so serious—so grown-up now. And you look so good! So handsome!" she exclaimed with admiration. I knew that on this day she would have been happy to see me no matter how I looked! It was so good to see ma again, too—to be alone with her, as we soaked in each other and felt the years we were apart melt away!

My memory had dulled over the years. I forgot how much a force of nature my mother could be! She appeared smaller than I remembered—not delicate, but somehow, more fragile. Her tears dried for the moment, as we sat at the kitchen table, sipping tea. It was like we used to do before school some mornings—mother and son—tea and empathy.

I said I was sorry again, this time face-to-face. Could I ever apologize enough? "I'm so sorry, ma. I'm sorry for everything!" It sounded pathetic, but sincere.

"We all make mistakes," she said calmly. "All is forgiven now," she went on. "You're home— safe and sound. That's all that matters. My William is home!" she proclaimed.

I sat at the table while ma put away the food that nana sent with me. She kept talking, catching me up on all the missing years' events. I watched her and listened, uttering only a word here and there. It was her time, and I understood that. It was important for her to verbally deal with her competing emotions. I felt that I knew her now, probably better than she knew herself! We were so much alike in some ways. We both had flashes of personality—full of charm and grace—or we could become sullen and mean spirited, hiding our fear and anger! I was learning how to love her. She had done the best she could with who she was, and she deserved my nonjudgmental love.

When I did speak, I conveyed my plan to return to California. I explained that with the money from nana, I could buy a car, learn to drive, obtain my license, and resell the car before returning to the West Coast. Ma could tell from my tone and plan details how determined I was to meet each objective toward my goal.

Those were the only quiet moments we enjoyed for the next few days. People came by to see me once the word was out that I was home. Charter Oak Terrace hadn't changed much and seeing my boyhood buddies was special! They promised to teach me to drive. We went to a used-car dealership, and I brought a Ford Falcon for two-hundred dollars! Charlie drove the car home, and soon, I took lessons with old pals in parking lots and on neighborhood roads.

The automatic transmission made it easy for me to master driving. I studied the Connecticut *Drivers Manual*, and my mother quizzed me. Within two weeks, I had a vehicle and was prepared to take the driver's test. I passed it easily. I was twenty-one-years old, and finally had a driver's license.

My other plans were moving just as smoothly. I applied and was accepted for training, as a temporary salesperson at the G. Fox & Co.

department store in downtown Hartford. My thrift-store suit came in handy for my interview. I looked like the salesman I wanted them to believe I could be! We were told to report to the former Kay Jewelers' building for sales-training classes. We would complete training before Thanksgiving. Then, we would be thrown to the shopping hordes on Black Friday, the day after Thanksgiving.

I shared the wonderful changes that occurred in my life with my family and friends. I talked openly about meditating without sounding preachy. As usual, everybody was happy for me. However, they didn't see the need for changes in their own lives. I wasn't surprised. I just wished I was a better example of what I believed.

When an occasion presented itself, I spoke up about the power and healing I discovered through the meditation. I was patient, forgiving, thoughtful, and kind most of the time. Whenever I had bad moments or gave into negative impulses, I ached. That's the way life should be. Life was about playing to learn!

I mastered the ultimate lesson, which was as follows: The old nature—that I grew up with and *thought* was me—was an impostor! It was an implanted alien identity that grew from my pride, fear, and anger. It was a conditioned self that resented any obstacle to self-gratification. This "enemy mind" was a shadow self, the counterfeit of my authentic self! The two were interwoven, yet the dark self flourished like a predatory weed, sucking the energy out of my life. The dark self fed on my anger and frustration; it trapped me into selfishness and guilt and flourished from my anxieties. It would hide in my egos' dark, confused and busy mind!

Awareness frustrates the alien self; it needs the host to stay asleep to its presence, so it whispers in your mind. It tries to echo your true thoughts with its own hypnotic words of seduction and comfort. I realized it would be a lifelong struggle—a struggle of surrender to the godly light that was shining in my darkness.

What a sweet science it was! My tormentors—would become my mentors! Within life's poison was the antidote! What a wonderful God this was; I was learning to know! I was learning to release self-defeating thoughts and ideas! I was learning to breathe more and whine less!

————•◆•————

The family was together for Thanksgiving that year. Nana came from New Rochelle, and my stepfather joined us, too. We all had something to be thankful for!

My dark journey brought me to a bright passage that I didn't know existed. I could not have imagined the wonderful world of possibilities that lay before me to discover. I was grasping that heaven was not only a destination, but part of the journey. Every moment lived in the presence of God in the present moment is a perfect moment. Then, all things work together for good— and all the way to heaven is heaven.

CPSIA information can be obtained
at www.ICGtesting.com
Printed in the USA
BVOW09s2342261017
498797BV00008B/51/P

9 781457 548277